MARTYRS

MARTYRS

INNOCENCE, VENGEANCE, and
DESPAIR in the MIDDLE EAST

JOYCE M. DAVIS

First published in hardcover in 2003 by Palgrave Macmillan
First PALGRAVE MACMILLAN™ paperback edition: November 2004
175 Fifth Avenue, New York, N.Y. 10010 and
Houndmills, Basingstoke, Hampshire, England RG21 6XS.
Companies and representatives throughout the world.

PALGRAVE MACMILLAN is the global academic imprint of the Palgrave
Macmillan division of St. Martin's Press, LLC and of Palgrave Macmillan Ltd.
Macmillan® is a registered trademark in the United States, United Kingdom
and other countries. Palgrave is a registered trademark in the European Union
and other countries.

ISBN 1-4039-6681-8

Library of Congress Cataloging-in-Publication Data

Davis, Joyce M.
    Martyrs: innocence, vengeance, and despair in the Middle East / Joyce M.
Davis.
        p.   cm.
    Includes bibliographical references and index.
    Hardcover ISBN 0-312-29616-9
    Paperback ISBN 1-4039-6681-8
    1. Martyrdom (Islam)   2. Jihad.   3. Terrorism—Religious aspects—
Islam.   4. Muslim martyr—Middle East.   5. Islam and politics—Middle
East.   6. September 11 Terrorist Attacks, 2001.   I. Title.

BP190.5.M3D39   2003
297.7—dc21
                                                                    2003041327

A catalogue record for this book is available from the British Library.

Design by Letra Libre, Inc.

First PALGRAVE MACMILLAN paperback edition: November 2004

10 9 8 7 6 5 4 3 2 1

Printed in the United States of America.

This book is dedicated to the memory of my brother,
Albert Othel Davis Jr.,
whose sudden death at the age of thirty-eight
inspired me to complete this work.

And to my darling son, Cole.
May he always cherish life more than death.

CONTENTS

ACKNOWLEDGEMENTS

DEVOUT MUSLIMS ALWAYS BEGIN ANY WRITTEN WORK WITH A statement like: "In the Name of Allah, Most Gracious, Most Merciful." As a practicing Christian, I am compelled to do no less, acknowledging God's guidance above all in the completion of this work.

I am also indebted to Knight Ridder for allowing me the time off to complete the travel, research, and writing needed for this book. But it must be stressed that this is an independent work that in no way is connected to the editorial policies of Knight Ridder newspapers.

This book is the culmination of years of research, but its completion would not have been possible without the skill, talent, and patience of David Pervin, my editor at Palgrave Macmillan. His contributions are truly immeasurable.

I must thank the Journalist in Residence Program of Johns Hopkins School of Advanced International Studies for its support of my work and the publication of this book's second edition.

On the personal side, I extend sincere thanks to the Reverend and Mrs. Carson Wise, the Reverend Willie Crenshaw and the members of Shiloh Baptist Church of McLean, Virginia, for their prayers and care of my husband and son during my difficult and sometimes dangerous travel through the Middle East. My sister Ann Davis Duplessis, as well as her husband, Virgil, and their daughters Brooks, Lyndsey, and Heather, also were vital sources of strength for my family. And I must thank Gene and Cathy Goodman, my loving in-laws, who supported my commitment to this work despite their fears.

Finally, it is a gross understatement to say that I could not have completed this book without the love and devotion of my husband, Russell, who not only took care of our son during my extensive travels but also served as my sounding board, first reader, first editor, and, as always, first friend.

1

A MINISTER'S QUESTION:
WHAT HAVE WE DONE THAT
THEY HATE US SO?

INSIDE THE FIRST BAPTIST CHURCH OF VIENNA, VIRGINIA, IN suburban Washington, D.C., a hush fell over the congregation as the Reverend Kenny Smith's voice echoed over the pews like the pounding of a cannon.

"We should ask ourselves," he thundered, "what have we done that these people hate us so?"

It was January 21, 2002, only four months after September 11, when the earth shook from the tremors of the fallen World Trade Center and the fiery wreckage at the Pentagon. Americans were living a nightmare. U.S. soldiers were bombing Afghanistan, and Osama bin Laden, the Saudi millionaire believed to have helped finance many attacks against the United States, was showing up on television, threatening to unleash hell's fire from sea to shining sea. The FBI was sending out warnings about terrorists on the loose in the United States, and to Americans, it looked like the world had become a cauldron of evil. People avoided airports, shopping malls, and even their mailboxes, afraid that letters might contain anthrax, the white powder that someone had spread through the mail, killing five people in the United States, infecting dozens of others around the world, contaminating Washington's bastions of power, and paralyzing the snow-sleet-rain-or-shine U.S. Postal Service. And Americans, like the Reverend Kenny Smith, were asking, "why?"

Why would anyone so viciously attack the United States? What would make anyone kill himself and thousands of other people in so brutal a fashion? And does Islam really condone that type of holy war and martyrdom?

Since that awful day in September, many Americans who had thought little about the Middle East except in Sunday School suddenly found themselves wanting to know more about the region in the modern world. Many, like evangelical Christians, felt a kinship with Israel, the land of the Bible, but they knew little about the countries around it. And they certainly knew little about the people who called themselves Muslims, even though several millions lived in their midst.

Suddenly Americans were being confronted with words such as *jihad* (holy war) and *shaheed* (martyr), and with strange names such as Osama bin Laden and Ayman Zawahri. And they had come to realize that these new enemies were unlike any they had encountered before—enemies who embraced dying as a way to kill.

And Americans, like the ones gathered at First Baptist, did not understand why. Was it religion or politics that motivated Mohammed Atta and his band of hijackers to meticulously plan and carry out an attack that they knew would kill thousands of people, including themselves? Was it envy of the United States? Why did they hate Israel? Were they simply deranged fanatics? And why would anyone call such people *shuhada*—martyrs?

These were the questions on the minds of the people gathered inside First Baptist Church, a congregation of middle-class African Americans, although many probably only a generation removed from rural poverty. Many of its members were transplants from places deeper South. They are fiercely patriotic but also keenly aware that even a country built on democracy and equality could stray from its principles, with tragic results. As a people, they had experienced both the beauty and brutality of American life, surviving slavery, lynchings, the Ku Klux Klan, Jim Crow, separate but equal, the backlash against affirmative action, and what many knew as the hypocritical superficiality of northern liberalism.

Now, however, many of the people gathered inside First Baptist were financially comfortable, if not well off. They were Bible-thumping believers in the power of nonviolence as a weapon of conscience. And they had come together to celebrate the birthday of their paramount symbol of the power of peace, a man they revered as a martyr, Dr. Martin Luther King, Jr.

Yet they also knew the word "militant." They knew that in their history, militants among their own people had tried to lead them down a path of violence and revenge—a path their parents and grandparents had firmly rejected. They had seen people succumb to such hatred and had watched it ruin them.

There was Nat Turner in Southampton County, Virginia, in 1831 and the "Death or Liberty" revolt of John Brown at Harpers Ferry, Virginia, in 1859. Both Turner and Brown and their followers thought they had been led by God to avenge the suffering of black slaves, but neither bettered the conditions of blacks one iota. Before he was hanged, Brown, a white abolitionist, went so far as to declare, "The crimes of this guilty land will never be purged away but with blood." Most of the people in this church believed otherwise.

Despite the bitterness of centuries of slavery and oppression, African Americans, especially those rooted in the Christian church, had shunned their militants and rejected extremism. Despite the daily harassment of Jim Crow segregation in the South; despite the lynchings and bombings, even when they claimed the lives of young girls inside a Birmingham church, their people had fed, nurtured, and truly loved the children of their oppressors. And their most respected leaders were not extremists but men such as King, who had died a martyr for peace.

And as they sat celebrating all their nonviolent movement had achieved, they could not help but wonder why those men—whose grievances could be no greater than their own after centuries of slavery and oppression—had chosen another way. Why did the Arabs who attacked on September 11 take the opposite path—the path they called holy war, jihad? Why had they become suicide bombers and terrorists?

As their minds pondered these questions, emotions began to flow through the church with the ferocity of a breached dam. The gospel music mercifully provided a release from the fear and uncertainty that had gripped their lives, and their fears found expression in a lone voice, backed by the full throats of a choir, that pealed with the power of a steeple's bell.

"Through many dangers, toils and snares,
I have already come.
'Twas grace that brought me safe thus far
And grace will lead me on."

Tears flowed as the singer intoned the terror that had gripped the entire nation, thankful that somehow, if only through God's grace, the people in this church had not been trapped on September 11 in the World Trade towers or the Pentagon, the latter only a few miles away. Many still worried that the country would have to weather another attack, perhaps even more devastating than the first. And everyone feared that Americans were in for tougher times and wanted to know why.

It was the Reverend Smith, majestic in a long black robe, who unleashed the thunderbolt and spoke what was on the minds of everyone in the cushioned pews encircling his pulpit.

"We must ask ourselves," he demanded, "what is it that would make a person crash a plane into a building, killing himself and everybody else? And what is it that would make a person strap explosives to his body and blow himself up?"

They were simple questions, but asking them publicly from the pulpit and challenging God-fearing Americans to do the same was unusual at a time when Old Glory waved from the pinnacles of suburban mansions, from the antennas of SUVs, and was pasted onto the visors of Little League baseball caps. It was a time when many Christians, although advocates of the love-your-enemy theology, lusted after revenge. Even those who were not motivated by revenge wanted to make sure nothing so horrible ever struck this country again. The best way to do that, the Reverend Smith suggested, was to delve deep into the psyches of the attackers to find out why.

The Reverend's questions were not an attempt to justify terrorism or to suggest that there can be any excuse for the actions of the men who commandeered the airplanes on September 11 and flew them into the symbols of American power and wealth. They represented sincere bewilderment at how different Atta and his entourage were from the people inside that church, people who cherished life, peace, and freedom. Atta and the hijackers were exactly opposite. By committing suicide and murdering thousands of people, they expected to find a place in heaven. They expected to be saluted on earth as martyrs.

The Reverend Smith's questions inevitably lead to an examination of martyrdom and Islam's teachings about war. Atta and his hijackers thought they were acting in accordance with God's command. They thought they were defending their world from a superpower that had already declared war on both Muslims and Islam. Why?

Most Americans would be outraged at the suggestion that their government is against any religion. The United States is, above all, a bastion of religious freedom. But this is where the divide between the Islamic world and the West is perhaps at its greatest.

Many Muslims, especially the extremists, are convinced that the U.S. war on terrorism that Bush declared after September 11 is really a war on Islam. The hijackers said they were carrying out a "martyrdom operation," and they believed they were acting in the highest principles of Islam. Even before September 11, many Muslims believed that by militarily supporting Israel and despotic Arab regimes, U.S. policies in the Middle East were oppressing Arabs. In wide-ranging interviews with Palestinians, religious scholars, political analysts, and even teenagers in Lebanese discos, many people in the Middle East said they thought America was against Islam, noting that Muslim groups were the primary ones on the U.S. terrorism list. They also complained about the Bush administration's threats to go after Iraq, Iran, and Syria, all predominantly Muslim countries, for their support of groups Arabs considered fighters for freedom.

While many Muslims feared the United States was blaming Islam for the sins of Osama bin Laden and Mohammed Atta, most argued vehemently that the attack was outside of the bounds Islam sets for a "just war."

The Islamic scholar Yusef al Qaradawi, who commands considerable respect among Muslims, was so outraged that the September 11 attackers claimed to be vanguards of Islam that he issued a *fatwa*, or religious ruling, declaring that bin Laden could not call himself a Muslim.

Muslim scholars throughout the world agreed and rushed to cite widely accepted interpretations of Islamic law regarding what is permitted and forbidden in war. But even as Islam's most learned men quoted from the Qur'an about injunctions against harming the innocent and the weak, extremists claiming to represent Islam ignored their admonitions and threatened further violence. In the West, many wondered just who spoke for Islam and whether the religion was really at war with itself. As moderate Muslims moved to clarify Islam's teachings and publicly repudiate the extremists, they represented potentially powerful allies for the United States in its war against global terrorist networks. Far from being a war against Islam, as bin Laden argued, the United States could counter that it, along with moderate Muslims, was engaged in a war to defend Islam.

Israelis warned that Americans were fighting the same war of terrorism that they were confronting in their conflict with Palestinians extremists. Many Israeli analysts were careful not to castigate all of Islam even as they called Israel and the United States to cooperate in an all-out assault on Palestinian and Muslim extremism. But an essential question remained: Were Americans really facing the same threat of suicide bombers and other acts of terrorism as the Israelis? Was the threat against the United States directly related to its support of the Jewish state? Were there lessons to be learned from Israel's tactics in fighting Islam's *istishhadi*, "one who martyrs himself," the Arab term for suicide bomber? Or were Americans facing a different, pervasive threat, one that would persist even after the resolution of the Israeli-Palestinian conflict?

This book attempts to address these questions as well as those raised by the Reverend Smith from his pulpit on that cold January morning. Based on dozens of personal interviews with Islamic scholars around the world, this book looks at what they say are Islam's teachings on martyrdom and how extremists have twisted those teachings to justify attacks against innocents. And from personal interviews throughout the Middle East, it also examines the lives and deaths of some of the people considered by Muslims to be legitimate martyrs, as well as some whose right to the title is disputed.

Chapter 2, devoted to the story of Mohammed al Dirrah, the Palestinian boy the world watched die on television, and members of the Israeli Schijveschuurder family who died from a suicide bombing, looks at the innocent as symbols of martyrdom. It shows how the conflict in the Middle East has degenerated into tit-for-tat murders of children, both Israeli and Palestinian, making martyrs of children, even infants, and fueling the conflict.

Chapter 3, the story of Mohammad Hosein Fahmideh, another child-martyr, looks at the child-soldier and the role of martyrdom in the world's only Shia state. (Sunni and Shia are the main branches of Islam, divided by differences over who had the right to become leader of the Muslim world after Muhammad's death.) Chapter 4 looks at a different type of martyr in the region—a Christian woman suicide bomber who was the precursor of the Palestinian women who took that path in early 2002.

The heart of the book deals with Islam's teachings on suicide bombers and terrorism, as seen through the stories of Izzidene al Masri, who blew himself up inside a Jerusalem pizzeria, and Mohammed Atta, the leader of the September 11 hijackers. In Chapters 6 and 7, the book offers a provocative look at the people who nurture martyrs—their mothers and their trainers. Chapter 8 offers arguments from counter-terrorism experts on how to defend against martyrdom as a weapon. Finally, Chapter 9 focuses on the real hope—that moderate Muslims will win the ideological battle they are now waging with militants for the soul of Islam.

The book offers insights into the families and societies of the region's martyrs based on interviews with the mothers, relatives, and friends of youths who died as suicide bombers or in battles with Israel.

Some of the most provocative and chilling interviews I conducted were with Palestinian guerrillas in the refugee camps of Jordan and Lebanon, with young men in Gaza and Jenin who said they were prepared to die as martyrs, and with the steely commanders who decide when a young man is ready to become one.

The book also shows the grief and anguish such actions cause innocent people. The death of most of the Schijveschuurder family in a suicide bombing is a symbol of the vulnerability of Israeli children to the vicious inhumanity of bombers who target civilians.

Martyrdom in the Middle East is a phenomenon that engulfs the innocent as well as the warrior. Arabs argue that it is wrought from the misery, oppression, and desperation that is the modern Middle East, but it also fuels that state of misery and desperation. When an innocent child dies, whether Israeli or Palestinian, people lust for revenge and justice, which often leads to a counterattack. When Palestinian gunmen killed ten-month-old Shalhevet Pass in Hebron on March 26, 2001, Jewish settlers there were determined to exact revenge, and they did. Two months later, they killed Dhiya Tmaizi, a three-month-old Palestinian boy. And the death of the eleven-year-old Palestinian boy Mohammed al Dirrah in his father's arms in October 2001 under a hail of Israeli bullets set off a wave of attacks against Israelis to avenge his death, which in turn led to Israeli reprisals and more misery.

Al Dirrah, huddled and crying against his father, clearly was not a willing martyr. He did not want to die. CNN showed the terror on his face as the bullets flew around him. His death has come to symbolize the vulnerability of the Palestinian people, who honor him as a shaheed.

In this book, I quote from my interviews with key Islamic scholars to offer insights into the religious underpinnings of the glorification of martyrdom in the hope of shedding light on the ways that Islam's teachings may also be used as a force for peace and not only for jihad.

But in dozens of interviews with Islamic scholars, youths, and avowed militants, I have learned that there is clearly a crisis between the Islamic world and the West. It is a conflict Muslim militants expect to last for generations.

"Our grandfathers participated with Saladin in the twelfth century when the Europeans attacked this area . . . the same as they are doing now [through] the Jews," said Ibrahim Ghosheh, spokesman for the Palestinian Islamic group Hamas in Amman, Jordan. King Hussein silenced him after Jordan signed a peace treaty with Israel in 1994.

"I am sure that the result will be the same [as when Saladin defeated the European armies]," Ghosheh continued. "This land will be freed and liberated as it was liberated 800 years ago." Saladin's army exacted revenge for the Christian crusades and returned Jerusalem to Muslim control. Some Muslims are still looking for a modern-day Saladin to reinvigorate their culture and save them from western domination.

Atta and his group saw themselves in just such roles and used Islam to justify the attacks that killed thousands of people and traumatized the world. But in examining Islam's laws, history, and traditions, it is clear that most respected Muslim authorities believe Atta was wrong. They say the September 11 crew was not the latest in the venerable lineage of Islam's martyrs, but were ruthless criminals. Atta and his band were murderers, Islam's leading scholars agree, *not* martyrs.

Webster's New Universal Unabridged Dictionary defines a martyr as "a person who chooses to suffer or die rather than give up his faith or his principles; a person who is tortured or killed because of his beliefs; a person who suffers great pain or misery for a long time." In the West, a martyr is generally a pacifist who suffers and dies but does not kill. Christian history is filled with officially proclaimed saints who withstood persecution and willingly died out of loyalty to their faith, people such as St. Stephen, John the Baptist, or Christ himself.

Jewish history is filled with stories of people who died for their faith. One of the best known is that of Masada, in which Jewish zealots decided to kill each other rather than face capture by the Romans in the first century. All of the estimated 1,000 men, women and children inside the fortress over the Dead Sea were killed or committed suicide in the siege.

Christian history also offers an example of the zealot-martyr, one that is close to the Islamic ideal of the warrior-martyr. Joan of Arc, an undeniable fanatic who killed and was willing to die on the battlefield to defend her God and her dauphin.

In Islam, the definition of a shaheed also includes several types of death. The word *shaheed* is commonly used to describe everyone from innocent children killed in war to gunmen opening fire in a crowded marketplace, even if such usage may not adhere to the religion's true teachings. Martyrdom is a powerful concept in the modern Muslim world, one that summons the earliest days of Islam's turbulent history in the seventh century, when followers of a man called Muhammad died defending their new, persecuted faith. In fact, the word for martyr in Arabic has the same root as the word—

shahida—meaning to witness or testify. In a testimony of faith, each Muslim publicly states what is known as the *shahada*, proclaiming that there is no God but God and that Muhammad was His prophet.

But although Islam's definition of martyrdom is different from that of the Christian West, there are nevertheless certain criteria that must be met before someone can be legally declared a martyr. Many of the Islamic scholars I interviewed for this book said a shaheed is anyone who is killed as a result of oppression or persecution. They said everyone who dies in the midst of battle defending his homeland or fighting evil is worthy of the ranks of the shuhada. Shuhada abide by Islam's teachings on just war, which exclude harming women and children and which some authorities contend exclude suicide. The *Islamic Desk Reference* defines a martyr as someone who "seals his belief with his death."[1]

Ayatullah Mohadghegh Damad, an Iranian Islamic jurist of considerable repute, especially among Iran's Shias, said Islam has clear rules for war and "everybody who is killed is not a shaheed." His teachings do not differ significantly from those held by many scholars of Sunni Islam, which is the religion's largest branch. According to Damad, a shaheed should be killed in battle when there is fighting or by the enemy when its soldiers invade Muslim territory. A shaheed is also someone who dies in a battle under the order of an *imam*, an acknowledged religious leader, Damad said.

In some ways, western and Islamic definitions of martyrdom are not that different; both respect those who are willing to lay down their lives for their principles, their faith, or their religion. The divergence comes when martyrs claiming to represent Islam also maim and kill. The issue of martyrdom in extreme forms is a manifestation of the Western-Islamic divide, and it is a key component of the terrorist threat facing the United States.

Americans may have a hard time equating suicide bombers with anything sacred. To Americans they are the personification of evil; they do not deserve any attempt to understand their motives. But when dealing with an enemy as ruthless as bin Laden and Atta it is important to fully understand them, to analyze their philosophies and their motivations, in order to develop the most effective tactics to defeat them. We Americans are ill served by half-truths or false stereotypes that would lead us to pursue policies destined to failed. For that reason, I offer unvarnished, uncomfortable, and sometimes disturbing information about the perspectives of Islamic militants. I do so in the hope that, by better understanding them, we will be more able to defeat them.

The regrettable truth is that it will not be an easy victory. Militants find easy recruits in the dust and dilapidation of refugee camps in Jordan, Lebanon, and Gaza and in the rat-infested squalor of Egyptian slums. And many who would never join them, who recoil at the use of Islam to defend such horror, much as Christians recoil at the Ku Klux Klan's claim to be followers of Jesus, say they share the rage that nurtures such evil, that turns young men and women into shuhada. Martyrs.

It is the word that Iranians used to describe the suicidal waves of youths they sent against Iraq in their eight-year war, 1980 to 1988, against Saddam Hussein. And it is the word that Palestinians used to praise the young men who die fighting the Israelis, including those who strap on explosives and obliterate their own bodies.

Shuhada. Martyrs.

The threat of martyrdom as a weapon against the United States would be dangerous enough if the threat came only from the world's poor and oppressed. But the people plotting and sowing vengeance against the United States are not only the illiterate desert nomads or Cairo's garbage-collecting *zebaleen* but part of the Arab elite. Bin Laden's wealthy family monopolized the construction industry in Saudi Arabia, and the reported brain of al Qaeda, Dr. Ayman Zawahri, was an established Egyptian physician-turned-holy warrior who fled his homeland to pursue a wider jihad against the United States from Afghanistan. Over the past few decades the Arab world's dispossessed and its educated elite have been moving closer together in their disdain of what they describe as the despotism of their governments and American domination of their world.

Even nonviolent and not particularly religious Arab intellectuals in the universities of Amman and Cairo, Pakistani businessmen, and Indonesian entrepreneurs speak with the same venom as the militants about the United States, embittered over what they see as U.S. indifference to the suffering of thousands of Palestinians and to the abuses of monarchs and despots that the United States is helping to maintain in power throughout the Arab world. They condemn acts of violence but also say they understand how a young Palestinian, Egyptian or Saudi, fed up with leaders who seemed to do the "evil" bidding of the United States, evolves into a gun-toting militant or into a single, determined, suicidal shaheed. Martyr.

At a conference on the Middle East that I attended in Washington D.C. shortly after September 11, one apparently well-educated and well-spoken

Arab intellectual put it succinctly: "America should understand how dangerous the situation is. When the vodka-drinking Arab and the Islamic militant
find common ground, you know there is a real problem."

In fact, it is hard to find anyone in the Middle East outside of Israel who
supports U.S. foreign policy in the region, even as they lambaste extremists
who are killing in the name of religion. Even Arab leaders such as King Abdullah of Jordan, Crown Prince Abdullah of Saudi Arabia, and Egyptian
president Hosni Mubarak, whose own regimes are threatened by Islamic militants, condemn the United States for what they see as a shortsighted foreign
policy in the Arab-Israeli conflict. They complain that U.S. bias toward Israel
is creating unrest inside their own countries as their people demand that
their governments do something to help the Palestinians even if it means
breaking with the United States.

On the Arab street, people are bitter over the apparent impotence of
their own leaders to pressure the United States to force Israeli prime minister
Ariel Sharon to pull Israeli tanks and troops out of the West Bank. But they
are also growing angrier at the lack of democracy and accountability in their
governments, which the United States supports both financially and militarily. In fact, many Arabs blame the United States for preventing the kind of
change the region needs to become democratic, open societies governed by
the rule of law.

Islamists, those Muslim scholars who want Islam's principles applied to
all aspects of life, want the United States to stop supporting dictators and
monarchs in the region and preventing the revolutions that they believe
would bring Islamic governments to power.

Islamic moderates have theories about a form of democracy based on the
Islamic concept of *shurah,* or consultation among elected officials, which they
are certain would cultivate an enlightened, tolerant, and moral society. Extremists want to see a strict Islamic state rule all of the Middle East, if not the
world, under a caliphate, or supreme leader, similar to the role the late Ayatullah Ruhollah Khomeini and that Ayatullah Ali Khamenei now plays in Iran.

Not everyone believes that if elections were free and fair in the Middle
East, people would necessarily vote in Islamic parties, but in most countries
there are very few viable alternatives. The regimes in control have quashed
their secular opponents just as they have tried to eliminate the moderate political religious groups. But they have been unable to eliminate the religiously
based opposition groups or the underground militants. While the govern-

ments can prevent secular opponents from holding meetings, they are unable to stop people from assembling in mosques, which is where the militants recruit their angry young men and women, who in turn recruit their own trusted relatives into tight-knit cells committed to jihad against their states even unto death.

Egyptian president Mubarak brutally pursued al Jihad and al Gamaa al Islamiya, the Islamic militant groups that wrecked havoc in his country during the 1980s. The groups' leaders, Jihad's Zawahri and al Gamma's AbuYasir Rifa'i Ahmad Taha, fled Egypt, then ended up uniting with bin Laden and leaders of other *jihadee*, or holy warrior groups in Afghanistan to unleash their terror on the rest of the world.

And while the prospect of Islamic governments throughout the Middle East may not seem an inviting prospect from a Western perspective, it is not so forbidding for many people there. Unlike in the West, many Muslims see much to admire in Iran's struggle toward a viable Islamic democracy that could stand up to the United States when their own leaders cowered. Many Arabs believe they could do no worse than current leaders such as Mubarak, who have kept their world in a state of perpetual decline, stifling dissent, rigging elections when they take place, lining the pockets of their cronies, and maintaining a system that provides few opportunities for smart, ambitious, and increasingly better-educated youths. All thanks to the United States, as many Arabs see it.

Analysts such as Abdullah Hassanat, the editor of the *Jordan Times* and a member of the Jordanian elite, warned about the anger building in the Arab world. Thousands of people in Egypt and Jordan were without jobs, living in poverty and unable to see the fruits of their countries' peace treaties with Israel and the United States, he said in an interview I conducted with him.

Islamic militants "are basically expressing in many ways a contention in the Arab and Muslim world that the deal we are having with the West in the region is not a fair deal," said Hassanat, who was widely castigated in his country after visiting Israel in October 1999. Although Jordan had signed a peace treaty with Israel, many people in the kingdom had not accepted it.

"The economy is bad everywhere in the region . . . the Saudis are even talking about imposing taxes for the first time in history," he said. "These are very stringent measures," which he warned were likely to increase the unpopularity of the regime and increase tensions. "Our oil is now worth nothing, and most of it goes back to the West to buy weapons," Hassanat complained.

Although Palestinians repeatedly have called for U.S. mediation, many Arabs believe the United States is against them in their dispute with the Israelis. And because the Israeli-Palestinian dispute involves land holy to Jews, Muslims, and Christians, the conflict is an international one that is not only about power, territory, and control, but about God himself.

Islamic militants from Egypt, Yemen, Saudi Arabia, and even Indonesia have taken up the Palestinian cause, just as they took up the Afghan cause, and rushed to help Muslim fighters evict the infidel Soviets from their land. But this time the land they are fighting to liberate is sacred. Muslims believe God spoke to them in Jerusalem and that they must control the sites that commemorate that event. According to Muslims, it was at the Haram al Sharif (Noble Sanctuary) that Muhammad ascended into heaven in his heralded "Night Journey," during which he received from Allah the basic tenets of the world's new religion.

But Jews also have a long and passionate connection to God in Jerusalem—one that evangelical Christians such as many inside First Baptist strongly supported. Jews and Christians also believed that the ruins of Judaism's holiest site, the Temple of Solomon, rest under the Haram al Sharif, which Jews call the Temple Mount. Below the Haram al Sharif-Temple Mount is the Western Wall, considered part of the foundation of Solomon's Temple, also called the Wailing Wall. Jews who pray at the wall, sticking their written supplications into the cracks between the ancient stones, present easy targets for rock-throwing Arab youths glaring down at them from the Haram al Sharif. The area has long been a flashpoint for Palestinian-Israeli clashes, which is why Israel had prohibited Jews from setting foot on the mount.

But Ariel Sharon, then leader of Israel's hard-line Likud party, stepped here on September 28, 2000, angering Palestinians who saw it as an act of provocation and touching off what became known as the second *intifada*, or uprising.

Palestinian militants are convinced that martyrdom is their ultimate weapon against the Israelis, whose very existence, they believe, depends on support from the United States. In the West Bank and Gaza, Hamas spiritual leader Sheikh Ahmed Yassin encourages young men to fulfill their duties as jihadees and suicide bombers in the war against Israel. Yet, like the futility of Jim Brown's rampage, martyrdom has not brought Palestinians any closer to achieving their long-sought state and has even worsened their condition, with Israeli troops bombing and reoccupying cities in the West Bank and the death toll growing. Somehow, though, Palestinian extremists continue to believe that bloodshed will help them reach their goals. Interviewed shortly before the Palestinian Authority placed him under house arrest in December 2001, Yassin and many other Palestinians, including those close to Palestinian leader Yasser Arafat, said Sharon's policies had fueled their conviction that the only effective dialogue with Israel was through war and martyrdom.

As if the Jewish-Muslim rivalry over this holy land were not enough, Jesus, whom Christians believe to be God incarnate, preached, and was crucified, buried, and resurrected in Jerusalem. Through the ages, Christians, too, launched brutal and bloody wars to control the city, until they were decisively routed by Saladin. It remained in Muslim control until the Ottoman Empire disintegrated after World War I. Then, in 1948, the western portion of the city became a part of the newly declared state of Israel in what Palestinians call *al Nakbah*, the catastrophe. The Old City and the rest of Eastern Jerusalem remained under the control of Jordan. In the Six-Day War of 1967, all of the West Bank and Gaza, as well as the Golan Heights, and all of East Jerusalem fell under Israeli control. East Jerusalem is predominantly Palestinian and holds the Haram al Sharif, site of the al-Aqsa mosque complex, one of Islam's holiest places. In 1973 the Arabs failed in their bid to recapture the land Israel won, leaving them demoralized and embittered.

After 1973—many would argue that it happened even before then—Arabs began searching for another solution to their problem with the Israelis and their powerful western backers. They looked back to the apex of their glorious history when they were the world's most vibrant civilization, stretching even into Europe. When Europe was still wallowing in the Middle Ages, the Islamic world boasted a civilization whose great poets, scientists, mathematicians, astronomers, and architects set new standards of genius. Muslims could not help but wonder what had happened. How did they come to be dominated by the West, unable to contain what they saw as the aggression of a tiny, hostile country in their midst, with their culture and religion under siege? Some argued that the solution to Arab misery could be found only in returning to the roots of Islam through a new jihad—both inner and outer jihad, they argued. The individual Muslim had a duty to purge both his inner self as well as his world of all signs of western culture and domination, even if it meant death and martyrdom.

This book explores the despair that has gripped the Middle East and why that despair has led many to embrace the concept of martyrdom, the biggest threat, according to some scholars, facing the United States and the Western world since the Soviet missiles of the cold war. Muslim militants from around the globe have taken a page from the recent history of martyrdom and have turned their shuhada against the United States. The attack on the World Trade Center was the second attempt to strike at the heart of American capitalism, although the first was not a suicide attack. In 1993 militants blew up a van in the garage of the World Trade Center, killing six people and wounding more than a thousand others. The men responsible for that act were caught and received life sentences. The next time militants struck the World Trade Center, they wanted to make sure it was exact and devastating. For that they needed martyrs.

Martyrdom has been used in other attacks against the United States. On April 18, 1983, a suicide bomber drove a small truck loaded with explosives into the U.S. Embassy in Beirut, killing 63 people, including 17 Americans. Only months later, on October 23, 1983, a smiling young man drove an explosives-laden truck into the army barracks at Beirut International Airport, killing himself and 241 servicemen and seriously wounding 80. It was not long before President Ronald Reagan decided to close the base and end U.S. military presence in Lebanon. Some argue that if the United States had stood its ground and declared war against terrorism at that time, events might have been avoided.

On August 3, 1999, the United States suffered one of its worst attacks. Suicide bombers attacked U.S. embassies in Dar es Salaam and in Nairobi, killing 11 in Tanzania and 213 in Kenya. A year later two men in a small boat pulled next to the USS *Cole* in Yemen and blew themselves up, killing 17 U.S. sailors and wounding 39 others. In retaliation for the *Cole* attack, President Bill Clinton bombed both Sudan and Afghanistan and sent hit squads to hunt for bin Laden, whom U.S. authorities believed was responsible for it. Not only did they fail to catch him, but they failed to prevent what years later would become the worst attack on U.S. soil in the nation's history.

Analysts such as Daniel Pipes, who has long urged aggressive action against Islamic extremists around the world, faults the United States for not taking Islamic terrorism seriously and not moving aggressively to fight it after its first manifestations in Lebanon. Pipes dismisses the idea that some Islamists are moderates and considers them all dangerous. Speaking at a conference sponsored by the Washington Institute, a policy think tank, that I attended in October 2001, Pipes said terrorists had more than hatred for the

United States, they had "contempt" for a country they considered arrogant, evil, and impotent.

But Arab analysts argue that terrorism cannot be defeated through military means alone. Many Arabs intellectuals insist that the United States needs to address the underlying issues that are fueling hatred of the United States in the Middle East and luring angry young men into martyrdom. And Arab analysts warn that the September 11 attack is but a painful symptom of an even more serious malaise that will threaten Americans and the western world until it is properly diagnosed and treated. Many in both the Arab world and the west believe that terrorism, especially that propelled by martyrdom, cannot be stopped without eliminating the motivation for such violence. The only way to tackle terrorism, some argue, is to make life more attractive to prospective shuhada than death—to give them more reason to live than to die.

It is true, as this book will show, that many young men and women, such as Izzidene al Masri, who blew himself up inside a Jerusalem pizzeria, are easy prey for the world's bin Ladens because the suffering they see around them daily makes them economically, emotionally, and spiritually vulnerable. Many of the people that al Masri met in the mosques of Jenin had urged him to kill in the name of Islam.

It is true that many people who become Islamic militants have strong religious convictions that make them unafraid of death. But some suicide bombers in conflicts in the Middle East are not even Muslims but Christians. In fact, a young Christian woman fighting the Israelis in Lebanon was among the first suicide bombers in the Middle East. Loula About was a leader, and not a follower, but by taking the path toward martyrdom, her life was both short and tragic. Her story is included in this book.

The issue of whether some youths are duped or coerced into becoming martyrs is an important one. In the video broadcast in the United States in which bin Laden bragged about the mayhem the attack wrought, he laughed that some of the men who participated in the attack did not know they were on "a mission of martyrdom." He was amused at the image of their sudden realization that they were not flying planes to Egypt, Iraq, or Afghanistan but into New York's World Trade Center.

Still, enough of the September 11 band had to be fully aware that they would die striking at the heart of American power. And they were eager to do so, believing that their rage was sanctioned by God. They believed they would be following in the footsteps of Hussein, the martyred grandson of Muhammad, who was killed in A.D. 663 in a famous battle at Karbala, now in Iraq, try-ing to uphold the principles of Islam. What they did not remember is that Hussein did everything he could to avoid fighting and to make peace, even walking onto the battlefield holding a baby in his arms and pleading for mercy.

Islamic militants idolize men such as Izzidene al Qassam, the guerrilla leader heralded as a martyr after he died in a shootout with the British when they ruled Palestine. The Palestinian group Hamas so admired al Qassam that its leaders named its military wing after him.

Extremists also look to the model of Hassan al Banna, the founder of the Muslim Brotherhood, the grandfather of Muslim activist groups. It was founded in 1928 in Egypt and spread throughout the region despite attempts by the power elites to crush them. As the Muslim Brothers aged and grew more moderate and politically savvy, many of its more militant members broke away to form groups committed to armed struggle.

But for Atta and his men, the paramount Islamic ideologue was Sayyid Qutb, who had spent the years 1947 to 1950 in the United States earning a master's degree in education. While Arab leaders such as Egyptian president Gamal Abdel Nasser were advocating Arab unity based on culture and lan-guage, Qutb, one of the Muslim world's most radical thinkers, was preaching Islam as a basis for one *umma*, or Muslim world community. Like many Arabs, Qutb was outraged at the state of the Islamic world and its sub-servience to Western powers. He believed the fault lay with Muslims who had compromised on the principles of their religion and were being ruled by corrupt, greedy, and godless leaders. Through his writings, he roused the Muslim masses to shake off the oppression of their leaders and the West through jihad and return to a strict adherence to Islam's teachings. Islam, he advocated, should be the basis of a new world order. His ideas were so provocative and so dangerous to the region's secular rulers that Nasser had him hanged for subversion.

The names of al Qassam, al Banna, and Qutb are as well known in the Muslim world as Thomas Jefferson or Winston Churchill in the West. Their lives still galvanize millions of people around the world and their deaths still inspire jihad and martyrdom. This book looks at these key figures in the an-cient and recent history of martyrdom in the Islamic world to examine their deep roots in the Muslim consciousness.

Since September 11, Muslim scholars have struggled to clarify Islam's teachings and to explain the difference between terrorism and self-defense, between murder and martyrdom. And they have not always agreed on some of the key questions now dividing the West and Islam. Unlike the role of the pope in Catholicism, there is no leader who speaks for and to all Muslims. Shias, the minority branch of Islam, are expected to take their guidance from learned scholars. The majority Sunni Muslims look to the rulings of acclaimed jurists like Sheikh Qaradawi, based in Qatar, or to authorities like Abdulaziz bin Abdallah al-Sheikh, the leading Islamic scholar in Saudi Arabia. The opinions of these people are important because they shape the thoughts and actions of 1.2 billion Muslims throughout the world.

Now Islam's scholars are heatedly debating issues that affect every American: Were the men who struck at the heart of the greatest power on earth really martyrs to anyone but bin Laden and his colleagues? Were they really the vanguard of Islam, as he proclaimed, brothers in a worldwide network of shuhada who have honed their trade in the region's wars and perfected it in the Arab struggle against Israel? Or were they apostates who defamed Islam and whose actions caused the deaths of thousands of innocent people? This book shows that mainstream interpretations of Islamic texts do not support such actions.

Islam burst upon the earth in 610 when the Archangel Gabriel ordered the illiterate Muhammad to read as he stood shivering in a cave in Mecca. It is rooted in both Judaism and Christianity, and Muslims believe it is actually the perfection of both religions. Through Muhammad, Muslims believe that God spoke again to the world, as he once had through Abraham, Moses, David, and Jesus, all of whom revealed a divine message that Jews and Christians had twisted and adulterated into half-truths. God's love goes out equally to all of mankind, not to a chosen few, they argue, distancing themselves from the exclusionary religion they believe Jews practice. Muslims believe Jesus was one of the greatest prophets who ever lived and Mary was his virgin mother, but to liken Jesus to God and to kneel before a statue of Mary, as some Christians do, is nothing short of heresy, they insist.

When Muhammad ascended into heaven in his "Night Journey" from Jerusalem, he spoke with the biblical prophets who advised him in how to establish the new religion and correct the wrongs of the previous two. It was Moses who pushed him to negotiate with God to reduce the number of prayers he originally mandated for Muslims from a hundred a day to five. And they even discussed whether that number of prayers would be too much, since Jesus' followers had been unable to keep the injunction to pray a mere three times a day.

Through Muhammad, Muslims believe God redirected his faithful to the right path, correcting the abuses that had befallen both religions. Yet Muhammad also saw "the People of the Book," as he called Jews and Christians, bound to Muslims by their descent from Abraham and their profession of belief in one God.

Muslims believe their religion came through the descendants of Abraham through Ishmael, Abraham's son with Hagar, his wife's Egyptian handmaid. As the Bible explains, Sarah had been unable to bear a son, so she urged Abraham to sleep with Hagar, planning to adopt as their own the child she would bear. Hagar did indeed bear Ishmael, but later God answered Sarah's prayers and allowed the elderly woman to bear a son. And that is when the trouble began. Sarah asked Abraham to send away Hagar and Ishmael, not wanting Abraham's oldest son to compete with her son Isaac as heir to their father's wealth. God tells Abraham to do as Sarah asked, promising in Genesis 17:20 to protect Hagar and Ishmael: "And as for Ishmael, I have heard thee: Behold, I have blessed him and will make him fruitful and will multiply him exceedingly; twelve princes shall he beget and I will make him a great nation."

Muslims have a different version of the story. Abraham did not abandon Hagar but escorted her to live in what is now Mecca even building her and Ishmael a house—the Kaaba, the focal point of Muslim worship during the annual pilgrimage known as the Hajj. And, they say, it was Ishmael, not Isaac, whom God asked Abraham to sacrifice. To back this up, Muslim scholars note repeated references in the holy texts that the boy offered for sacrifice was Abraham's "only son," who could only have been Ishmael before Isaac's birth.

Despite the differences, Muslims hold many of the same basic beliefs as Jews: There is one God, the God of Abraham, Ishmael, Isaac, and Jacob; belief in the biblical prophets and their teachings; and reverence for Jerusalem as a holy city. Muslims also refuse to eat pork, and conservative, devout women fully cover their bodies and their hair to preserve their modesty.

Although Muslims also share similarities with Christians in their belief in one God, they differ from Christians in one key respect. As the Reverend Dr. Martin Luther King Jr. so often reminded his people during the Civil Rights movement, Christ called on Christians to "turn the other cheek," and "do good to them that hate you." But Islam has no such teachings. For Muslims, seeking revenge is not forbidden and exacting justice against one's enemies on earth is not only permitted, but desirable. And while many Muslims insist

Islam is essentially a religion of peace, it is also not afraid of war. The Islamic scholars interviewed for this book repeatedly pointed to one verse in the Qur'an, Surah 2:216: "Warfare is ordained for you, though it is hateful to you; but it may happen that you hate a thing which is good for you, and it may happen that you love a thing which is bad for you. Allah knows, you know not."

The message, they explained, is that God understands things that men do not. And that man may fulfill God's purpose even through war. It is not unlike Christian teachings that hold that God can use what may seem like an unbearable misery to work a greater good; and that he can create beauty from even the greatest evil. Death and war may seem tragedies, but for Muslims, they also lead the way to paradise.

In fact, Islamic scholars say Muslims have a duty to struggle against evil, both within themselves and in the world around them. Militants, including the ones interviewed in this book, argue that because their leaders are corrupt and Muslim land is under siege, each individual is compelled to declare his own personal jihad to liberate that land from western control and to overthrow their corrupt governments. This is a radical departure from traditionally held views that jihad must be declared and directed by a religious leader or by an established Islamic government. But extremists believe that even religious institutions such as Cairo's al Azhar University and rulers of their holiest cities of Mecca and Medina are not truly Islamic and indeed are apostates and thus could not be counted on to defend Islam. Thus it falls to each devout Muslim to fight them. This was clear in the 1998 communiqué that bin Laden and his colleagues issued, a copy of which was faxed to me from the offices of Sheikh Omar Bakri in London: "The ruling to kill the Americans and their allies—civilians and military—is an individual duty for every Muslim who can do it in any country in which it is possible to do it, in order to liberate the al-Aqsa Mosque and the holy mosque [Mecca] from their grip, and in order for their armies to move out of all the lands of Islam, defeated and unable to threaten any Muslim. This is in accordance with the words of Almighty God, 'and fight the pagans all together as they fight you all together,' and 'fight them until there is no more tumult or oppression, and there prevail justice and faith in God.'"

For Muslim extremists, the message is clear. "We are going to have now many freelance Islamic movements who want to attack America, and they will not distinguish between military and civilian targets," said Bakri, shortly after bin Laden's statement was distributed around the world. Bakri once served as the European spokesman for bin Laden's World Islamic Movement.

But bin Laden's philosophy of freelance jihad was a departure from what many moderate Muslim scholars held was Islam's true teachings on the subject.

"The statement attributed to Osama bin Laden that Islamic law makes no distinction between civilians and soldiers in war is flagrant contradiction to generally held Islamic jurisprudence," said Imad-ad-Dean Ahmad, contacted after bin Laden sent his message. Ahmad is president of the Minaret of Freedom, a Maryland-based Islamic think tank that collaborates with Islamic scholars around the world. "The bombers of the U.S. embassies in Kenya and Tanzania are wrong if they think that Islamic law permits the killing of civilian envoys in a third country as a means of war against foreign soldiers on their home territory."

As John Kelsay noted in his book *Islam and War*, " . . . almost all important discussions of jihad over the last 150 years have stressed that it is a war in defense of Islamic values. This is so for Sunni and Shiite scholars alike."[2]

Iran's Ayatullah Mohadghegh Damad said that Islam's teachings on jihad and just war are clear and that it should be defensive. "Everybody who is killed is not a shaheed," he said. "This is very important. . . . If somebody himself attacked the enemy society and the enemy came and killed him, he is not a shaheed." The Qur'an says a shaheed is someone "killed in the way of God," Damad said.

In their early history, Muslims had been called to jihad and martyrdom most often to defend their territory. The first jihads were conducted against the rulers of Mecca who had so persecuted the first of Muhammad's followers and had confiscated the homes and property of those who fled with him to Medina. But some believe as Qutb taught, that jihad could also be conducted to extend the territory of Islam, to bring what is called the *jahilliyah*, those hostile to or ignorant of God's law, under his rule. Traditional Islamic scholars say this type of war is not an individual obligation but a collective, communal responsibility that should be conducted only under the leadership of an established Islamic governing authority. However, Muslim militants engaged in modern jihad are not trying, as Qutb envisioned, to bring the jahilliyah under Islamic law. They believe they are defending Islam from the more powerful jahilliyah. And they argue that there is no legitimate Islamic government in existence that can order a jihad, so individual Muslims are compelled to fight on their own authority.

In Islam, martyrdom is not something to be feared, Muslim authorities agree. In fact, it is to be welcomed as the most beautiful testimony of faith. Muslims scholars have written extensively on the duty of believers to fight and to be ready to die to overcome oppression and corruption in the world. And Muslims around the world, especially in the Middle East, regularly hear imams extol the virtues of martyrdom at Friday prayer. Damad pointed to Surah 4:74 in the Qur'an: "Let those fight in the way of All who sell the life of this world for the other. Whoso fighteth in the way of Allah, be he slain or be he victorious, on him We shall bestow a vast reward."

According to Damad, Islam teaches that the martyr need have no fear of death because he feels no pain as he leaves this life and is transported immediately into the next. Damad also cited Surah 3:169: "Think not of those who are slain in the way of Allah as dead. Nay, they are living. With their Lord they have provision."

In order to understand the new danger facing the United States, Americans must examine Islam's reverence for martyrs and its teachings about war. We must understand how the problems of the Middle East have burned their own shores with all the destructive rage of a volcano's eruption. Only by truly understanding the forces behind terrorism will we be able to develop appropriate strategies to protect our homes and families from the threat of martyrdom.

Israelis warn that Americans are facing the same kind of fear that had made them afraid to put their children on the school bus, afraid to stroll in a shopping center, afraid even to eat pizza in a downtown restaurant. Suicide bombers have struck in all of those places with startling regularity. In the eyes of many Israelis, the region was overrun with religious fanatics willing to commit suicide to terrorize Jews.

But to fully understand the reality of the threat facing Americans, it is important not to be lulled into racist and misleading stereotypes that can thwart real attempts to prevent a repetition of the horror of September 11. Whatever causes, the kind of human suffering rampant in the Middle East is a breeding ground for hatred and anger. Any serious attempt to address the causes of terrorism cannot ignore the reality of life for Palestinians in the West Bank and Gaza, nor can it can ignore the Israelis' valid fears and vulnerabilities in an area they see filled with people willing to commit suicide to "drive them into the sea."

"We are not suicidal," said Labib Kamhawi, a Jordanian political analyst whom I interviewed in Amman during the winter of 2001, less than two months after the attack on the United States. "We are just desperate. And desperate people do desperate things." That is not always the case, as the African American experience has shown. But desperation in the Middle East has frequently led to acts of aggressive martyrdom, not only in the Israeli-Palestinian conflict but in other regional wars, especially the eight-year Iran-Iraq war. It was desperation that the Iranians felt when Iraqi tanks were rolling into the towns of Khorramshahr and Abadan and dropping biological and chemical bombs on the Majnoon Islands and on other towns as the West watched in silence. In fact, Iranians were so desperate to win the war with Iraq that they sent women and children among the "human waves" of martyrs to stop Saddam Hussein.

Many Muslims accuse the United States of policies that have not only wreaked havoc in their societies, but that have perpetuated a similar climate of desperation.

Those who seek a real solution to this problem do themselves a disservice by simply writing off the desperation that is fueling martyrdom in the Middle East as fanaticism or barbarism. It is a dark side that can engulf any people, any race, any religion. Martyrdom and holy war are not exclusive to Islam or to the peoples of the Middle East, as Jewish terrorism expert Barry Rubin argued in an interview for this book.

Kamil Saleebi, head of the Institute for Interfaith Studies in Amman, Jordan, tried to explain the human sources that have propelled so many Muslims toward martyrdom in recent times. "Really there's no difference between us and any other people," Saleebi said in an interview with me only months after September 11. "There is something in any person that respects someone who dies for a cause, who dies for his country."

Marwan Barghouti, head of Yasser Arafat's Fatah group in the West Bank whom Israelis imprisoned during their siege of the West Bank in early 2002, said something similar about Palestinian martyrs when I interviewed him in the Palestinian town of Ramallah on the West Bank only a few months before his arrest: "Everywhere in this world, everyone appreciates people who sacrifice their lives for their homeland; everywhere, not only in Palestine. These people are like holy things, because they gave up their lives for us. They died so that others will have a better life."

The concept of martyrdom is not exclusive to the Middle East. It has been used both in desperate protest and as a weapon elsewhere. For example, the Tamil Tigers used human bombs in their fight for independence from Sri

Lanka. At the end of World War II, fearing they were losing the war they started, Japan sent kamikaze pilots to attack the United States. In South Vietnam during the early 1960's, many Buddhists shocked the world by burning themselves to death in public to protest government oppression of their religion. Even in China, a Falun Gong supporter and her young daughter set themselves on fire on January 23, 2001, to protest China's persecution of the group. And in Northern Ireland, zealots on both sides of the Christian divide have slaughtered with the full recognition that they risked the same fate. Even Catholic and Protestant children were not immune from the brutality.

Christians, with the blessing of their religious leaders, bloodied Jerusalem with thousands of innocent deaths, as Karen Armstrong recounts in her book Jerusalem: "For three days the Crusaders systematically slaughtered about thirty thousand of the inhabitants of Jerusalem. Ten thousands Muslims who had sought sanctuary on the roof of the Aqsa (mosque) were brutally massacred, and Jews were rounded up into their synagogue and put to the sword. There were scarcely any survivors. At the same time, says Fulcher of Chartres, a chaplain in the army, they were cold-bloodedly appropriating property for themselves."[3]

In all-too-recent history, people calling themselves Christians have been guilty of repeating such crimes, slaughtering thousands of Muslims in Bosnia and Kosovo in acts that outraged the world. But even closer to home, the stories of David Koresh in Waco, Texas, and of the Reverend Jim Jones of the Jonestown tragedy provide clear examples of how Christianity, like any religion, can be contorted to lay the foundation for fanaticism and virtual insanity.

Many would argue that virtual insanity has gripped the Middle East, and that, unlike the fringe heresies of Jones and Koresh, it actually has become part of the mainstream, seriously threatening world stability. The region is looking to the United States for leadership, guidance, and protection even as many accused it of promoting injustice, despotism, and terrorism.

As we seek answers to the questions that are now at the core of the post September 11 American psyche, many argue that we must be dispassionate, resolved not to allow our anger at the atrocities committed against us to lead us to wrong conclusions or to an excessive, inhumane response. In the aftermath of the Afghanistan bombings, people around the world are starting to question whether the United States risks becoming the evil it was determined to annihilate. Reports that U.S. bombs struck innocent civilians, including children, tainted the victory that the Bush administration had claimed against al Qaeda. And there are allegations that Americans are mistreating the Taliban and al Qaeda prisoners they captured in the Afghanistan raids, prompting criticism from our European allies.

A poll taken by the Pew Research Center in late 2001 showed that American attitudes toward their government and their relation with the world had been significantly affected by the events of September 11. "While the 9/11 attacks gave Americans a renewed sense of nationhood, they also changed the way the public views the world," Pew's research concluded. "Rather than retreating to a position of increased defensiveness and isolationism, Americans have become more committed to U.S. involvement in the world, and to a multilateral approach to international affairs."[4]

The attacks, according to Pew, "brought unparalleled national unity, and patriotism, but perhaps more importantly and more enduringly, they have once again elevated the importance of nationhood. Washington, the federal government and even its political leadership have new relevance post 9/11." According to the poll, the attacks renewed public trust in government, which had been low prior to the attacks, even as Americans continued to criticize the government for being too wasteful and controlling. Yet clearly Americans were feeling a new sense of unity and patriotism, which tended to stifle criticism of efforts to prevent a recurrence of terrorism in the United States and to punish those believed responsible for it.

But some American religious leaders were starting to speak out against U.S. military action. On January 23, 2002, on the eve of an international gathering of religious leaders in Assisi, Italy, that Pope John Paul II had convened to pray for peace, a coalition of American religious leaders called upon the United States and its allies to work toward solving the political and economic problems that caused terrorism. Among them were the Right Reverend Richard Shimpfky, chair of the Episcopal Church's Standing Commission on Anglican and International Peace with Justice Concerns and bishop of the California Central Coast, Diocese of El Camino Real; Bishop C. Joseph Sprague, Chicago Area of the United Methodist Church; Sister Kathleen Pruitt, CSJP, president of the Leadership Conference for Women Religious, which represents 12,000 congregations of religious women (approximately 76,000 Catholic nuns); and Rabbi Arthur Waskow, director of the Shalom Center in Philadelphia.

"Monstrous situations produce monstrous results," Sprague said in a press conference shortly after the January 23, 2002 meeting. "Military actions provide a kind of seedbed for more fanatical actions from a fringe of persons who are driven at least in part by the actions of the dominant powers."

While avoiding criticism of the Bush administration's decision to go after the terrorists who attacked the United States, Rabbi Waskow, speaking at the same press conference, called attention to the pervasive hostility toward the United States that existed in the Muslim world. "Many act as if there is a choice between dealing with the terrorists themselves and dealing with the pools of despair and anger out of which terrorism can [grow] and has grown," he said. "It is like dealing with malaria; you attempt to end the epidemic with medicine, but you also must drain the standing water. . . . If we want to end terrorism in the long-term, then we must eliminate the pools of cultural deprivation, poverty, and despair."

The rabbi's warnings echoed those that Reverend Smith offered at the King commemoration in his church. As Americans seek to bring the September 11 terrorists to justice, we must be wise enough, he said, not to replicate the evil we so despise. In our quest for justice and understanding of what led to September 11, we must not lash out in anger at Muslims or Jews in our own country and in the Middle East, peoples whose genius, philosophies, religions, and history are at the very core of western civilization, but whose centuries-old conflict is now churning like a hurricane toward our shores.

In the end, the questions posed by religious figures such as Reverend Smith, Rabbi Waskow and Bishop Sprague have served as the basis for this book:

- What have we done that these people hate us so?
- Why would anyone kill himself and thousands of people so brutally?
- And were Mohammad Atta and his partners the vanguard of Islam, as bin Laden claimed? Were they indeed its holy shuhada? Martyrs?

2

THE INNOCENTS:
MOHAMMED AL DIRRAH AND
AVRAHAM YITZAK SCHIJVESCHUURDER

THE COMMON DEFINITION OF A MARTYR IN THE WEST IS SOMEONE who willingly sacrifices his life for a cause. But in the definition that is common in the Middle East, anyone who dies in the midst of battle is considered a martyr. By that definition, Mohammed al Dirrah, Mohammed Hamad Daoud, Dhiya Tmaizi, Shalhevet Pass, and Avraham Yitzhak, and Ra'aya and Hemda Schijveschuurder are all martyrs. And they are all innocents—the most tragic victims of the war between Israelis and Palestinians, or of any war. These martyrs are all children. Two were babies whose fragile bodies were torn apart by snipers' bullets.

Al Dirrah, Daoud, and three-month-old Dhiya were Palestinians. Ten-month-old Shalhevet and the three Schijveschuurder siblings were Israelis. Despite their innocence and their weakness, the youngest of them were targeted for death in calculated revenge killings that both Islam and Judaism repudiate.

The deaths of such innocents have been reduced to a commodity on both sides—used as tools in their propaganda war to win the hearts and minds of people around the world. That is not to minimize the sincere sorrow, bitterness, and anger that Palestinians feel over the death of baby Dhiya or to diminish the outrage that Israelis feel over tiny Shalhevet's murder in her father's arms. But it is also true that both Israelis and Palestinians have tried to advance their causes in the global arena of public opinion by capitalizing on the deaths of their innocents. And, what is perhaps worse, people on both sides have used such tragedies to fan the fires of rage and revenge among their people and to incite further bloodshed and martyrdom.

Al Dirrah may be the best known of the region's child martyrs. His photos were plastered on all of the walls of the alleys leading to his family's home in Gaza's al Bourij refugee camp. There little boys in faded pants several sizes too small and little girls clutching tattered dolls spend their days playing in the dirt streets, dodging donkey carts and rusting, banged-up Mercedeses. The only decorations on the streets of al Bourij are the red, green, and black graffiti deliberately dribbled down dingy, whitewashed stone walls to look like dripping blood. The words scream a simple message—"Mohammed," Palestine's shaheed.

But Mohammed al Dirrah did not intend to die a martyr at age twelve, even though he became for Palestine a perfect shaheed. He died in battle, but he did not die fighting. He was killed, but he attacked no one. And his death won more international support for the Palestinian people than the dozens of suicide bombers who had struck Israel during the second intifada. Many Israelis also have expressed sorrow at the boy's death.

Yet the tragedy on September 30, 200, coming on the second day of eruption of Palestinian unrest in the West Bank and Gaza, enraged Palestinians and helped fuel the uprising and many of the dozens of suicide bombings that came afterward. Hamas, Islamic Jihad, and even members of Arafat's own Fatah organization vowed revenge as al Dirrah's death rallied world sympathy for the Palestinians, especially for their children.

In November 2001, more than a year later, Palestinian militants were still talking about the need to avenge the fifth-grader's death, as if killing more people could restore the boy's life or even erase the horror from his father's memory. For militants, al Dirrah's fate had come to represent more than just one child's suffering. He represented the Palestinian child, crouching beneath his helpless father, who tried but could not save his son. "For the love of God, protect me, Baba," Mohammed cried out as the bullets hit him, according to his father.

People all over the world watched the tragedy of September 30 unfold with their own eyes after a French television crew captured it on film. They watched a boy in faded blue jeans and a T-shirt die, even as they hoped against hope that this drama would have a happy ending. Millions saw Mohammed al Dirrah terrified and sobbing as he huddled with his father in front of a brick wall, shielded only by a water barrel that provided no barrier from the hail of bullets exchanged between Israelis and Palestinians. Mohammed's father was left paralyzed and mentally scarred for life. But Mohammed died where he fell, on Shuhada Road, Martyrs' Road, named for the hundreds of Palestinian martyrs, many as innocent as he.

Mohammed al Dirrah would be only the first of dozens of Palestinian children to die in what many have dubbed the al-Aqsa intifada. The world was appalled at the killing that was engulfing children on both sides. Less than a month after the boy's death, United Nations Secretary General Kofi Annan issued this statement after another bloody day of clashes: "The news of the West Bank violence this morning was chilling. It comes on top of two weeks of tragedy, during which over 100 people were killed and 1,000 wounded—mostly Palestinians, but also Israelis. We are at risk of seeing a dangerous situation escalate to a crisis that could destabilize an entire region.

"I appeal to all—leaders and citizens alike—to stop and think about what they are doing today and what kind of tomorrow they want for their children. Violence breeds violence. I urge you to opt for restraint."[1]

Annan's words fell on deaf ears.

On March 26, 2001 Palestinian gunmen opened fire on Jewish settlers in the divided city of Hebron, striking ten-month-old Shalhevet Pass as her father cradled her in his arms. This attack also outraged many people around the world and reinforced Israel's charges of the inhumanity of Palestinian terrorism.

Raanan Gissen, spokesman for Israeli Prime Minister Ariel Sharon, told reporters that the baby's murder was deliberate. "This was a premeditated murder in which a sniper put his crosshair on the head of a baby girl and blew it off." Israeli and Palestinian gunmen exchanged fire after the baby's killing, and Jewish militants from the community of Qiryat Arba even clashed with Israeli troops as the former tried to enter Abu Sneina, the Palestinian neighborhood from where they believed the shots had been fired.

Benjamin Ben-Eliezer, the Israeli defense minister, called on the settlers to control their anger. "The cruel murder of Shalhevet Pass is a hard blow," he said, "but we cannot lower ourselves to the level of her murderers." Noble sentiments, but not everyone felt that way. Jewish extremists cried out for revenge, and a Palestinian baby became their next victim.

Dhiya Tmaizi was only three months old when Jewish settlers killed him; his twenty-year-old uncle, Mohammed Tmaizi; and another relative, Mohammed Salameh Tmaizi, also twenty. The three were riding in a car near the village of Ethnam, not far from Hebron, in July when gunmen sprayed their car with bullets. Five other people in the vehicle also were wounded. The Committee for Road Safety, a militant Jewish group believed to have organized in 1989, claimed responsibility for the baby's death.

Israel's foreign minister, Shimon Peres, was outraged at the shooting, as were many Israelis, who look with disdain on the group, "Without warning, these terrible people came and made us look ridiculous," Peres said on an Israel radio station shortly after the incident. "They have brought shame upon the Jewish people."

The Committee for Road Safety was linked to the Kach movement that had been led by Meir Kahane, a U.S.-born rabbi who was killed by an Egyptian in New York in 1990. Kach advocated expulsion of Palestinians from the West Bank. Most Israelis despised such extremists, and Israel had outlawed the group.

Dhiya Tmaizi was the youngest person killed in the first two years of the second intifada. His martyrdom provoked Palestinians to launch another wave of suicide bombings and shooting attacks to avenge his murder, which in turn provoked Prime Minister Sharon to send troops into the Palestinian villages of Jenin, Ramallah, and Beit Sahour to hunt down militants. Within months the suicide bombings had escalated so much that Sharon had ordered Israeli troops to reoccupy portions of the West Bank where many remained for months. President George W. Bush had severed diplomatic contact with Palestinian leader Yasser Arafat, blaming him for not doing more to stop attacks against Israel; according to Palestinian militants, this confirmed their contentions that the United States was not an honest broker in the Middle East dispute. They accused Bush of caring more about Israeli dead than the larger number of dead on the Palestinian side. As much as Israelis and their children had suffered from the suicide bombings of the intifada, more Palestinians and their children had died from Israeli attacks, they argued. But Israelis countered that repeated Palestinian attacks and suicide bombings had created conditions that put Palestinian children at risk, and they called on Arafat to rein in the militants. It was not clear if Arafat wanted to do so or even if he could.

The Defence for Children International, an international non-governmental organization based in Geneva, Switzerland, estimated that between September 2000 and March 2002, more than 230 Palestinian children under the age of 18 had been killed in the Israeli occupation of the West Bank and Gaza. The organization said that more one-third of the Palestinian children killed in the year 2001 were under the age of 12.[2] Some were babies; Iman Hijo was only four months old when she died amid Israeli shelling of the Khan Yunis Gaza refugee camp on May 7, 2001. Her nineteen-year-old mother and several other children were wounded. While the slaughter between Israelis and Palestinians has killed innocents on both sides, the violence has claimed the lives of at least three times more Palestinians than Israelis, many of them children.

"It seems we will not get independence or freedom without the sacrifice of martyrs," said Marwan Barghouti, head of Fatah in the West Bank, said in an interview in Ramallah a few months before he was captured and imprisoned by Israelis during their assault on Palestinian towns in early 2002. "I have attended sixty-four funerals since the second intifada and many of them were small children. It's not something you can really describe with words." Israelis accused Barghouti of orchestrating attacks against Israel and using Palestinian youths to continue the intifada.

Barghouti clearly supported the intifada and he did not deny that children had a role to play in it. "Burying children is painful," he said, "but this is part of the Palestinians' sacrifice. "You know the intifada means painful sacrificing, suffering. It's not an easy thing; it's a war. And we are the victims always."

But Israelis charged it was leaders such as Barghouti who were to blame for the large number of deaths among Palestinian children. There are accusations that families are being paid huge sums of money to send their boys out to throw stones at Israeli soldiers and to get shot and killed in the process. Some Israelis even accuse the Palestinians of deliberately putting their children in harm's way as a propaganda tool against Israel. In an article entitled "The Use of Palestinian Children in the Al-Aqsa Intifada" published by the Jerusalem Center for Public Affairs, Justus Reid Weiner, a human rights lawyer and Scholar-in-Residence at the center, charged: "The Palestinian Authority has intentionally mobilized Palestinian children to man the front line in its struggle against Israel, frequently using them as shields to protect Palestinian gunmen." Weiner, also an adjunct lecturer at Hebrew and Tel Aviv universities, contended: "This mobilization of Palestinian youth has . . . been facilitated by the long-term impact of Palestinian Authority curricula, government-controlled media, and summer camp programs, which indoctrinated the youth for armed confrontation with Israel even prior to the current crisis."[3]

In effect, Weiner and other Israelis charge that Palestinians are deliberately allowing their children to die for their own political purposes and that Israel was not to blame for the large number of children killed in the confrontations with its soldiers. Palestinian leaders such as Barghouti acknowledge that Palestinian youths are among their fighters, but they blame Israel for the oppression that compels such "sacrifices."

Yet some respected Islamic jurists disagreed with Barghouti. Sheikh Saud Ibn Muhammad al Aqili, a lecturer at the King Fahd National Library in Saudi Arabia, went so far as to issue a fatwa against the use of Palestinian children in the intifada that was published in the Arab newspaper al Hayat on April 16, 2001. Al Aqili argued that neither women nor children were obligated to participate in jihad, even defensive jihad. In the early days of Islam, he said, Muhammad did not allow children to fight, no matter the circumstances. They would always be behind the front lines and protected. Al Aqili argued that the "Prophet did not allow them to fight" even in battles that "endangered Islam itself." And he said, "Moreover, Islam defended the souls of non-Muslim children when it forbade the killing of the enemy's women and children."

The contrast between the actions of Muhammad and the Palestinians was clear, al Aqili suggested: "Today . . . we see in the Intifada, children who are less than the age of maturity, thrown unarmed and undefended to be targets for the Jews who are armed from head to toe so that they can hit these children as they wish. The Prophet even forbade the use of animals as targets. So what is there left to say about the Palestinian people who have turned their children into targets?"[4]

Palestinians accuse Jewish settlers in the West Bank and Gaza of similar acts, of deliberately exposing their children to extreme danger by bringing them to live in the midst of thousands of angry Palestinians bent on reclaiming land. Even if Jewish settlers are willing to risk death to take over the land, some argue, bringing children into a war zone is gross negligence. While it is virtually impossible for Palestinian youths to avoid Israeli soldiers inside their own towns and villages, Palestinians say, Jewish settlers do not have to expose their babies to the front lines of the Israeli-Palestinian war. Such arguments seem senseless, however, when confronted with the harsh truth: Extremists on both sides have targeted children and used deaths of innocents to promote their political goals.

Both Palestinian and Israeli children have suffered not only physical but emotional trauma from the war their parents pursue. Israel offers extensive mental and physical health care for its young and for families affected by the violence but Palestinians had few such resources. The Young Men's Christian Association (YMCA) in Beit Sahour, just south of Bethlehem, operates one program to try to help Palestinian children and families with free counseling. As part of the activities of the emergency program, the YMCA has issued a number of publications to guide parents, teachers, and social workers in how to deal with children affected by the daily violence. The YMCA also declared its offices throughout the West Bank to be emergency centers for counseling and documented the torment that many Palestinian children are experiencing as a result of living through war. In addition, it has compiled case studies and put them on its web site for the world to read: Some examples:

Tala is a Palestinian four-year-old child from the Bethlehem area. Upon witnessing her parents' watching the incidents on the TV and noticing that the talk of her parents and neighbors is limited merely to these incidents, she has screamed at her mother, asking her to turn off the TV, since the only things it shows are murder and blood. Tala, who [keeps] close to her mother and refused to play inside or outside the house, has blamed her father for not protecting her since . . . he frequently leaves the house and cannot be found when she is in need for him.

In the village of Ya'bod, Um Mahmood and her family are living in the area of the confrontations with the Israeli Army. Like many other houses of the village, their house is exposed to the shooting and tear bombs. Um Mahmood said that when exposed to the tear gas, her nine-month-old child begins coughing and does not stop until becoming unconscious. "Finding my baby in such a horrible situation, I really feel much horror and fear," said Um Mahmood.

She added, "As soon as the confrontations begin, Bader, my five-year-old child, begins yelling and crying for continuous hours even after the ceasing of these encounters. Besides, Bader has lately refused to play and go anywhere. He does not want to be away from me; actually he keeps holding the edge of my dress. During the night, Bader wakes up saying that he has seen the soldiers entering from the windows, although our house is located in the third floor. We try to relieve his fears and make him feel safe; nevertheless, our attempts have unfortunately never been crowned with success. And when he wakes up in the morning, Bader begins looking for his plastic gun and asks me to fill it with bullets in order to kill the soldiers when they come to our house." Once, when Bader heard his parents' discussion regarding doing shopping for the house, he shouted, "No, don't use the money to buy such things, instead buy a gun for each one of us; we want to defend ourselves." It seems obvious that Bader is indeed so much afraid and has begun looking for means of feeling safe."[5]

In a BBC Online article published April 27, 2002, Dr. Rita Giacaman, associate professor and director of the Institute of Community and Public Health at Bir Zeit University in the West Bank, said that even young Palestinian children who live in the midst of daily warfare are increasingly being motivated to acts of violence out of a sense of desperation.[6] After the Israeli raids on Palestinian towns in April 2002, Palestinian children lived with constant fear and "feeling totally helpless and incapacitated," the report said.

And Mona Zaghrout, who helps run rehabilitation centers in the West Bank and East Jerusalem, said that "children hear houses being shelled at night, they hear of neighbors being killed and fathers who can't work and something goes inside them." Many Palestinian children were showing signs of trauma, Zaghrout said, "such as nightmares, bed-wetting and psychosomatic symptoms—stomach aches, high fevers and rashes—when there is nothing physically wrong with them."[7]

The second intifada, fueled by Palestinian children, had hurt them most of all. Their second Palestinian uprising broke out in September 2000 after Sharon, who only months later would become Israel's prime minister, set foot on what Muslims call the Haram al Sharif (the Noble Sanctuary), the complex that holds the Dome of the Rock and the al-Aqsa mosque, one of Islam's holiest shrines. Muslims believe Muhammad ascended into heaven in his "Night Journey" from the Dome of the Rock. Jews call the same area in Arab East Jerusalem the Temple Mount, as it was originally the site of Solomon's Temple, which the devout believe will be rebuilt before the Messiah comes. The Israeli government had forbidden Jews from stepping onto the Temple Mount to avoid inflaming Muslims. Palestinians had long hated Sharon, Israel's former defense minister, whom they blamed for the deaths of hundreds of Palestinians in the Sabra and Shatilla refugee camps in Lebanon in September 1982. That memory was why Palestinians were so enraged by his stepping onto the Haram al Sharif and declaring that every Jew had "a right to visit the Temple Mount."

Mohammed al Dirrah died in clashes two days after Sharon's visit to the area; he was one of the first children to die in the al-Aqsa uprising. On October 1, Mohammed Nabil Daoud was shot in the head as he ran from Israelis soldiers in Ramallah, about 10 miles north of Jerusalem. Daoud's family lives in a large, comfortable house in al Bireh, near Ramallah, and they had draped a large Palestinian flag over the entrance, a sign of the strong passions within. As in the homes of most Palestinian families that have lost loved ones in clashes with Israelis, the Daouds' freshly painted living room, with its overstuffed chairs and family photos, is a memorial to their thirteen-year-old martyr.

Daoud's mother, forty-two-year-old Munabrahim Daoud, said her son was not involved in throwing stones, but he was near some boys who were doing so. Some of Mohammed's friends told reporters that he threw some stones as well. They said Israeli soldiers struck him twice with rubber-tipped bullets, but that he kept throwing stones. Then an Israeli sniper with live bullets shot him, killing him instantly.

Munabrahim's story was a bit different. "It was the third day of the intifada," she said, "and children were not expecting a lot of trouble." Daoud and a friend were walking near their home when they saw a confrontation developing. As boys will, they ran toward the trouble instead of away from it, eager to see what was happening. It was not the first time Daoud had been curious about clashes between Israeli soldiers and rock-throwing boys. Munabrahim said that sometimes her son had thrown stones with and taunted Israeli soldiers, but not that day, she insisted. That day Daoud was dressed nicely in tailored pants and a pressed shirt, and when he found himself in the middle of trouble, he worried that he would get his clothes dirty and upset his mother.

"He had rolled up his pants legs and sleeves so that they wouldn't get dirty from the mud in the street that day," Munabrahim said. "He hadn't gone there planning to do anything that day, but he got caught up in the trouble." Although Munabrahim said she had been worried about her son going into the streets due to the possibility that Israeli troops would enter the area, she had been unable to keep him at home. The day before, schools were closed, and she had kept her son busy helping her in the garden. "I did it consciously so that he wouldn't go out." But it was too much to expect an adolescent boy to busy himself around the house for a second day. Palestinian boys do not have Nintendo games or nonstop television to command their hours outside of school and to keep them within the relative safety of their homes. At Daoud's age, their youthful adrenaline propels them into streets that can be quiet one minute and filled with Israeli soldiers the next. Boys also are impressed by gun-toting militants they see fighting Israeli soldiers. The boys consider it a mark of patriotism to join the gangs throwing rocks at soldiers armed with machine guns.

When Daoud's school was closed a second day, Munabrahim urged him to study indoors. He did that for a while, but soon he grew restless and told his mother he was going for a walk.

"Two hours later I heard the ambulance sirens," she said.

Daoud had walked to Ramallah's main street and ran into the funeral of a man who had been killed in fighting with the Israelis. A demonstration broke out. Israeli troops were spotted nearby, and some boys started throwing stones at them. "He would get excited. He was a bit of a daredevil," his mother said. "He didn't take it all very seriously."

Suddenly Israeli troops opened fire on boys near Daoud and two were hit. Daoud ran away and tried to jump over a wall to get back home, but he was hit in the head, according to his mother.

Her son was not involved in any militant organizations, she said. In fact, he was a Boy Scout who took school seriously and who excelled in his English studies. The youngest of five children, he also loved being the center of attention. "He was close to me. He would go with me on visits to my friends. He liked to be close to me," she said. "He often used to sleep with me. He was very affectionate. He would come and help me in the morning. He had that innocence of a child. And just at that age when he was coming closer to me, he left us . . .

"He used to write the names of girls that he liked and put it on a piece of paper," she said. "He was a young man in the body of a young boy."

Munabrahim Daoud criticized the world for what she saw as its indifference to the suffering of the Palestinians and to its refusal to enforce UN resolutions that would restrain Israel. In fact, Palestinians consistently criticize what they see as a double standard in international law, with the United States using the United Nations to garner international support against Iraq's invasion of Kuwait but ignoring UN resolutions that called for Israel to withdraw from the West Bank.

On November 22, 1967, the Security Council passed Resolution 242, which called for the withdrawal of Israeli armed forces from territories occupied during the Six Day War. The withdrawal was intended to be in exchange for the "termination of all claims or states of belligerency and respect for and acknowledgment of the sovereignty, territorial integrity, and political independence of every State in the area and their right to live in peace within secure and recognized boundaries free from threats or acts of force."

On October 22, only weeks after 1973 war began on October 6, the United Nations General Assembly passed Resolution 338, calling for an end to the fighting and for negotiations between Israel and the Arab states on the basis of land for peace, which was also the foundation of Resolution 242 and has been the basis for all of the subsequent negotiations. But in November 1975, the United Nations also passed a resolution equating Zionism, the movement that promoted creation of the Jewish state of Israel, with racism, and calling it "a threat to world peace and security." (The UN rescinded that resolution in 1991.) In addition, the UN Commission on Human Rights passed several resolutions in April 2001 condemning what it described as Israel's "disproportionate and indiscriminate" use of force against the Palestinians, which had resulted in many deaths.[8]

The commission also passed a resolution calling on Israel to stop settlement activity in the West Bank and Gaza as well as the expropriation of land, the demolition of houses, and the confiscation of property. It urged Israel to cease these activities and comply with earlier resolutions on these issues. This resolution was approved by a roll call vote of 50. The United States voted against the resolution and Costa Rica abstained.[9]

On December 5, 2001, in Geneva, Mary Robinson, UN High Commissioner for Human Rights, called the world's attention to the gravity of the situation and demanded that international monitors be sent to the region. Robinson called on Palestinians to stop suicide bombings and other attacks against Israelis. But she also criticized Israel for what she described as actions that violated UN resolutions and for policies that ignored internationally accepted standards for the protection of human rights. She pointed to Israeli policies of "collective punishments, such as prolonged siege and closures of the territories and destruction of homes and agricultural land." Such policies had led to "increased poverty and a steady economic decline in the West Bank and in Gaza," conditions that fuel desperation and extremism. And she pointed to Israel's continued building of settlements, which she described as a "catalyst for violence." Robinson noted: "Today there are more than 150 settlements in the West Bank and Gaza inhabited by approximately 380,000 settlers, of whom some 180,000 live in East Jerusalem. Although resolutions of the Security Council, the General Assembly and the Commission on Human Rights have stated that these settlements violate article 49 (6) of the Fourth Geneva Convention, the settlements have undergone considerable expansion since the start of the Oslo Peace process in September 1993."[10]

Robinson called for an international monitoring force in West Bank and Gaza, a proposal that Israel repeatedly rejected. The demands for such a force intensified with the deaths of children such as Daoud. But it was the televised death of another child, Mohammed al Dirrah, that doomed the Oslo peace process and galvanized Palestinian outrage into a second intifada.

Even though the world watched her son die on the nightly news, al Dirrah's mother did not learn of what happened to her husband and son until hours later, when she saw a phalanx of neighbors heading for her home.

"I just started screaming. I realized something had gone wrong," said Amal Zaki Ahmad, a woman in her mid thirties, with fine, dark features and olive skin. "I kept asking them what has happened? What has happened? But no one would tell me."

Interviewed at her tin-roofed home in a narrow alley deep inside a refugee camp in Gaza, Amal sat in a room lined with pillows and mattresses just off the large living room that contained only two cots, a table, and some plastic flowers. The living room was the domain of four small children and their television set blaring out an old American cowboy movie dubbed into Arabic. That room also served as al Dirrah's shrine, with one wall dedicated to a large oil portrait of the boy and photos of both him and his family. Gilded verses from the Qur'an hung near a small plastic bird cage; posters of Arafat, the al-Aqsa mosque; and Iraqi president Saddam Hussein completed the decorations.

But Amal wanted to talk about her son in the room away from the blaring television, in the room where they had placed his body when the shooting stopped and he was brought home for the final time. A few pillows served to soften the cold floor where she sat looking back over her son's short life. It was the same floor on which al Dirrah slept with his brothers and sisters every night. He would simply roll out one of the mattresses when it was time for bed and grab a pillow from the heap along the wall.

Amal said she still didn't know exactly where her son was killed or exactly what time that day. No one had the strength to tell her the details. In fact, she said, no one has said the words "Mohammed is dead" to her to this day. "Mohammed just never came home," she said.

"I was trying to think back over what happened," she said. "It was all so confusing. The house was full of people and someone stepped toward me and said, 'You must have faith in God. You must trust in God. God gave you something and he took it back. Trust in God.'"

Then, they brought al Dirrah's body and laid it in the sitting room facing Mecca. "That was around 3 P.M.," she said. "I don't know when he was killed. Maybe around 11:30 A.M. or 12? The whole family knew but I didn't."

She showed how the body lay diagonally across the room, in the same position she had found him napping only hours before he died. She thought that detail extremely important, meaningful, as if the heavens had sent a warning. As if his death were preordained, part of some master plan.

"He died on a Saturday, the day before was Friday. He had the day off. He didn't have school on Saturday and he gets to play and go out." Amal remembered the smallest details about Mohammed's last days, and like the community around her, she had come to idolize him as "the most special child." She remembered big and little things, how he was the easiest of her seven children to deliver, coming in just ten minutes. How he would put gel in his hair like his father and pretend to shave. And how he seemed to be growing faster during his last months alive.

"In his last days, he had gotten quite tall and he was acting like a young man. It was like he grew up all of a sudden. He liked looking smart and he did all the things all the other boys did, but he did them faster. He knew he didn't have time." At that, Amal dissolved into tears. It took a while for her to regain her composure. Then she was moved to talk about his last night with her, how he ate popcorn before going to bed—"He loved popcorn"—and all the little things he said as he fell asleep.

"He lay with his head on my lap in this room," she said, "and he asked me to massage his head. I did and then I tickled him. That's when I told him to go to sleep. That's enough." He woke up early the day of his death, she said, and grilled onions and tomatoes for breakfast.

"He had a great meal. When I woke up the kids were taking bread from the kitchen and going outside to eat what he had grilled. He had created a picnic outside the door. My children and some neighbors children were eating bread with tomatoes and onions.

"Mohammed's hands were all black from the grilling and he wanted to do more. He went to an aunt's house. . . . All of our family lives in one neighborhood, and they gave him some meat to grill."

After al Dirrah had been to the mosque for prayers, he returned home and took a nap, lying in the sitting room in the same position they placed his body after he died.

"It was strange, as if he was practicing for his death."

Suddenly, Amal remembered it was Ramadan, the holiest month of the Islamic calendar when Muslims fast all day and, and she begged to break away for morning prayers. She returned after only a few minutes to continue her monologue about her youngest son, adjusting a green-flowered scarf to hide her thick, dark hair. Her children scurried near her. Bassam, her youngest at three years old, abandoned the television to sit in her lap, brandishing a toy gun carved out of wood. He used it alternately to scratch at the wall's peeling paint and to shoot at visitors with a mischievous chuckle. In the United States, where adolescent boys have gone on shooting rampages in schools, many parents have forbidden their children toy guns and discourage aggressive games that psychologists say desensitize children to the reality of violence. But in Gaza, where death is pervasive, parents such as Amal gave little thought to the subliminal lessons such games teach. Children there are taught to be tough and they grow accustomed to violence and death long before they reach puberty.

"To me, he was the most beautiful of my children," Amal resumed. "He was generous with his aunts, his friends and all of his family. Whenever he had nuts, he would always hand out some to his family. "For days now, I have been thinking about him," she said. "He was a happy child and at Ramadan he brought life to the house."

Mohammed also was a prankster who loved his home and his family, she said. "He loved to stay in the house and he played a lot. He liked to play tricks and practical jokes."

Amal and her husband were always worried for their children. During these violent days, he had forbidden the children to go outside. Amal seemed the dutiful wife, quiet and obedient to her husband, who often laid down the law to his wife and to his family.

"One night my husband told me to put the door key under my pillow when I slept," she said. It was his way of trying to make sure that none of the children left the house in the morning before their parents had awakened. "So I slept with the door key under my pillow and the next day I awoke to find all the kids outside, except Mohammed." Despite their stringent precautions, Palestinian parents like Amal often find it impossible to protect their children. Most live with the constant threat that their child could be the next to die.

Mohammed was very close to his father Jamal and loved to be with him, Amal said. When her husband announced that he was going to look for a used car, Mohammed jumped at the chance to go with him. "I was cleaning windows when he asked me where his father was going," Amal said. "I said your father is going to buy a car." He was going to ask one of his male relatives to go with him to look for the car, she said, but Mohammed and his father ended up going alone.

"I really didn't know where they were going or where he would buy the car. He didn't usually take the boys to buy a car but this time he did. That day there was a strike and I knew there would be demonstrations and shooting. I thought it was good he would be with his father."

They were in a taxi on the way home when Jewish settlers from the area blocked the road with a demonstration. The two were forced to leave the cab and take another route home. Al Dirrah and his father were walking down Shuhada Road when they found themselves in the middle of a gun battle between Israeli troops and Palestinian gunmen.

Jamal yelled at the Israelis to hold their fire, that there was a child with him, but in the shooting frenzy, they had no way of knowing if Mohammed and his father were innocent passersby or part of the Palestinian gunmen. Jamal al Dirrah yelled to the French camera crew for help, but they could do little more than record the events for history.

The father told reporters afterward that his terrified son nevertheless kept trying to reassure him that they would be okay, even after they both had been struck repeatedly by bullets. Finally, the boy was struck in the chest and collapsed. While Mohammed was dead in a matter of minutes, the shooting continued for three-quarters of an hour, according to his father. In the hail of gunfire, it was really not clear whose bullet actually killed Mohammed al Dirrah.

Initially, Israeli authorities denied responsibility for the killings and said Palestinians shot al Dirrah and his father. Ultimately, however, they conceded that Israeli soldiers had fired the fatal shot and the government issued an apology. The apology offered no comfort for the al Dirrah family or for Palestinians who vowed to avenge his death with more blood.

Only days after al Dirrah's death, another Palestinian child would be killed. Two-year-old Sara Abdelhaq was killed as she rode in the backseat of her father's car near the West Bank town of Nablus. Her father, Abdelazzim, said Israeli gunfire struck his car at least ten times, also injuring his niece who was in the car.

Yet Israeli children also have suffered at the hands of Palestinian gunmen, and suicide bombers have created many martyrs and orphans on the other side. The case of the suicide bombing at the Sbarro Pizzeria on August 9, 2001, is one of all too many examples.

In the Sbarro explosion, eight-year-old Haya Schijveschuurder lost both of her parents, Mordechai and Tzira Schijveschuurder, forty-three and forty-one respectively; her four-year-old brother Avraham Yitzhak and her sisters Ra'aya and Hemda, ages fourteen and two respectively. Haya was lucky, if you can call it that. She was among the estimated 130 wounded, suffering severe burns and cuts from the bomb that Izzidene al Masri, the 23-year-old suicide bomber, packed with nails, bolts and scrap metal. When he walked into the restaurant, he must have passed the baby carriages and heard the cries and laughter of unsuspecting children. In fact, he probably timed his fatal trip to ensure the restaurant would be packed with families.

Many of the people in the Sbarro were "happy" children, as Haya described herself that day during an interview with Israelis authorities shortly after the explosion. They were giggling over hot, gooey cheese pizzas in an afternoon scene not unlike one that might take place in the United States. Except Haya and her family had the misfortune to be in Jerusalem that Thursday at 2 P.M. when al Masri walked in.

As she lay swollen and bandaged in a hospital bed, Israeli authorities filmed Haya and put the video on the Internet for all to see.[11] Clearly, the Israeli government was using her story to sway international public opinion against the Palestinians. The pictures indeed were a powerful testament to the brutality of suicide bombings and the suffering they have brought to Israeli children. Haya talked about seeing her little brother Avraham Yitzak on the floor and of wanting to say good-bye to him because, she said, "I knew we wouldn't be in the same hospital." She called out his name, but little Avraham Yitzak did not respond.

"He didn't answer me," she said. "He just lay there and didn't do anything."

She talked of running out of the building as fast as she could, never believing that she would die in the explosion. And with all the wisdom of a prophet, she talked as if God were speaking directly through her.

"The Lord knows what he's doing," she said. "Nothing will be just for nothing. He wants to tell us that. We need to behave a little better. . . . In the end, soon the Messiah will come. Then all the dead will rise up."

It was startling and moving to see a little girl, her faced scarred, her mouth swollen and bruised, clinging to her belief in God and the resurrection after living through such a nightmare. But what was even more startling was how similar her beliefs seemed to be to those of al Masri, who walked into the restaurant and obliterated her family in the name of God. Both had a strong faith, both were confident that God was aware of their suffering, and both were convinced that death was not the end of life but the path to a new beginning. But al Masri was the killer and Haya's family were among his victims.

The Sbarro bombing was one of the most gruesome attacks ever against Israeli civilians. Knight Ridder newspaper reporter Nomi Morris, was one of the first journalists to get to the scene of the explosion, described the carnage at the Sbarro restaurant as "surreal." Here and there people were sobbing, she said, as sirens wailed. But it was the empty baby carriages that touched her the most. Some were singed from the heat of the explosion, and others lay overturned amid the wreckage of shattered glass, twisted metal and bloody limbs.

"The bodies of the dead and wounded, some without limbs, lay strewn across Jerusalem's busiest intersection at the corner of Jaffa and King George streets," Morris wrote. "The glass front of the pizzeria was blown out, and twisted metal and concrete littered the area. People, some with blood streaming from their faces, ran crying and screaming from the scene."[12]

According to Israel, more than 300 Israelis were killed in Palestinian attacks between September 2000, when the second intifada erupted, and the spring of 2002. The government was providing financial and other help for survivors and for the families of people killed in the attacks.

For his part, Prime Minister Sharon resolved to crush the militants responsible for the carnage, believing peace negotiations were not possible while Palestinians continued to attack Israelis. In a speech he made to the Israeli Knesset (parliament) on April 8, 2002, Sharon took the opportunity to send a strong message to the Palestinian people:

On behalf of the people of Israel, I tell you: we have no quarrel with you. We have no desire to control you or to dictate your fate. We want to live side by side with you in peace, as good neighbors, helping and respecting each other.

But in order for this to happen, you can and must take your fate into your own hands. If you want to seize a place of honor among the family of nations, you must eschew terrorism, the murder of children and the elderly, the terrible violence, the murderous hatred and incitement. Do not surrender to those elements among you who have brought you one disaster after another over the past 55 years, because those same forces—they and not us—will guarantee your next disaster.[13]

Far from soothing Palestinians, however, Sharon's words only inflamed them. That spring saw Israeli troops storming into Palestinian villages in the West Bank and Gaza. In the refugee camp in the town of Jenin, Palestinians alleged that Israeli troops massacred hundreds of innocent civilians. Other reports indicate the number of dead, while significant, was probably under 100. Israel has refused to allow a UN commission to investigate how many people were killed and how they died.

A few months later, Israeli troops laid siege to Arafat's headquarters in Ramallah and arrested dozens of Palestinians believed to be members of Hamas, Islamic Jihad, and Fatah's militant al-Aqsa Martyrs Brigades. Israeli officials even threatened to send Arafat into exile, take over Palestinian areas, and establish new leadership. Still, no one could envision how replacing Arafat would bring more moderate leaders. Despair and rage were fueling not only the militants, but had taken hold of most Palestinians, who saw no point in trying to make peace with a government headed by Ariel Sharon. And the rising toll of innocent martyrs on both sides did nothing to push Israelis and Palestinians back to the peace table. In fact, the tragedies of children such as al Dirrah and Avraham Yitzhak Schijveschuurder seemed only to reinforce the mutual hatred that had caused their deaths.

3

THE CHILD AS SOLDIER-MARTYR:
IRAN'S MOHAMMAD HOSEIN FAHMIDEH

Red death is much better than black life.

—*Ayatullah Ruhollah Khomeini*

THE LONG ENTRANCE HALL TO THE MARTYRS MUSEUM IN TEHRAN is carpeted in blood red and a giant sign overhead proclaims: "In the Name of God of the Martyrs and the Honest." Soft music, hypnotic and monotonous like the lapping of ocean waves, envelops the museum, which is hushed, dimly lit, and somber. Room after room offers photos of fresh-faced boys, some smiling and shown with their mothers; dark-haired, handsome young men and earnest women clothed in the *chador* (black cloak), all killed defending Iran in the war with Iraq or fighting the despotism of Shah Reza Pahlavi.

Along every wall, bits of clothing and personal items are clustered behind glass cases, with copies of the Qur'an, remnants of weapons, and prayerful tributes to lives cut short. The museum is a chilling testament to Islam's warrior-martyrs who died in the revolution against the Shah of Iran and by the thousands in the country's eight-year war initiated by Iraq; each name is typed and catalogued with dates of birth and death.

"The purpose of this museum is to keep alive the stories of the brave people who sacrificed their souls for the goals of the Islamic Revolution and the war with Iraq," said the director of the Martyr's Museum, who identified himself as Javad. "The families donate the items, and we're always in close contact with the families of the martyrs."

Among thousands of names on the museum's list of martyrs is one that has come to symbolize the ideal of martyrdom in modern Iran: Mohammad Hosein Fahmideh, one of the thousands of Iranian volunteers known as the Basiji, the Popular Mobilization Army or People's Army. The Basiji fought to hold off Iraq's invasion of Khorramshahr in September 1980 and they were known for their "human wave" assaults in which youths as young as nine years old as well as middle-aged men volunteered to use their bodies to clear mines that Iraqi soldiers laid along the border.

In Iran, martyrdom is a powerful weapon that is directed not only against the infidel West but against another Muslim country, albeit one ruled by a man Iranians considers an infidel: Saddam Hussein. Yet there are signs that Iranians are preparing to turn the ultimate weapon of martyrdom against themselves. Iran's increasingly freedom-hungry and angry youths are growing bolder in opposing the country's stridently conservative *mullahs* (religious authorities), who are resisting peaceful attempts to reform the government and make them accountable to the people, not only to Allah. Iran's moderates are finding it more and more difficult to prevent what many fear will be an inevitably bloody clash between Iran's militant clerics and the youths who are growing increasingly disillusioned with the go-slow approach to reform.

Few places on earth so revere death and martyrdom as Iran, perhaps because the horror of what they call the "Imposed War" with Iraq is so fresh and the fact that the Shia branch of Islam was founded in the martyrdom of Hussein (also spelled "Hosein" in Iran). While lithe women modeling designer jeans, swimsuits, and even underwear adorn the billboards of American cities, in Tehran, Isfahan, and Qom, public spaces promote religious values and the remembrance of martyrs. Pictures of young men and many women martyrs hang from lampposts or are plastered across walls in cities throughout the country, and artists use public spaces to create memorials to those proclaimed martyrs for Islam. Streets and alleys are named in their honor, and the country's religious leaders are careful to regularly pay homage to those who died helping to create their Islamic republic.

Numerous cemeteries are dedicated exclusively to their memory. In Isfahan alone, the Goleston-e Shohada, the Rose Garden of Martyrs, holds the graves of thousands of people who died in the war. Many of the photos atop the graves show smiling youths, as Iran's army would accept volunteers as young as 14, although, as mentioned earlier, there are reports that children as young as nine were admitted into the Basiji.

Tehran holds what is said to be the world's largest cemetery, the Behesht-e Zahra (Zahra's paradise), named for the Prophet's daughter, who was the mother of the martyr Hussein. With more than 27,000 graves, Behesht-e Zahra is located near the gold-domed mosque that holds the body of Khomeini, and so the whole area has become a pilgrimage site of Iranians from all parts of the country. Memorials at the cemetery, as most in Iran, are startlingly graphic in the photos and depictions of death scenes. Many display photos of bloody corpses and describe the battles in gory detail.

From a Western perspective, Iranians seem obsessed with the macabre. For years one of Tehran's main thoroughfares contained a fountain in which red water overflowed to symbolize the spilled blood of the country's martyrs. It was meant to be a constant reminder of the martyrs' sacrifice. And during the Muslim celebration known as Ashura, Iran's Shias used the commemoration of Hussein's martyrdom to rededicate themselves to the memories of the martyrs of their recent history.

But unlike veterans memorial ceremonies in the West, which might include a marching band, the reading of a poem and maybe a moment of silence in honor of the dead, in Iran, Ashura events are brutally emotional and passionate. Ashura (meaning "tenth") commemorates the tenth day of the Islamic month of Muharram, the fatal day when Muhammad's grandson Hussein met the forces of the ruler Yazid at Karbala. The story of Ashura is tragic and gruesome, inspiring revulsion and anger among all Muslims, especially Shia.

It began with Hussein's move to take over leadership of the Islamic world in A.D. 680 when it had become a position of considerable power, prestige, and wealth. After Muhammad's death in A.D. 632, there had been continuous conflict over who should rule. Some believed that Muhammad's mantle should have passed to Ali, his closest male relative and the husband of his daughter Fatima. The majority voted for Abu Bakr, the first person outside of Muhammad's household to accept the new religion and the man they considered most capable of leadership. Ali eventually became *caliph*, or leader of the Islamic world, only to be assassinated in the continuing power feuds among Muhammad's followers. Ali's son Hasan relinquished his claim to rule, accepting a generous pension from the ambitious and ruthless Muawiya ibn Abi Sufyan, who seized power and founded Islam's Umayyad dynasty. It was Muawiya's son, Yazid, who succeeded to the throne on his father's death and sent his forces to stop Muhammad's second grandson, Hussein, from mounting a challenge to his authority.

Unlike his brother Hasan, Hussein did not turn away from the calls for him to assume what Shias argue was his rightful place as head of the Muslim world. When the people of Kufa, in Iraq, asked Hussein to assume leadership of their town, he reluctantly accepted. Hussein and an entourage of about seventy armed men, along with some women and children, left Mecca for Kufa to begin gathering support for an insurrection against Yazid. But on the tenth day of the month of Muharram, Yazid's forces met Hussein at Karbala and attacked.

Hussein fought like a madman. Before he was killed, an arrow pierced his infant son's brain as he held him in his arms and he saw a favorite nephew's arms sliced off and all of the men in his party killed. Yazid's soldiers then surrounded and tortured Hussein, a direct descendant of the man they revered as God's greatest prophet. In fact, many historians say Hussein even looked like Muhammad, handsome, with olive-brown skin and a serene countenance. Despite the resemblance, Yazid's men were not content to merely kill Hussein. After piercing him with dozens of arrows and slashing him repeatedly, they finally cut off his head and mutilated his body. Some accounts say that Yazid, upon receiving Hussein's head, struck it with his fists or with a stick. A man named Abu Barzah reportedly saw those actions and warned, "Gently, O Caliph! Have I not seen those very lips kissed by the Messenger of God?"[1] Other accounts say it was actually Ubaydu'llah, Yazid's commander in Kufa, who struck the lips of Hussein's severed head and who was reminded about Muhammad's love for Hussein.[2]

Whatever the details, Hussein's death at Karbala split Muslims into two distinct sects, Sunni and Shia, and set the standard of martyrdom in Islam. While today, Sunni Muslims lament Hussein's brutal massacre and are inspired by his example of self-sacrifice, it is the Shia who lament his death as if it happened yesterday.

According to leading Islamic scholars, there are no gradations of martyrdom in Islam, nevertheless, many consider Hussein the preeminent Muslim martyr. During passion plays known as the Taazieh, which re-enact Hussein's death at the battle at Karbala and are held during Ashura commemorations, Iranians express their emotions openly. And in Ashura street celebrations, women in the ubiquitous black chador wail and men beat themselves bloody with chains to share in his suffering. It is similar to the scenes of Jesus' crucifixion reproduced in some countries around the world, and like the graphic depictions of the stages of the cross, in which old women crawl on their knees to share in Christ's suffering. In Iran, even the young flail themselves and fall prostrate in grief.

Ashura mourning sessions are regularly held in Iran to remember Hussein's suffering and death and to promote the reverence of martyrdom. Iran's late Ayatullah Ruhollah Khomeini, who ruled Iran until his death in 1989, encouraged such events for political as well as religious purposes. In a speech he gave on June 20, 1982, to fellow Shia clergy, Khomeini said, "These mourning sessions have developed young men and youths who voluntarily go to the war fronts seeking martyrdom and feel unhappy if they don't achieve it. These Ashura mourning gatherings develop such mothers who urge their sons to go to the war fronts and if they do not return, the mothers wish they had more sons to send or say we have other sons to send to the war fronts."[3]

Shias identify strongly with the death of Hussein, and his martyrdom set the tone for everything that has happened since in their world. Shias are a majority in Iran but a minority within the Islam world and they often have been persecuted by their fellow Muslims because of their insistence that Ali, Muhammad's nephew, was his rightful and chosen successor. The martyrdom of Hussein and the historical persecution of the Shias are at the root of why Ayatullah Khomeini seemed such a dour man. He frowned on cheerful decorations and bright colors and decreed that good Shias should not decorate their homes lavishly. Khomeini believed Muslims have to pay constant homage to Hussein's suffering at Karbala and must be ever mindful of their duty to battle evil within and without.

"An Islamic regime must be serious in every aspect of life," Khomeini said in a radio broadcast in August of 1979, shortly after he led the revolution that ousted the Shah and brought him to power. "There is no fun in Islam. There can be no fun or enjoyment in whatever is serious."[4]

Young Mohammad Hosein Fahmideh, who died in the Iran-Iraq war, represented the best of Shia Islam and its martyrs. Streets throughout the country were named in his honor, as were hospitals, schools, even sports stadiums. Like the death of Muhammad's grandson Hussein, Fahmideh's death symbolized the holiness of self-sacrifice through martyrdom, even for a child. Ayatullah Khomeini bestowed upon Fahmideh the ultimate honor, referring to the adolescent shaheed as "our leader." And he encouraged other youths to follow in his footsteps. "Our leader is that 12-year-old child who threw himself with his little heart against the enemy. He is worth more than a hundred pens and a hundred tongues," Khomeini said.[5]

In September 1980, Iraq sent five armored and mechanized divisions across the Shatt al Arab waterway to invade oil- and mineral-rich southern Iran. Capturing this region would have been a great prize for Saddam Hussein's army. Iran has an estimated 9 to 11 percent of the world's oil reserves and was the fourth largest oil producer, at 3.6 million barrels of oil per day. And Iran, a country about the size of Alaska, is rich in minerals, containing the world's second largest reserves of copper, located largely in the south.

The Iraqis quickly seized several towns in the area, and on November 10, captured Khorramshahr. Fahmideh was among those who tried to stave off the Iraqi troops in fierce house-to-house battles in which thousands of Iraqis and Iranians were killed. A skinny, innocent-looking boy, Fahmideh seemed an unlikely hero. But in the frenzy of men and boys running to meet the Iraqis, he decided to do something rash. He stuck a hand grenade under his shirt, threw himself under an Iraqi tank, and pulled the grenade's pin. His single act emboldened the men around him and inspired the entire nation to risk death rather than see their young republic fall to Iraq's Saddam Hussein.

Almost twenty years later, Iranians were still praising Fahmideh, and his last act was the focal point of Tehran's Martyr's Museum. His story had been heralded by Iranian leaders from the late Ayatullah Khomeini to President Mohammed Khatami and it is retold every year when Iranians commemorate the death of Hussein at Ashura rituals and again when they celebrate the end of their war with Iraq. Iranians believe he represents the noblest values of their culture and of Islam. His death has become a symbol of Iran's determination to defend the state founded in revolution, devoted to Islam, and ostracized by the United States, the country Khomeini once called "the Great Satan."

Fahmideh was one of thousands of boys who were martyred during the Iran-Iraq war. In Iran, there was no draft and there was no need for one. Iraqi troops had invaded the country, and anyone who could fight, did. Yet much of the world was horrified at the sight of young children facing Iraqi tanks and being sent to clear minefields. A culture gap exists between those in the developing world and those in the West, with regard to the role of children. The Western world lambastes child labor and demands that children go to school rather than work long, hard hours. But in India, Pakistan, and even Iran, families often need every member of the household working to stave off starvation. In Thailand and Indonesia, some parents even sell their daughters into prostitution to try to ensure that the rest of the family survives. And when a society's existence is threatened, as Iran's was in its war with Iraq, even children are summoned to the ultimate sacrifice—martyrdom.

Iran's leaders do not see the prevalence of so many child-martyrs as shameful, however. They take pride in the fact that young boys willingly offered their lives to defend their country. And they think every Iranian youth should be prepared to do the same, if not in martyrdom, in dedicating his life to the principles of Iran's Islamic revolution and eschewing what they see as the foolishness of Western youths.

During the Iran-Iraq war, mothers were encouraged to prepare their sons for battle and for martyrdom, which is in keeping with the example set by Hussein. In Khomeini's last will and testament, he heaped special praise on the mothers of martyrs. "Often we hear our women . . . cry out loud, saying that they have given children in the path of God and Islam and are proud of it. They realize that what they get in return is far above the blessings of Heaven, let alone the material things of this world."[6]

Thousands of Iranian youths went to their deaths clearing mines, rushing toward Iraqi soldiers, or exploding themselves against Iraqi tanks. In the long list of names kept by the Martyrs Museum, the dead are categorized by age—under ten years old, between fifteen and nineteen and over sixteen. Although women did not serve on the front lines, scores volunteered to help as nurses or aides, and scores of women also became martyrs, all sanctioned by the Ayatullah. The museum has recorded the martyrdom of 69 women. If some Islamic leaders have reservations about a woman's role in jihad and martyrdom, Khomeini did not. He praised the participation of Iran's women in war:

> We are proud that our women, young and old, regardless of their status, are present and active, side by side with the men, often more active than men, in all scenes including cultural, economic, and military areas. They strive, sometimes more effectively than the men, for the propagation of Islamic teachings. Women who are capable of fighting take military training, which is a major prerequisite for the defence of Islam and the Islamic state. Our women have extricated themselves from the deprivations imposed on them by the enemies of Islam and by the inadequate knowledge of friends of Islamic tenets. They have bravely discarded the superstitions created by enemies through some ignorant preachers. Those women who are unable to fight in the war fronts serve behind the front lines with such ardour and courage that makes the hearts of their men tremble with delight and it

throws fear in the heart of enemies and makes ignorant individuals who are worse than foes shake with anger and fear.[7]

Far from western stereotype of Iranian women as meek and docile, they are involved in all aspects of Iranian society, as lawyers and judges, doctors, engineers, university professors, even soldiers. And they are well represented in Iran's roster of martyrs.

During the Iran-Iraq war, Khomeini often summoned the memory of Muhammad's martyred grandson Hussein, urging Iranians—male and female, children and adults—not to fear death in battle against the evil of Iraq's Saddam Hussein. "Seeing that a cruel ruler is over the people, his holiness clearly stated," Khomeini said in one speech quoting Hussein, "one must rise and oppose that and halt the infliction of cruelty alone, if he must, or with many like-minded men, even if it means fighting a multitude, an army."

The Iran-Iraq war ended when Iran accepted UN Security Council Resolution 598, leading to an August 20, 1988, cease-fire. Conservative estimates are that as many as one million people died, and many more were injured on both sides. The Iraqis suffered an estimated 375,000 casualties, and another 60,000 were taken prisoner by the Iranians. At least 300,000 Iranians were killed and an estimated 500,000 were wounded, out of a total population of, by the war's end, nearly 60 million.

In homage to the sacrifice of Iran's martyrs, Khomeini imbued his Islamic republic with a philosophy of sobriety and asceticism, which he embodied even at the height of his power in Iran. He argued that all leaders should eschew the trappings of luxury and prestige, as did Muhammad and his companions. In one of his speeches before the Iranian revolution, Khomeini drew a sharp contrast between the ostentatious luxury of the Shah and the lifestyle of Muhammad and Ali. Khomeini said:

Whoever has written about how the Holy Prophet himself actually lived has told of how he in fact led a life more simple than that led by the ordinary people in Medina at the time. The Prophet lived in a home built from mud; he lived in a mud-built room within the mosque. He used to ride a donkey and would seat a passenger behind himself. He would discuss religious issues with his passenger during their journey and would give him instruction and guidance.

And then there was Hazrat Amir [Ali, the Prophet's nephew, whom Shias believe should have been his successor]. . . . According to written accounts, Hazrat Amir owned a pelisse made from sheepskin on which he and his wife would sleep at night. During the day he would use this sheepskin on which to scatter grass for his camels to eat. . . . He probably never once ate a wholesome piece of bread in his life . . . the Hazrat's diet was such that he would seal the lid of the container in which barley bread was kept in order to ensure that no one would open it up and add something to bread to make it more pleasant to the taste.[8]

Khomeini's small and sparsely furnished apartment in Tehran has become a virtual shrine since he died on June 3, 1989, from heart disease and stomach cancer. Khomeini and his wife shared a kitchen, a bedroom, and a tiny living room that contained a sofa and table. A round mirror hung behind the sofa, some books on a shelf, and on the table was a microphone in which Khomeini recorded his sermons. The one allowance to beauty was on the floor, an exquisite green-and-red Persian carpet with an elaborate medallion design at its center.

"He lived very simply," explained Hussein Nikoufal, an elderly man who has the honor of showing visitors around Khomeini's home. He had a passion for learning and for staying informed, Nikoufal said. "Every day he read all the newspapers in Iran."

Khomeini also regularly listened to the radio and picked up broadcasts from the United States, Great Britain, and Israel, Nikoufal said. But unlike his image in the West as a close-minded fanatic, Iranians consider Khomeini a man of keen intellect and tolerance who was greatly interested in other cultures. Much like George Washington is considered the father of the United States, Khomeini is considered the father of modern-day Iran; unlike Washington, he has the added benefit of being a symbol of holiness.

"He really wanted dialogue among people. He wanted a dialogue with Christians," Nikoufal said. "His idea was renewal of all religion, not just Islam."

A corridor led from Khomeini's apartment over an alley into a balcony of the mosque where he led prayers and offered guidance to his followers. After his death, pilgrims and schoolchildren regularly visited the mosque where he preached and prayed, studying his words and trying to gain insights from his teachings.

Khomeini's attitude toward asceticism and seriousness in life is evident in his country. In public, Iranians talk in hushed tones; any outburst of public laughter is discomfiting and emotions are reserved for serious matters such as protests, revolutions, and Ashura celebrations.

Khomeini frowned on the lavish living that once went on inside the palaces of the Shah's elite families in Tehran. After the revolution, the palaces were transformed into government offices; only the elaborate architecture and grand rooms attested to a former grandeur. Khomeini discouraged Iranians from spending money and effort decorating their homes, believing such activities were mere frivolity.

The campaign against fun and pleasure seems to be a losing battle in some quarters, however. There are signs everywhere that many of Iran's youths are eager for more freedom and are growing weary of their elders' preoccupation with suffering. In order to deal with such heresy, the Basiji have found a new post-war role and they use the memories of their martyrs to increase the power they exert in everyday life. They are desperately trying to hold the strict conservative line, determined to preserve their version of the pure Islamic state they have fought so hard to defend.

Because so many Basiji have been martyred, the volunteer force has earned both respect and fear in Iranian society. They have also become a religious police, prowling the streets looking for any behavior, dress, or speech that violates what they see as Islam's teachings. The Basiji have the power to intimidate, threaten, and arrest, and they use that power to keep Iranian youths in check. On Fridays, when the young people of Tehran head into the mountains over the city to "picnic," their term for eyeing the opposite sex, clandestinely meeting boyfriends and girlfriends and listening to pop music—guards are always posted in strategic locations to watch for the Basiji.

One Iranian woman from a well-connected and respectable family remembered how the Basiji had been responsible for her being beaten for not having her hair covered in public. She said she was working in a travel agency, and the women had grown used to simply taking off their scarves in the back offices. One day the Basiji burst into the offices and found her uncovered. Confident that her family connections would protect her, she answered the summons to appear at a government office for her punishment. She was mortified when a stern woman greeted her and asked her if she had any explanation for not wearing her scarf.

"I told her no, I didn't have any explanation," she said a bit cockily; she was still sure she would not face any punishment. The woman then told her to lie down, and she proceeded to lash her several times with a thick leather strap. "They let me keep my chador on, so my clothes actually protected me," she said. "But it was humiliating. I was hurt more from the humiliation than from the blows."

The experience was so sobering that she never again took off her head-scarf outside of her home. She makes sure her oldest daughters are always adequately covered and as soon as her youngest daughter turned nine, she insisted that the girl don a scarf outside of the home to ward off any overzealous Basiji.

Despite their place of honor in Iran's history, the Basiji have become a major nuisance to many Iranian youths who do not feel that devotion to Islam or to their country should mean depriving themselves of fun or occasional youthful public frivolity. Iran's young people did not live through the revolution and many have no real memory even of the war with Iraq. They are well aware of how American and European teens live and many yearn for that kind of freedom.

Two decades after their parents revolted against the excesses of the then-ruling Shah's pageants and palaces, Iran's young people are increasingly risking jail, fines, and official beatings for things Western youths take for granted: wearing makeup, slow dancing at a party, dating and holding hands, and more. In fact, some of Iran's teenagers get drunk, smoke opium, and shoot heroin—even in public downtown shopping malls. Many parents lament the drug epidemic that seems to be sweeping through their country even as they assure themselves that their own children are good Muslims.

Romance between unmarried men and women is illegal in Iran—a couple can not even get a hotel room without producing a marriage license. Late one night, a young man in Tehran approached a car containing a married couple and asked if they would help him get a room for himself and his wife. He explained they were visiting the city and had forgotten to bring their marriage license with them. No hotel would give them a room.

"It could be that it's a true story," the couple in the car said, "but it's also possible that he and his girlfriend are trying to get a room." They decided not to help him.

Despite the obstacles, many young people in Iran find ways to date, even though it, too, is punishable by whipping or a jail sentence. It is also common for Iranian girls and boys to dance together—and even drink—at parties in private homes, even though the feared Basiji have been known to burst in uninvited and arrest everyone in sight, beating them even before their sentencing.

In fact, young people have become more daring since Mohammed Khatami was elected president in 1997 on a platform of moderation and democratic reform—as his conservative critics have noted. Many girls wear as much makeup as an American rock star, exposing more and more hennaed hair under flowered Chanel scarves and showing off painted toenails under black chadors. An increasing number do not even bother with chadors and have created a new Islamic fashion industry around loose coats and slacks.

Nowhere is the new atmosphere clearer than in the mountains around Tehran, where young people hike to escape the city's pollution—and their parents. One morning at a café high atop the mountains, dozens of teenagers listened to music and even flirted. Iran's government has forbidden unmarried men and women from touching, but one girl playfully slapped a boy who tried to pull down her scarf. They ended up chasing each other into the mountain brush.

Under one tree, a girl arched her back against the trunk and smiled into the eyes of her boyfriend, close enough to feel his breath on her face.

On the other side of the tree, the girl's young cousin was equally enthralled with a curly-haired, green-eyed lad in tight blue jeans, the perfect Iranian John Travolta. "We come here to relax and to have some fun," 18-year-old Marah said with a giggle, glancing at Korosh. "He's my boyfriend. We've been dating for seven months."

Korosh and Marah met at a Tehran shopping mall that's popular with young people, especially with those looking for drugs, they said. "We don't use drugs, but we know a lot of kids who are addicted," Marah said. "I think more and more are doing it."

Older people, those who well remember the misery of life under the Shah and the bloody war with Iraq, complain that Iranian youths have lost their sense of purpose. They don't seem to care about religion, and many are obsessed with imitating the clothes and "cool" of their Western counterparts. But parents have few answers to what is widely considered a problem. Iran's smart and sophisticated youths have no problem easily deceiving their parents, who are still reeling from the trauma they lived through years ago.

Marah's parents don't know she is dating Korosh. When she goes to the mountains each weekend to see him, they never question her. They don't even seem to notice the flowery scarf and the layers of makeup she painstakingly applies before each rendezvous.

"My parents know about Marah," Korosh said coolly. "Boys don't have much of a problem. Fathers are getting more relaxed with boys having girlfriends, but not with the girls having boyfriends." Yet neither Korosh nor Marah seem worried about anyone seeing them so close together.

They don't even seem concerned about a surprise visit by the Basiji, with so many young men and women joking and frolicking or paired off along the mountain cliffs. Yet Marah confessed to almost having experienced the wrath of the Basiji.

"I have been beaten before," she said with a sullen defiance. "I was caught at a party. They took us all in."

"I was almost caught once," said Amid, who was standing with her cousin on the other side of the tree. "I was driving a car and I had been drinking. I guess the way I was driving caught the attention of the Basiji and they followed me. I knew I had to run away. I would have no chance if they caught me."

Many of the young men clustered in groups on the mountain did not have the diversion of girlfriends. Instead, they use the Friday picnics as a sort of political salon. Young intellectuals with slicked-back hair and dark sunglasses huddled and spoke in whispers, talking about the need to confront Iran's hard-liners and support Khamenei and his efforts at reforms.

"We have to go slow and take one step at a time," said one young man who was the most outspoken, at least in English, of his group. "We can't just go in and try to overthrow everything all at once. That would backfire on us. We have to first get control of the parliament and then move to start stripping their power little by little."

He explained that issues such as whether women cover and whether young people are allowed to date are not as important for Iranians as changing the country's political system so that the mullahs would not have a veto over who could run for office. Once that is achieved, the young man said, change would come rapidly. Yet even this young rebel was not sure that Iranians wanted to be a duplicate of the West. Iran's youths were not against Islam, he said, but are trying to find a system that blends true democracy with Islam's moral principles and that allows more freedom and "fun."

Of course, not all of Iran's youths are so rebellious or so eager for things to change. Mariam, a plump, pleasant girl of sixteen, was eager to practice her already-fluent English and was clearly curious at the sight of an African American reporter in Iran. She was escorting her aging parents to see the famous "shaking towers" near Isfahan. She watched a skinny man climb to the top of one of a pair of brick minarets flanking what is believed to be the tomb of a hermit named Amu Abdollah Soqla, who had them built in 1316.

She and her parents exclaimed with delight when the man began shaking the minaret, causing its twin to shake, as well. The show lasted all of five minutes, but Mariam and her parents seemed quite satisfied and were prepared to wait the twenty minutes to watch the towers shake again.

Iranian youths "are so silly," she grumbled. Mariam, with her kindly, round face and thick eyeglasses, said she preferred to study and read. "If God helps me, I want to be a doctor one day. I'd love to study abroad and come back to Iran to serve my people, but since my parents are both disabled, I don't want to leave them alone."

Mariam said she is among a core of Iranian youths who are "more serious"; they understand the vital role they will play in Iran's future and still revere the martyrs who defended their country.

"We're a Third-World country. We should be reading as much as possible, acquiring as much knowledge as possible and be ready to use that knowledge to improve our country." Sadly, she said, such views were not popular among most of Iran's youths. "They don't care much about morality. They just care about fashion. It's confusing to me that young people here are so irreligious and we're a religious state."

Mariam echoed a refrain familiar even in the West: "Children don't care about their parents' approval anymore. They don't tell their parents about their friends—even about their boyfriends. But I blame the parents. They don't even ask."

Iran's newly rebellious youths are increasingly presenting a problem for the conservatives in government. New young martyrs have already been made in clashes between police and students demanding free press and democracy, and many Iranians fear that there will be more bloodshed between the hard-line conservatives and Iran's youths, who are becoming impatient with President Mohammed Khatami's slow moves to open society and with the conservatives' ability to repeatedly check him.

Attacks on Iran's vibrant press are particularly disturbing to many Iranians, who see the press as the battleground between the nation's conservative clerics and the growing tide of "reformists." The reformists want to bring accountability to government and reduce the power of hard-line conservatives who oppose democratic openness in government. The political situation in Iran is in flux, but in late 2002, conservatives controlled enough branches of government to close newspapers and magazines they considered offensive, still, Khatami's reformists were in enough places of power to issue licenses to have the same people reopen them under a different name.

One big showdown came with the closing of the newspaper *Salam*, whose publisher was then forbidden from opening another newspaper for three years. On July 9, 1999, Iranian police stormed a Tehran University demonstration in which students were protesting *Salam*'s closure. Police killed 4 students, wounded an estimated 200, and arrested 500. As student protests continued, there was real fear that hard-liners in the government would use the opportunity to crush the students. Khatami and other reformists moved to calm the students to prevent further bloodshed, but they were concerned that the conservatives would try to provoke the students to launch another crackdown.

Yet the reformists had some powerful supporters in their ranks, including many who could play the martyrdom card. Iran's Islamic state was founded and preserved on the blood of young martyrs, and many of their families have joined the ranks of the reformists, showing the same determination and courage that their relatives had shown on the battlefield. Many are staunchly demanding openness in government, and they insist that its leaders be accountable not only to God but to the people. The same determined, impassioned spirit that had been directed against the enemy is now being turned against Iran's ruling clerics, especially against the hard-line conservatives who believe that political power is best kept out of the hands of the people and in the hands of the country's religious potentates, whom they deem to be closer to God.

Hamidreza Jalaie-Pour had three brothers who died as martyrs, and he is prepared to face the same fate in his role as one of the government's most ardent critics. He owned a series of popular newspapers that were closed one after another by conservatives in powerful branches of government. But that didn't stop him.

"When they close down one newspaper, we simply open another," Jalaie-Pour said in an interview in 1999 in his Tehran office. "All we are calling for is more transparency in government." He is among Iran's reformists who believe its leaders, whether religious authorities or not, need to have checks and balances and should have to explain their rulings to the electorate.

"Some conservatives here say the Islamic government is responsible only to God. We say it should also be responsible to the people." Iran's conservatives argue that their first responsibility is protecting Islam, not promoting democracy. "They think the press should not question their actions. But for us reformists, religion is good, but there is politics and then there is religion, and everyone who comes to power should be held accountable."

For such views, Jalaie-Pour spent eleven months in prison. He credited his mother, the mother of martyrs, with helping get him out of his one-room cell in solitary confinement. Any mother of a martyr in Iran enjoys considerable prestige and moral standing, and Jalaie-Pour's mother had lost three sons defending Iran.

"My mother had an interview with a national newspaper," Jalaie-Pour said, in which she argued on behalf of her imprisoned son and reminded the country's leaders that her family had already paid the highest price of loyalty and patriotism. "She had enough influence on their consciences that they let me out."

Yet Jalaie-Pour also knows that he could be walking the same road as his brothers by defying Iran's conservatives, people who, like the martyrs of the Iran-Iraq war and the revolution, are radical, passionate and not opposed to using violence to silence any threat to their vision of the Islamic state. In 1998 Iran's intellectual elite had already been terrorized by a series of murders of writers, artists, and journalists, and they suspected the country's radical conservatives were behind the crimes.

One of the most outrageous incidents occurred on November 21, 1998, the same day that a mob attacked a bus carrying thirteen Americans in Tehran, breaking its windows and shooting into the air, terrifying the passengers. That night, Dariush Forouhar and his wife, Parvaneh Eskandari, were murdered in their homes. The couple was among Iran's best-known political activists and were considered critics of the government. But they were not the only intellectuals killed in an apparent backlash against dissent. Priouz Davani, Majid Sharif, and Mohammad Moktari, all writers, disappeared. The bodies of Sharif and Moktari were found later. Apparently, they died from strangulation. In a January 5, 1999 article, *Salam* had carried a commentary entitled "Seek the Roots of the Sedition," which accused Iran's security forces of being involved in the killings. Shortly after the article appeared, Judiciary Chief Ayatollah Mohammad Yazdi announced the arrest of several people inside the Intelligence Ministry who were described as "rogue elements." In January 2001 an Iranian court convicted three former Intelligence Ministry agents for four of the murders and sentenced them to death. Five others were sentenced to life imprisonment. Another seven received jail terms of between thirty months and ten years.

Even though Yazdi announced the arrests, he was no proponent of free press or free speech. In a 1999 sermon marking the start of the Iranian new year, the Iranian Times quoted Yazdi as saying, "There is no freedom for you to write and say anything you like. Our people do not want such freedom if it is against the tenets of Islam."[9] He even threatened free speech advocates, saying, "The ruling institutions are overseen and they will take action when necessary and will not listen to what others. . . . Don't come out tomorrow and ask why you were not warned in advance. Don't cry out when we arrest someone."

Many Iranian reformists fear that bloodshed is inevitable, even as they disavow all violence in their opposition to the government's conservative power brokers.

Jalaie-Pour and other reformists saw two classes of conservatives in Iran: the "rational conservatives and the fanatic conservatives." Reformists believe that the fanatics are bent on ending all dissent, resorting even to assassinations and purposefully stirring up students to provoke the army to crush them.

"I cannot predict that the rational conservatives will control the fanatic conservatives," Jalaie-Pour said. In fact, he is convinced that eventually there will be a showdown.

"There are 4 million M.A.s and Ph.D.s in this country, with 20 million students in high school. The level of education is getting higher," he said. Iranians, especially the youths, are demanding change, and they are determined to get it.

"We are in a very important period of social movement, of political movement, of reform in religion," said Mehrangiz Karr, a female Iranian attorney who is known for her outspoken opposition to Iran's conservatives.

We are rethinking Islam. We cannot claim that everything is changed after Khatami, but we can claim that society has gotten more aware about the political issues. There are new religious thinkers who are saying Islam is against violence. We didn't have something like that in our history before. We are opening every door . . . we are examining every taboo. Maybe this is the way toward a renaissance in Iran.

Yet the question is whether Iran's renaissance will come without more bloodshed, either from internal or external threats. The Bush administration has issued a direct threat to Iran, as well as to Iraq, warning that it could be a target of its war on terrorism. Iran is one of the most strident opponents of

Israel and supports Islamic groups dedicated to jihad against the Jewish state. In fact, Iran believes that Israeli Prime Minister Ariel Sharon should be put on trial for war crimes in connection with the 1982 refugee camp massacres in Lebanon.

In March 2002 Iran's supreme leader, Ayatollah Ali Khamenei, Khomeini's successor, rejected a peace proposal that Saudi Arabia had offered to try to stem the bloodshed between Israelis and Palestinians. Khamenei declared, "Only the continuation of the intifada could unravel the tangle of the Palestinian people," according to the IRNA, the official Iranian news agency.[10] Khamenei cited the example of Hussein as inspiration for Palestinian martyrs and he spoke with pride of a Palestinian woman that he saw in a televised news report.

The woman was saying good-bye to her son as he headed off to fight the Israelis. Khamenei said, "That mother was saying that, 'If I had a hundred sons like this one, I would sacrifice them all for this cause." Such was the attitude all Muslims should have toward martyrdom and jihad, Khamenei said, when they are faced with the kind of oppression and humiliation that the Palestinians were suffering under the Israeli occupation.

The United States has accused Iran of being a state sponsor of terrorism by sending money and arms to support the Palestinians and for encouraging Palestinian youths to become martyrs. Iran had provided military and financial support for Hezbollah's mostly Shia guerrillas and suicide bombers who pushed the Israelis from southern Lebanon, emboldening Palestinian Islamic groups such as Hamas. Iran also provided funding for hospitals and other social services to aid the Lebanese fighters. Even after Israel's withdrawal from southern Lebanon, Iran had maintained close ties to the country's Shias. In the Shia section of Beirut, photos of Ayatollah Khomeini hung on the same lampposts as those of Sheikh Fadlullah, who was considered one of the founders of Hezbollah and its spiritual leader. Many shops also sported photos of another famous Shia martyr, Sheikh Abbas Musawi, killed by Israelis in 1992. He was commander of Hezbollah's Islamic Resistance and later the party's secretary-general. Musawi was believed to have ordered the 1988 kidnapping and murder of U.S. Lieutenant Colonel William Higgins.

And like Hamas and Islamic Jihad, Iran's leaders believe that Palestinians are compelled to wage jihad against Israel and to continue their uprising against Israeli occupation of the West Bank and Gaza.

The Foundation of Khordad 15, an important Iranian charity, in October 2000 announced plans to build schools in honor of Palestinian martyrs. The foundation is a charitable association set up after the Islamic revolution of 1979 to commemorate an anti-Shah uprising on June 5,1963, which was the fifteenth day of the month of Khordad in the year 1342 of the Persian calendar.

"We are going to build 1,000 schools . . . and each one will carry the name of a martyr of the intifada," Ayatollah Hassan Sanei, head of the Foundation, told Iranian TV.[11] Students at the school would study the "struggle against the Zionist enemy," he said.

Iran also has flown injured Palestinians for medical treatment into the country and provided financial assistance to families of those killed in clashes with the Israelis. But more than just charity work, Israel has accused Iran of militarily and financially supporting Hamas and other militant groups. Both the United States and Israel believed Iran was responsible for a ship carrying an estimated $100 million in arms that was destined for the Palestinians in the Gaza Strip, a Hamas stronghold. Israel seized the *Karine A* in January 2002 in the Red Sea, about 300 miles south of Eilat. Israeli officials put on display 50 tons of missiles, mortars, and mines, along with machine guns, Katyusha rockets, grenades, AK-47 assault rifles, and more than a half-million rounds of ammunition for assorted weapons—all allegedly from the *Karine A*.

U.S. and Israeli authorities have long known about Iranian arms shipments to Hezbollah but since 2000 there have been growing signs that Iran is also sending weapons to the Palestinians, and that it is attempting to coordinate the activities of Islamic groups to increase their effectiveness in their war with Israel. In its support of Israel, the Bush administration considers Iran's backing of Hamas and Hezbollah to be supporting terrorism, even if Iran, the Palestinians, and all of the Arab regimes believe such groups to be legitimate freedom fighters, defending Islamic holy land from the Israelis.

"There's no question but that the Iranians were deeply involved in the *Karine A* ship that was captured by the Israelis that had tons of equipment that was being sent down into the occupied areas of that part of the world for the purpose of conducting terrorist attacks," said U.S. Secretary of Defense Donald Rumsfeld at a Washington press briefing in April 2002. "There's no question but that the Iranians work with the Syrians and send folks into Damascus and down to Beirut and then into south Lebanon, so that they can conduct terrorist attacks."[12]

Clearly Rumsfeld's definition of terrorism and the Iranian definition of terrorism are two different things, but there is agreement on one key issue. Iranians accept that September 11 was an atrocity and President Khatami expressed his deep sorrow and sympathy for the American people. "On behalf of the Iranian government and the nation, I condemn the hijacking attempts and terrorist attacks on public centers in American cities which have killed a large number of innocent people," he said in a public statement shortly after the attack. "My deep sympathy goes out to the American nation, particularly those who have suffered from the attacks and also the families of the victims."[13]

Mohammad Javad Zarif, Iran's deputy foreign minister, speaking to the United Nations shortly after September 11, denounced the attacks as "heinous" but qualified his words somewhat, saying that the atrocity is a by-product of U.S. foreign policy based on the principle that "might makes right."[14] And Iran has refused to cooperate in the U.S. war on terrorism, insisting that the United Nations had to lead any such international campaign.

"One can make a decision on how to fight terrorism only in a healthy society that is not controlled by superpowers." Iranian defense minister Admiral Ali Shamkhani said during a state visit to Moscow.[15]

Iran's leaders, like many Islamic leaders around the world, could denounce as terrorism the September 11 attacks against the United States, but praise Palestinian suicide bombers as holy martyrs. Yet Iran has denied accusations, including those from the Palestinian Authority, that it is aiding and abetting the suicide bombings and financially supporting Hamas and Islamic Jihad, the two Palestinian groups outside of Yasser Arafat's control that claimed responsibility for suicide attacks against the Israelis.

In 1999 Palestinian police chief Ghazi al Jabali, no friend of Islamic militants in the Palestinian Authority, had accused Iran of giving Hamas $1 million and of helping Hamas stage suicide attacks, allegations which Iran and Hamas denied. But it is not unreasonable to assume that many people in Iran, if not the government itself, are committed to helping Palestinians wage jihad against Israel and that they will provide any means available to do so. This fact is at the root of tensions between Iran and the United States, which considered Iran's leaders to be major sponsors of terrorism around the world.

"Murderers are not martyrs," Rumsfeld contended at the April 2002 briefing, in which he sent a threatening message to Iran and other Middle Eastern countries. "Targeting civilians is immoral, whatever the excuse. Terrorists have declared war on civilization, and states like Iran, Iraq, and Syria are inspiring and financing a culture of political murder and suicide bombing.

Despite the threats from the United States, Iran is unlikely to back down from its support of Palestinian fighters. Khamenei has been a key voice rallying the Muslim world to stand with the Palestinians and recapture Muslim holy land. At a conference held in Tehran in April 2001, to which an estimated thirty-five Muslim and Arab states sent representatives, press reports quoted Khamenei as declaring: "Supporting the Palestinian people is one of our important Islamic duties."[16]

In his last will and testament, a document his followers consider almost sacred, Ayatullah Khomeini denounced not only the United States but also the leaders who had signed peace treaties with Israel as well as Morocco, which was considered less hostile to the Jewish state:

> The USA is the foremost enemy of Islam. It is a terrorist state by nature that has set fire to everything everywhere and its ally, the international Zionism, does not stop short of any crime to achieve its base and greedy desires, crimes that the tongue and pen are ashamed to utter or write. The stupid idea of a Greater Israel urges them to commit any shameful crime. The Islamic nations and the *mustazafeen* [the meek, the oppressed] peoples of the world are pleased to have Hussein of Jordan, a professional, itinerant criminal; Hasan of Morocco; and Hosni Mubarak of Egypt . . . as enemies. These are fellow-criminals with Israel and commit any act of treason against their own nations to serve the USA.[17]

While President Khatami is believed to back improving relations with the United States, there is little indication that his views toward Israel and its U.S. ally are any different from Khomeini. Khatami has frequently met with leaders of Palestinian groups who opposed the peace process with Israel and assured him of Iran's support.

At one such meeting in May 1999 in Damascus, Khatami met with the former chairman of the Palestinian National Council, Khaled al-Fahoum; the leader of the People's Front for the Liberation of Palestine, General Command, Ahmad Jibril; and Ramadan Abdullah Shalah, secretary general of the Palestinian Islamic Jihad. Arabic News.com reported that Khatami criticized Yasser Arafat and his negotiations with Israelis, saying those "who proceeded in the process of negotiating with Israel and giving it concessions have to consider the results."[18]

Yet Iran's leaders contend that they will accept whatever decision the Palestinians make about their future, even as they insist that any peace treaty should be a just one that guarantees Muslims sovereignty over Islamic holy places in East Jerusalem. This is Iran's main concern in the Israeli-Palestinian conflict, a concern shared by more than 1 billion Muslims around the world. Muslims consider the Haram al Sharif (Noble Sanctuary) a trust of the entire Islamic world, not just the Palestinian people. Any agreement that does not guarantee Muslim sovereignty over the al-Aqsa mosque would be rejected by Muslims far and wide. Yasser Arafat knew this when in October 2000 he walked away from a peace treaty that did not guarantee such sovereignty, angering both Israeli prime minister Ehud Barak and President Bill Clinton. Arafat was worried about what he called "an Arab bullet," should he sign such a treaty. But it is not be hard to imagine Muslims around the globe dedicating themselves to jihad and martyrdom to regain control of the site where Muhammad ascended into heaven, despite any peace treaty.

And it is not hard to imagine Iranians at the forefront of an Islamic al-Aqsa jihad, raising the banner of the "Master of Martyrs," to rally the world's Muslims to defend Islam's sacred land.

4

THE WOMAN AS SOLDIER-MARTYR
AND SUICIDE BOMBER:
LOULA ABBOUD

*The participation of women is not needed. We can't meet the grow-
ing demands of young men who wish to carry out martyr operations.*

—*Sheikh Ahmed Yassin*

THE ROAD TO THE TINY VILLAGE OF AOUN WINDS TIGHTLY AROUND
the craggy Lebanon mountains, then plunges deep into the Bekaa Valley. It is
a treacherous route, with hairpin curves around jagged cliffs and potholes so
deep they bite into tires with the ferocity of a thunderbolt. In the unlit night
and blinding rain, even with a careful driver like Mohammed, the road to
Aoun is more than merely dangerous, it seems a certain path to death.

This road, with its startling but majestic views over the Bekaa, leads to
the home of Loula Abboud, a young woman who decided to take up arms despite cultural and religious prohibitions against women soldiers. She died
after exploding her own body in a battle against Israel soldiers in her home-
town of Aoun.

Aoun claims only a few miles of the road but its small, central square
holds both the giant dome of the village mosque and the soaring steeple of an
Orthodox Church. When Christmas and the Muslim holy month of Ramadan coincide, the square is a carnival of colored lights as the mosque and
church compete in celebration. Everyone in Aoun, Christians and Muslims

alike, knows the story of Loula Abboud. So do many people in Lebanon and throughout the Middle East.

In fact, Loula Abboud may have been the model for the first Palestinian women who became suicide bombers in 2002. It is a good bet that Wisal Idris, the Palestinian woman who made headlines in January 2002 by blowing herself up in an attack against Israelis, knew Abboud's story. And Abboud is a legend among the Palestinians in the refugee camps near Beirut. They call Loula Abboud an ideal martyr, seeing her as a courageous woman who fought for her land and for her people, and who went to her death willingly.

But Loula Abboud, the dark-eyed, petite girl of nineteen with the shock of thick, black hair caressing a soft, oval face, was an unlikely martyr in Lebanon's battle against Israel. Loula Abboud was a Christian. She was also the military leader of a resistance group that fought the Israeli occupation of the Bekaa during the 1980s to force out guerrillas of the Palestine Liberation Organization. Abboud's avowedly militant Christian family had already produced a long line of warrior-martyrs.

"Loula isn't the first martyr in the family," explained Dr. Fouad Elias Abboud, Loula's brother, in an interview in November 2001. A soft-spoken, contemplative man, his hulking frame belies his quiet, easy-going manner. Dr. Abboud now lives in a modern apartment building about midway along the road between Beirut and Aoun. Seated in the comfortable living room of the home he shares with his wife and two small sons, Dr. Abboud was eager to talk about Loula and about the family that produced her, before we continued down the road to visit his mother in Aoun.

"In 1973 the first martyr was my cousin, Jihad Asaad. He died at the Bank of America. There was a branch of it in Lebanon. This bank had given $10 million to the Israeli state." So, Dr. Abboud said his cousin Jihad and a group of people went to the Lebanese branch of the bank and demanded $10 million for an Arab state.

"When they refused, they took hostages," he said. "In the end, they surrendered to police and the Lebanese government executed them." The Abbouds consider Asaad a martyr, but Lebanon's government then simply called him a terrorist.

"Then came the Lebanese war. My brother Nicholas died in 1976 during the civil war. He was also nineteen when he died, like Loula. There also was Khalid Bishara, our cousin, who died after Nicholas, fighting the Israelis in his village of Deir Mimees. Marwan Bishara, another cousin, also died a martyr. Loula died in 1985. She was our family's last martyr." The doctor reeled off the names of his dead relatives as though he had told the story many times before. He spoke of one, Suha Bishara, as though she were an international celebrity. She almost usurped Loula's spot as the family's last martyr.

As the afternoon stretched into the dusk of evening and the clouds grew angrier, Dr. Abboud pursued the path through his sister's life and death, smoking cigarette after cigarette and paying little notice to the sudden darkness that enveloped us every half hour or so. His wife, a tall, striking woman with intense dark eyes, sat like a sentry on the edge of one of the two sofas that dominated the room, apologizing for the rolling blackouts and alert to subtle changes in her husband's mood. Perhaps she knew that, as with his sister, Dr. Abboud's tranquility and self-control were only a thin veneer to hide inner emotional and intellectual turbulence; only a mask for the deep sorrow at the loss of his sister and anger at the way, and the reason, she died.

In fact, Dr. Abboud did not discuss the details of Loula's death for a long time. Not about how she opened fire on unsuspecting Israelis soldiers marching through Aoun on April 20, 1985. Nor about how she allowed her comrades in arms to escape as she kept firing to give them cover. Nor about how the Israeli soldiers surrounded her and moved in to arrest her. Nor how she patiently waited for them to come closer and closer. And it took a long time for him to describe how she blew herself up after carefully calculating when the Israelis were close enough to die with her.

Before he told Loula's story, he wanted to offer a rationale for her death. So he went into great detail in talking about the panic that he said people in Aoun felt seeing Israeli soldiers heading toward their villages, burning down homes and carting off young men to die or to prison camps. He wanted to make sure it was clear that Loula did not go to Israel to kill Israelis. They came to her.

It is hard to know if the details of the doctor's story are true or if they are exaggerated. He was not a witness to the events himself, did not really know how many Israeli soldiers were there or what they did in the village. His recounting of the events are pieced together from the reports of the people who fought with his sister but survived, and from his own sympathetic imagination. Dr. Abboud's version is only one side of the events in Aoun that day. The other side is lost with the young Israeli soldiers who died with Loula Abboud.

ideology

"A person is willing to die for his cause if it's a question of his very existence," he said quietly, puffing on his cigarette and speaking more to himself than to anyone else. "Americans don't have that problem. They don't have to fight for their existence, and maybe that's why they don't understand or don't accept the concept of martyrdom."

Dr. Abboud's two sons, two and a half and five, broke the heavy stillness as they ran through the room, laughing and teasing each other. Mrs. Abboud ushered them out again, returning later with cups of sweet tea and pastries. But Dr. Abboud remained in deep and calm concentration.

"All cases of martyrdom are cases of fighting for your existence," he said. "You can find cases of martyrdom in your own history with the American Indians who were fighting for their existence. And if Americans ever feel they have to fight for their existence, they will become martyrs, too.

"In the Second World War, the Japanese thought that their existence and culture was being threatened, and the result of that was the kamikaze," he said. Here, Dr. Abboud was either ignorant of or consciously ignoring the fact that it was the Japanese who helped start the war and were the cause of their own desperation. "Now, we in the Middle East are being threatened by the West, which is embodied by the Israeli presence. Of course, the attack is not from the people of the West but from the *governments* of the West. But we are being forced to fight for our very existence. Every martyr of ours was a martyr who died in self-defense. We never went to Europe or killed Jews there. We were defending our own children."

Dr. Abboud could not accept that some Israelis believed the same thing about their invasion of Lebanon, that it was necessary to protect their land and their children from Palestinian guerrillas who continued to attack the country from their base there. Although Dr. Abboud is a Christian who also believes in the Old Testament and therefore the long history of Jews in the Middle East, it is clear that he believes that the Jewish state is a Western transplant and a continuation of European colonialism.

While there have been no reports of Christians going on suicidal missions against Israelis in the West Bank and Gaza, in Lebanon Christians have been among the suicide bombers and the soldiers who fight Israelis and their proxies, the South Lebanese Army in southern Lebanon. Lebanon's suicide bombers have been effective against Israel, according to Boaz Ganor, an Israeli terrorism expert and executive director of the International Policy Institute for Counter-Terrorism. In an article published by Ganor's institute on

April 25, 1998, he said that suicide attacks during the 1980s led to the Israeli withdrawal from southern Lebanon and had even broader consequences:

> This served as proof for the Palestinian-Islamic organizations that a readiness for self-sacrifice, determination, and long-term vision, together with the correct use of terrorist strategies (and with reliance on the influence of the mass media on western opinion), can lead to far-reaching military and political achievements. Activists in the Islamic organizations quickly learned that suicide missions are extremely effective. (A relatively small number of high-impact suicide missions succeeded in ousting from Lebanon the French, the Americans and eventually the Israelis.)
>
> The Palestinian-Islamic organizations, relying on a fundamentalist ideology similar to that of Hezbollah, started to learn and imitate the new terrorist methods, and preached daring and self-sacrifice in preparation for suicide missions.[1]

It is not hard to see the connection between the success of such operations in Lebanon against both Israel and the United States to the September 11 attack against the United States. But Dr. Abboud insisted that there is a big difference between a terrorist, like Mohammad Atta, who attacks civilians far away from his home, and his sister Loula Abboud, whom he described as fighting for the liberation of her own homeland.

Loula and the rest of the family had already safely evacuated Aoun and were ensconced in Beirut when they learned of the Israelis approach. Loula had spent weeks in Beirut meeting with her friends from Aoun along the corniche, singing patriotic songs and performing her village's traditional dances, to keep up their spirits. Then she decided to return to Aoun. To fight.

It seems Loula Abboud had no other access to information other than the rumors that were rampant in Lebanon about Israeli atrocities in the Bekaa. She did not hear balanced news reports about the reasons why Israeli troops were in her village, so she may have thought that they were there to stay, even to take over her land. But for a young woman to leave the relative safety of Beirut, where her family had fled, to return to a battlefield meant she was either insane or desperate. Dr. Abboud believed she was simply heroic.

"The freedom fighter chooses death as a final choice. He doesn't choose it from the beginning. It's after he can not fight anymore that he decides to kill himself," he said, his voice rising only slightly with emotion. "And she was fighting the Israelis within her own village. She was not fighting Israelis in Israel."

But Loula Abboud did not have to fight the Israelis herself. She went looking for a fight. A woman in this area, Christian or Muslim, is not expected to strap on a gun and lead men into battle like a modern-day Joan of Arc. The average woman in the Arab world is not as confined by tradition as many westerners may believe, and in conservative Muslim countries such as Sudan and Iran, women have served in the armed forces and even on the front lines, but primarily as nurses. But it's fair to say that Loula Abboud's actions exceeded all expectations not only for women in war, but for men as well. While her older brother was away at school studying to become a doctor, Loula made her decision to lead a resistance group. The whole thing still baffles her mother, Antoinette, who prefers to be called Um Walid, mother of Walid, after her eldest son. Yet Um Walid should not have been baffled. She herself said she raised Loula to be "liberated," an independent, strong-willed, deep-thinking girl who did not have to get her parent's approval for everything she did, even at the age of nineteen.

"It was the day after Easter when she decided to go back to the village," Um Walid said, settling into one of the large, cushiony sofas along three walls of her large living room, not far from a large photo of her daughter.

"She came to me and said, 'I want to go to the Bekaa.' And I asked her, 'What do you want to do there?' But she just said, 'I want to go to the Bekaa and I'll be back on Wednesday.'"

It had taken about an hour to travel from Dr. Abboud's apartment in the Bekaa Valley to his mother's house, and the rain had begun to fall hard, bringing with it a decided chill. But Um Walid's living room was warmed by a sizable kerosene heater. Its metal smokestack stood like a black column in the center of the room, jutting through the roof. Except for a large television, it was the room's only distraction from the collage of photos that served as Um Walid's memorial to her daughter. The most striking photo showed Loula with a thin smile, her heavy brows arched over wide, oval eyes and a dark curl cascading over one eye. Around her neck hung a sliver of gold with a tiny cross.

It was in this simple stone country house, with its wood-shuttered windows, outdoor toilet, and hodge-podge kitchen that Loula lived with her family. And it was this house and her family's right to live there that she thought she was dying to defend.

Um Walid is a short but sturdy, no-nonsense, rebellious spirit who had raised her children to have strong convictions. She did not acknowledge it, but she had shaped the woman who died a suicide bomber. In her day, Um

Walid had been a rabble-rouser and probably more outspoken and controversial than Loula. As youths, both mother and daughter had decided to work through the Lebanese Communist Party to act on their convictions.

"I'm from the South. Not from this village," Um Walid said brusquely. "I was born in Der Mimees. Suha Bishara is my niece." Her tone implied that the world must know of Suha's daring feat to attempt to kill General Lahd whose South Lebanon Army helped Israel occupy southern Lebanon. Bishara also came from Der Mimees and like Loula Abboud and Um Walid, had allied herself with the Lebanese Communist party. Bishara was fifteen years old when she joined and was nineteen when she became a member of its military wing, the National Resistance Front. And like Loula, she did not tell her family of her mission.

Bishara spent a year getting close to Lahd and his family. She tutored his children and became friends with his wife. Then, at 8 P.M. on November 7, 1988, she pulled out a Soviet-made handgun and fired three bullets at the general, prepared to die herself. He was wounded in the arm and jaw, and was partially paralyzed as a result, but neither he nor she died. Bishara had dubbed the assassination attempt "Operation Loula Abboud," in honor of her dead cousin.

Um Walid said Bishara spent the next ten years of her young life in the notorious Israeli Kyam detention center in southern Lebanon, then under Israeli occupation, although she was never charged or tried. Bishara told her family she spent most of her time in solitary confinement, deprived of food, abused and tortured. During her first four months in detention, her family said she slept on a bare mattress and was not allowed to bathe. Despite the misery of her ten years in Israeli custody, after her release Bishara proclaimed to the world that she had no regrets about trying to kill Lahd and that she would do it again if she had the chance.

In the Arab world, Suha Bishara became a symbol of Lebanon. Through her, Loula Abboud's story also became legend. International human rights organizations and activists, especially those in France, championed Bishara's cause and it was the French who ultimately succeeded in getting her released from prison on September 3, 1998.

When she rushed into the arms of her family, she flashed a smile and a victory sign for the phalanx of cameras documenting her role in Lebanese history and proceeded to accept the personal congratulations of Lebanese prime minister Rafik al-Hariri. That day, she proclaimed to her adoring countrymen:

I was liberated today but I am still there [Khyam detention center] with my friends, fellow detainees. I hope the Lebanese resistance will achieve the liberation of our land soon. This morning they [the Israelis and their allies] moved me to another room . . . they opened the door and they told me I was being released they [the Israeli allied militia] said through their radio station that I was being freed for humanitarian reasons . . . and that I paid enough for my crime. . . . But I am sure what I did was not a crime . . . this is our right, our duty is to fight for the liberation of our land.[2]

That spirit runs through her family, Um Walid boasted. "We're all freedom fighters. My brother's son is a martyr. He died fighting the Israelis. My cousin's son was killed by the Israelis. His name was Marwan Bishara. Khalid Bishara was also my nephew. He's also a martyr. That's my family."

Um Walid, with a sharp and penetrating frankness, also laid bare her own past. "I grew up in the Communist party. My father was a Communist. The Communist party used to be called the Workers Party. My father was with them when they were called the Workers Party. And I was a member of the Communist party. And my husband was also a member of the Communist party. We got married because we were both Communists."

Loula's father, the late Elias Abboud, was a fairly prominent journalist who was one of the founders of the Lebanese daily *al-Safir*, which is known throughout the Middle East. He also wrote several books, the last about his daughter's martyrdom.

Um Walid and her son both had a good chuckle at what must have been an inside family joke, that she and Elias Abboud married because they both were Communists. Then she continued soberly. "We both loved our country. I was an activist and I used to take part in demonstrations. I've been in jail twice myself."

She related all of this without emotion, as if she were detailing the ingredients for her family's tabouli. But for all of her bravado, when she started to talk about the last night she spent with her daughter, Um Walid broke down, and for a moment she could not speak.

"She slept next to me that night," Um Walid recalled, battling tears. "And all night she was kissing me and hugging me in her sleep and saying sweet things to me, how much she loved me."

Dr. Abboud handed her some tissues kept on a table under Loula's picture, but maintained his gentle stoicism.

"She left the house the next morning and we all thought she was going to the Bekaa that wasn't occupied by the Israelis. We have cousins in that part. But then, you know, she didn't call. She was late. And we got worried. So I went to the village to look for her."

Um Walid knew that the Israelis had withdrawn from Aoun and when she arrived, she joined in the celebration. Concerned about Loula's reputation, Um Walid didn't want to draw attention to the fact that her family did not know where her nineteen-year-old daughter was. So she discreetly asked only a few people if they had seen her. No one had. Most of the village people did not learn of her death until the next day.

These were days of immense joy in Aoun. People were celebrating and congratulating the various groups that had been fighting the Israelis. Young fighters with the Communist party had been at the forefront of the battles. It was the party's leaders who finally told Um Walid's neighbors that they had lost their leader, Loula Abboud. But no one rushed to break the news to her mother.

"They sent a boy from the village to tell me," said Um Walid. "I was at the home of some neighbors and there were a lot of people in the house. He took me aside and simply said, 'I want to tell you that our comrade Loula has died.'"

Maybe the news came too suddenly, or maybe it did not seem real, but Um Walid remained calm in the midst of the celebration around her. "I didn't say anything. I just told him to take me to where she was. I didn't cry. I just wanted to see where my daughter was."

But it seemed no one knew where Loula was buried. Her friends, the people she died trying to protect, buried her secretly, fearing that if the Israelis found her body and identified her, they would return to her village, destroy her home, and massacre everyone in the area. Days later Um Walid found her daughter's grave. She had the body exhumed and reburied in the family cemetery, which lies along the rugged path leading from Aoun's central square to her home.

Almost twenty years later, as she looked back over Loula's last days, Um Walid said she had no idea that her daughter was involved in the resistance against the Israelis. Many mothers of youths who kill themselves in suicide attacks or who die in a whirl of gunfire with the Israelis also said they knew nothing of their children's activities. In the United States, where often both parents work and teenage children are often alone, it is easy to imagine that a parent might not be aware of her son's drug habit or her daughter's pregnancy. But in the Arab world, where families are still close knit, where it is hard to keep even family secrets from the rest of the village, where even adult children are expected to obey their parents, and where young women generally do not walk the streets alone, it took a great deal of subterfuge for Loula to hide her activities from her family. It is hard to believe that she really did and that even her brother suspected nothing when he was home.

Dr. Abboud, who was close to Loula, ultimately admitted that he knew she was involved in something, although he said he did not know the specifics.

Once, when Dr. Abboud was home on summer vacation from his studies in Bulgaria, Loula asked him to take her to the movies. "But as soon as we leave the house, she tells me, 'Well, you know, I have a meeting to go to and I needed to get out of the house. Will you cover for me?' Then she told me to go to the movie and wait about two hours and we'll go home together."

Ever the dutiful brother, Dr. Abboud waited for his sister and even told her what the movie was about, in case someone asked her what they had seen. But Loula did not tell him where she had been or what she had been doing. And he did not ask. Maybe he feared that his sister was involved with a boy and he could not bear confronting her. In this part of the world, it is not unheard of for families to ask brothers to kill wayward sisters to protect the family's honor. That was not the reason Dr. Abboud did not confront his sister, however. It is possible he knew the truth.

"Anybody who's engaged in a secret resistance isn't going to talk about it," he said. "And she didn't want the family to be worried about her."

And Dr. Abboud conceded that Loula's gender might have been an issue, even in their family, which prided itself on its independent, educated women. "During the war, my brother and I both were fighters. And we're men. We used to leave the house to go fighting and it was no problem. But it would have been very hard to accept a girl fighting. My parents had already lost a son. It would have been very hard for the family to accept that they'd lose another member, especially the youngest girl."

Um Walid remembered Loula as a religious girl, who used to attend church, pray and light candles for the Lebanese soldiers fighting the Israelis.

She was a smart, serious girl, good at math and science, who liked to laugh and have a good time, but she was not prone to foolishness. There was no hint that Loula was interested in boys or had a boyfriend. In this culture, such issues are not bandied about lightly. A young woman's reputation is everything, not only for her but for her family, which is why some families decide that the only way to restore the reputation is to kill a wayward daughter. But Loula had far more serious issues on her mind than flirting with boys.

"She was educated. We had a library. And we weren't a very conservative family," Um Walid said. She and her husband allowed Loula a lot of freedom.

"Loula had a friend," said Um Walid. "And she used to tell us that she was studying with this friend. And she used to tell us that she was sleeping over at the girl's house. And then she would ask the girl to cover for her. She told the girl, 'Trust me. I'm not doing anything wrong, but cover for me.'"

To the Western eye, Loula Abboud seems very much a deranged fanatic whose family should have stepped in to save her from herself, as there are reports that some Palestinian families are starting to do for their potentially suicidal children. But the people who knew her best said she showed no sign of insanity. In fact, they describe her as highly intelligent and more independent than other girls in her society, but still fully within the range of normal.

Palestinians say the same thing about their first female suicide bomber, Wafa Idris. She was nothing out of the ordinary. Just a twenty eight-year-old woman who ended up a suicide bomber.

But unlike Abboud, Idris attacked civilians. When Idris blew herself up on Jaffa Road in downtown Jerusalem in January 2002, she killed an eighty-one-year-old man and wounded more than 100 others. Idris, a volunteer medic with the Palestine Red Crescent Society, grew up in the al Amari refugee camp on the outskirts of the Palestinian town of Ramallah, only a short ride from Jerusalem.

It is not far-fetched to suspect that Idris may have been depressed and she may have felt she had nothing to live for. She had lost a baby during pregnancy and was unable to bear other children, a significant stigma in the Middle East. Her husband divorced her because of her infertility, and her chances of finding a man who would marry a barren woman were slim. Idris may have decided that life without her own family was meaningless. And she may have sought that meaning in her death, hoping to be heralded among her people as a martyr.

Friends and family said she loved children and was angry at the deaths of so many young Palestinians. They say Idris saw a lot of suffering and death in her job as a medic. "She used to tell me, coming home from work, about what she saw that day. Someone lost a leg, or a brain on the ground, or a child killed," said her oldest brother, Khalil Idris, told reporters shortly after her death. "All these things accumulated."[3]

Arab journalists, apparently unmindful of the message they might be sending to other young women, praised Idris as a heroine, comparing her to Mary, the mother of Jesus.

"From Mary's womb issued a child who eliminated oppression, while the body of Wafa became shrapnel that eliminated despair and aroused hope," the London-based Arab newspaper *al Quds al Arabi* quoted Dr. Abdel Sadeq, head of the department of psychiatry at Ein Shams University in Cairo.

Hussein al Amoush, a columnist with the Jordanian newspaper *al Dustour*, used her death to criticize what he saw as the superficiality of Western feminists, women who seemed to him more concerned about fashion and beauty than principles.

Wafa Idris, al Amoush said in *al Dustour*, "did not carry in her suitcase makeup, but rather, enough explosives to fill the enemies with horror."

In fact, the bag she carried on her back as she walked down Jaffa Road was filled with explosives as well as with bolts and pieces of metal, as is the norm for such attacks, which are designed to wound or kill as many people as possible.

After receiving word of her daughter's death, Idris' mother, Wasifyeh, said she was proud of her and urged more Palestinian women to follow in her footsteps. Of course, she may have simply been putting on a brave face in light of the tragedy of her daughter's life and death.

"If I knew that she was going there, I would have prevented her," Wasifiyeh Idris' mother told reporters after he death. But she added, "She is a hero. My daughter is a martyr."[4] Press reports around the world said Idris's family initially seemed confused at the reports that the young woman had become a suicide bomber. There were questions about whether she really meant to kill herself or whether somehow the package of explosives had been planted on her. But Idris's sister-in-law, Wissam, was quoted as saying she had often spoken of becoming a suicide bomber.

"Wafa was always saying, 'I hope I will be a martyr,'" Wissam told NBC News in a story it aired Feb. 4, 2002. Wissam quoted her sister-in-law as saying, "I'm going to carry a bomb."

Fatah's Al-Aqsa Martyrs Brigade claimed responsibility for Idris's attack and labeled it a "martyr operation." It was greeted with general jubilation throughout the Palestinian areas and there were reports that Iraqi President Saddam Hussein named a street in her honor. An Arab journalist wrote a column about Idris in which he compared her to the Mona Lisa and rhapsodized about her "dreamy eyes and the mysterious smile on her lips."

Saudi Arabia's ambassador to the United Kingdom, Ghazi Algosaibi, reaped both praise from the Arab world and condemnation from the West for a poem he wrote praising another Palestinian woman suicide bomber—Ayat Akhras, who blew herself up in a Jerusalem supermarket on March 29, 2002, killing two Israelis and wounding 25. "The doors of heaven opened for her," wrote Algosaibi, a highly acclaimed poet in the Arab world. In the West, it was hard to understand how an official of a country that has proposed a way to bring Palestinians and Israelis to the peace table could allow one of its highest ranking diplomats to wax poetic about a female suicide bomber.

Not everyone lauded Idris, however. Hamas's Sheikh Yassin, who supports suicide bombings against Israel, said Islamic law requires that women not take on such responsibilities as long as there are men willing to do it.

"I'm saying that in this phase (of the uprising), the participation of women is not needed in martyr operations, like men," Yassin told the London-based Arab daily *al Sharq al Awsat*, published on February 2, 2002. "We can't meet the growing demands of young men who wish to carry out martyr operations."[5]

While the streets may have proclaimed Idris a martyr, Islam's male-dominated jurists did not want to be seen encouraging women to line up for suicide operations. But like Israeli's secret service, they knew that Idris might be only the first in a long line of women who would follow the martyr's path in footsteps of Idris and Loula Abboud. In fact, Shin Bet, Israel's domestic security and intelligence service, had been warning that women would soon be joining the ranks of the more than 100 suicide bombers that had struck Israeli targets since the second intifada broke out in September 2000. The Shin Bet also knew that while Idris was the first Palestinian woman to detonate herself to kill Israelis, she was not the first female to do so. Women such as Loula Abboud had already paved that path in Lebanon.

As much as Loula's mother still grieved for her daughter, like Idris's mother, Um Walid took pride at what she saw as her courage and her leadership. And it was only in looking back that Um Walid saw the signs that pointed toward her daughter's death:

We used to be watching TV with the neighbors and some issue about the occupation would come up and I would be having a heated discussion with my neighbor over it. But Loula wouldn't say anything. She'd just look at us and smile. Now we know she was working on something much bigger. She was doing a lot more than we were doing. We would be discussing the situation, but she was actually fighting. She was actually contributing.

If any Christian were to become involved in an Arab resistance movement against the Israelis, he or she would be from a Lebanese Orthodox Christian family. Orthodox Christians identify strongly with their Arab roots and culture. Dr. Abboud patiently explained that in Lebanon, not all Christians have the same values or loyalties.

"The Christians haven't been able to figure out where they stand, culturally," said Dr. Abboud. "So some consider themselves Western. They're not better than anyone else, but the French gave them power."

As Sandra Mackey explained in her book *Lebanon:*

> Lebanon's Christians . . . are not a monolith but a collection of distinctive groups possessing marked diversities. They broadly divide into three major denominational groups—the Maronites and the Melkites, both Roman Catholic, and the Greek Orthodox, who are part of the Eastern Orthodox church. . . . The Maronites reject inclusion in the Arab world outright; the Greek Orthodox accept their status as part of that world; and the Melkites vacillate between the two attitudes. However, all Lebanese Christians perceive as imperiled their survival as a religious minority trapped in a sea of Islam.[5]

The modern nation of Lebanon was formed after World War I (1914–1918), when the defeated Ottoman Empire, which had controlled the area, was divided. France received a mandate from the League of Nations to rule Lebanon, and the French favored the Maronite Christians, granting them a great deal of political power.

Lebanon's Maronites harken back to a monk named Maron who lived in the fourth century near Antioch in Syria. Maron and his followers believed strongly that Jesus was both human and divine, which resulted in their persecution by Christian sects that contended Christ's nature was only divine, with some human attribute. Maron retreated from the Christian quarrels to lead an ascetic life in the mountains near Antioch, where he reportedly worked many miracles. By the time of St. Maron's death in A.D. 410, he had many followers in both Syria and Lebanon. To escape persecution from fellow Christians who opposed their belief in the dual nature of Christ, Lebanon's Maronites took refuge in the mountains of Lebanon. Later, their haven also would allow them to weather hostilities with Muslims in the region.

Under the 1943 National Pact, designed to keep peace among Lebanon's religious factions, a Maronite must be president of the country; this helps to guarantee that the Christian minority will not be overpowered politically or otherwise by the majority Muslims.

But the Maronites have a shady history, as far as many Arabs are concerned. They cooperated with the Christian crusaders who slaughtered their way through the Middle East, and even now many of them look more to the West, preferring to speak French and distance themselves from Arab culture. The Maronites allied themselves with Israel before the outbreak of the civil war in 1976, receiving arms and supplies as Israel looked for a way to work against the Palestinian militias that had fled to southern Lebanon. But it was an Orthodox Christian soldier by the name of Saad Haddad who organized the South Lebanon Army and recruited Christians to serve as commanders of what turned out to be an army of Shia mercenaries paid by Israel. Christian paramilitary soldiers known as Phalangists helped Israel invade southern Lebanon in 1982 and proceeded to massacre hundreds of Palestinian refugees in the Sabra and Shatilla refugee camps, with Israeli soldiers guarding the perimeter. Ariel Sharon was then Israel's defense chief, and, as mentioned, Palestinians held him ultimately responsible for the slaughter. But it was Christians who actually committed the acts, by Israeli accounts killing more than 700 women, children, and elderly people who had been assured international protection in the camps. The Palestinian Red Crescent claimed more than 2,000 people were killed in Sabra and Shatilla.

Dr. Abboud took pains to explain that Lebanon's Christians were a diverse group even within their own branches and that his family were neither Maronites nor supporters of their Phalangist militia. In fact, he said he found common ground with Muslim groups such as Hezbollah.

"I consider Hassan Nasrullah [leader of Hezbollah] as a national hero. He represents even me as a Christian. He respects my ideas, and I feel that he represents all Lebanese," Dr. Abboud said. "I am somebody who has put a lot of effort into liberating my country, and Hassan Nasrullah is somebody who was able to realize that dream for me. He was able to make it happen. He was responsible for the liberation of my country and I appreciate him for that."

While other Christians have called for Syrian troops to leave Lebanon and for Syria to stop interfering in Lebanese affairs, Dr. Abboud did not see things quite that way. "I live in the Bekaa, which is the region that is most populated with Syrians. We are not afraid of the Syrians. . . . The Syrians want one thing from Lebanon. All they care about is Lebanese foreign policy. They want Lebanon to be with them in foreign policy."

Dr. Abboud believed that the Lebanese needed Syrian intervention to keep from killing each other once again, but many other Lebanese believed that they could handle their own affairs without Syrian interference. And they believed that Syria was controlling every aspect of Lebanon, including domestic and foreign policies. Dr. Abboud offered this explanation: "All small countries are greatly influenced by large countries, and we can't avoid that. The Syrian presence is a lot less now than it was before. And we prefer the Syrian presence to another civil war. We experienced a war that brought out the animal in people. A Christian would kill a Muslim and vice versa just because they were of another religion."

Lebanon's civil war broke out in 1975 when Lebanese Muslims and those on the left began questioning Christian political power guaranteed in the 1943 National Pact and sought to put an end to it. The Maronite Christians panicked and civil war ensued.

The late Syrian president Hafez al Assad helped to broker an end to the civil war with the Taif Agreement, hashed out between September 30 and October 22, 1989, in Taif, Saudi Arabia. It was formally approved on November 4, 1989.

"The Taif Agreement restored the balance of power in the country," Dr. Abboud said. "And I believe the Taif Agreement is more to the benefit of Christians than any other party. Why? If you want to look at the statistics, 38 percent of Lebanese population is Christian; 61 percent of the Lebanese population is Muslim, including Shia, Druze (an offshoot of Shia Islam), Sunni. The Taif Agreement put in the constitution that the president must be a Maronite. Before that it was not a part of the constitution. Even if Christians shrink to 20 percent of the population, the president is still a Maronite."

The significantly higher Muslim birthrate represents a threat to Christians, which the Taif Agreement took pains to address. "They did it to reassure the Christians that they are not going to be eradicated because the Christians are a minority and they're always afraid they're going to be oppressed."

But the issue is actually a Christian problem, Dr. Abboud said, "especially for Maronite Christians," who well remember when their people were slaughtered during Lebanon's civil war of 1960 by the Druze, a secretive, clannish sect that broke from Shia Islam.

"Now, after the war, I believe the agreement is more than fair, but certain Christian leaders, because of their political stand and their anti-Syrian manifestations, certain leaders are serving Israeli interests," Dr. Abboud said, believing such disunity helps the Israelis, whom many Lebanese still consider their enemy. It is a common if underhanded tactic in the Arab world to accuse one's political opponents of serving Israeli interests. Yet many Lebanese Christians would argue that their country would best be served by promoting peace with Israel rather than continued war.

Some Lebanese Christians are particularly critical of President Emile Lahoud for what they see as his coziness with Syrian president Bashar al Assad, accusing him of not doing enough to push for Lebanon's independence.

"Isn't President Lahoud a Christian? Why should we consider the president is a traitor to Lebanon just because he has normal relations with Syria? Generally Lebanese Christian leaders have interests that conflict with the president and the government."

Dr. Abboud believed Christians wielded a great deal of power in Lebanon. "The minister of interior, who is a Christian, has a lot more power than the vice president, who is a Sunni Muslim. Despite the fact that there are a lot more Sunnis in the population than there are Christians."

Dr. Abboud feared that militant Maronites were pushing Lebanon toward yet another civil war and were forcing Christians to take sides. "The Maronite extremists are forcing the Christian population to make one of four choices. The first choice is . . . [to not] care about anything. Be apathetic. Stay out of politics. The second choice is to be an extremist. The third choice is to work with a foreign power against their country. And the fourth choice is to leave Lebanon."

"This is wrong because this is our country just as it is the Muslims' country. We should all accept each other. Each of us is free to worship God the way he wishes, but we are not free to treat our country any way we want. Christians should not say I will only belong to Lebanon if it is a Christian state. And the Muslim cannot say I will only be a Lebanese if it is a Muslim state."

Yet Dr. Abboud feared that the issues that plunged Lebanon into the last civil war are still unresolved. "If we don't fight for a united Lebanon, there will be another war. The victims of this war will be both the Christian and Muslim populations and the only ones who will benefit from this war with be the Israelis." And as he saw it, that would only make a mockery of his sister's martyrdom.

Neither Um Walid nor Dr. Abboud saw any conflict between Loula's death and their strong Christian beliefs, even though Christianity, like Islam, forbids suicide. Both said they were not opposed to an Israeli state nor to efforts to produce a peace treaty between Arabs and Israelis. But they insisted it has to be based on mutual respect and it has to guarantee a homeland for Palestinians.

"Christ tells us not to kill for the sake of killing," the doctor said. "But we can defend ourselves."

Dr. Abboud was aware that the United States had launched what the Bush administration was calling a global war on terrorism and that groups such as Lebanon's Hezbollah and other Arab groups that he considered freedom fighters might be caught up in the dragnet.

"We hope that western governments will not push us into a corner," he said. "And we hope Sharon does not impose the existentialist fight upon us. This land is big enough for all of us."

At the end of the interview, as the car sloshed through the muddy gravel streets toward the main road back to Beirut, Dr. Abboud stopped at his sister's grave. Hardly more than a slab of stone on the side of the road, it blended into the hills of Aoun as perfectly as the rocks and brush that surrounded it. As he stood in the steady drizzle, it was hard not to wonder if he and his martyr-laden family might once again be caught up in fighting in the Bekaa, if these hills would once again witness the sacrifice 19-year-olds such as Loula Abboud—and for what cause would they feel compelled to die.

5

SUICIDE BOMBERS AND SEPTEMBER 11: MOHAMMAD ATTA AND IZZIDENE AL MASRI

If one takes a life, it is as if one has taken the life of all humanity. If one saves a single life, it is as if he has saved the life of all humanity.

—*Qur'an 5:32*

WAS MOHAMMAD ATTA, THE ALLEGED RINGLEADER OF THE September 11 attackers, a martyr or a murderer? Was Izzidene al Masri, the youngster who blew himself up inside Jerusalem's Sbarro Pizzeria, killing unsuspecting women and children, a martyr or a murderer? Were they a part of the vanguard of Islam, as Osama bin Laden described the September 11 hijackers? Or were they manifestations of a horrific corruption of Islam's ideals?

Both Atta and al Masri killed innocent people, and both willingly died doing so. One struck far away from his native Middle East, while the other hit close to home. One is widely castigated among Muslim scholars as a murderer and an apostate, while the verdict on the other is somewhat murkier. Yet both thought they were devout Muslims who went to their deaths fully believing they would awake with God in paradise.

American authorities believe Muhammad Atta, age 33, was the leader of the September 11 hijackers. He was part of a terrorist cell based in Hamburg, Germany, where he was a graduate student and lived with his cousin, Marwan al Shehhi, who was from the United Arab Emirates. Atta spent months, maybe even years, planning the September 11 operation, authorities believe.

An Egyptian, Atta was the son of a lawyer and had several aliases, among them Mehan Atta, Mohammad al Amir, Muhammad al Amir Awad al Sayyid Atta, and Muhammad Muhammad al Amir Awad al Sayad. Egyptian authorities had no record of him and said they had no indication of his involvement with either of their two militant organizations, al Jihad and al Gamaa al Islamiyah (Islamic Group), which wreaked havoc in Egypt during the 1980s before their leaders fled to Afghanistan to wreak havoc on the world. People who knew Atta in Egypt described him as a nice, quiet youth. Atta's father stridently disavowed that his son could have any link to terrorists. Presumably Atta allied himself with Islamic militants after he left Egypt.

Mohamed Alameer Atta told reporters that his son even spoke to him by telephone after the attacks, so he could not have died in them. Like many Arabs after the September 11 attack, Atta's father did not believe that his son or bin Laden were involved. He believed it was Israel's work to discredit Arabs and that his son was framed and killed by Israeli agents. Many Arabs reasoned that bin Laden may be wealthy, but how could someone living among the rocks of Afghanistan with little more than a satellite phone and an M-16 stage such a sophisticated, detailed operation? How could he direct men thousands of miles away in an operation that involved hijacking three jetliners almost simultaneously and striking at the heart of the greatest power on earth?

The operation did seem well planned. At 7:58 A.M., EDT, United flight 175 departed Boston for Los Angeles; it was hijacked and diverted to New York City. At 7:59 A.M., American flight 11 left Boston for Los Angeles; it was hijacked and diverted to New York. At 8:01 A.M., United flight 93 left Newark, New Jersey, for San Francisco; it was hijacked and diverted south. At 8:10 A.M., American flight 77 left Washington D.C.'s Dulles Airport for Los Angeles; it was diverted to the Pentagon. All of the resulting mayhem occurred almost simultaneously within one hour.

Whether framed or not, Atta is believed to have organized and coordinated the operation, with the help of bin Laden and his al Qaeda network. Atta had met with several of the other suspected hijackers including his cousin, Marwan al Shehhi, whom American authorities suspected flew United flight 175 into the World Trade Center's South Tower minutes after Atta's American flight 11 crashed into the North Tower.

In May 2000, Atta and al Shehhi were studying at Hamburg Technical University where Atta had organized an Islamic student group, when both men secured tourist visas to visit the United States. German authorities said

Atta had reported his passport stolen and received a new one, possibly in order to hide his travel to Afghanistan, which might have prevented him from getting a visa to the United States. Authorities say he also met with an Iraqi intelligence agent in Prague before arriving in the United States in June 2000. Atta and several of the others suspected of hijacking the planes, including al Shehhi, took flight lessons in Florida from July until December 2000 and even tried to purchase a crop duster.

It seems that some of the alleged hijackers did not know they were on a "martyrdom mission," as bin Laden put it. And some of the men suspected of involvement, such as Ziad Jarrah, were not known to be religious, even though the FBI said he associated with both Atta and al Shehhi in Hamburg. In fact, Jarrah was known to be a womanizer and a drinker, and his father considers him one of the victims, not one of the hijackers. Whatever Jarrah's actual role or motivation, Atta and enough of the others clearly realized they would die in the attacks and hoped that many innocent people would as well.

Four days before the attack, authorities said that Atta and al Shehhi went to a sports bar, bragged about being pilots, and were seen drinking. While it's possible that the witnesses were wrong and the men actually were not drinking alcohol, such behavior would be bizarre for Islamic militants. Devout Muslims are not supposed to drink and fanatics would beat anyone caught with even a wine cooler. And one would think that the prospect of death would peel away the façade of a hypocrite. So either the witnesses did not see what they thought they saw, which is not out of the question, or Atta and al Shehhi were not devout Muslims who so firmly believed in Islam that the prospect of death meant only a step into a better life.

American authorities said that Atta left a death note in which he detailed the Qur'anic verses he used to embolden him for the operation. The note said:

Remind yourself of obedience. In this night you will face decisive moments. These moments require obedience (100%). Calm your soul, make it understand, and convince and push her to do that [the mission].

Increase your mention of God's name. The best mention is reading the Qur'an. All scholars agreed to this. It is enough for us, that [the Qur'an] is the word of the Creator of Heaven and Earth, Who we are about to meet . . .

Also do not appear to be nervous, be happy with a happy heart, be confident because you are doing a job that religion accepts and loves. And then there will be a day that you will spend with beautiful angels [hur'aen] in paradise. Oh young Man keep a smiling face. You are on your way to everlasting paradise.[1]

As early as April 11, 1996, Atta was preparing for death. In the presence of two witnesses, he penned a last will and testament. In it he made reference to the biblical story of Abraham, whom Muslims call Ibrahim, who was willing to kill his own son on God's instructions. But Atta did not envision that he would die so violently that there would be no body to prepare for burial, he wrote:

> This is what I want to happen after my death, I am Muhammad the son of Muhammad Elamir Awad Elsayed: I believe that prophet Muhammad is God's messenger and time will come no doubt about that and God will resurrect people who are in their graves. I wanted my family and everyone who reads this will to fear the Almighty God and don't get deceived by what is in life and to fear God and to follow God and his prophets if they are real believers. In my memory, I want them to do what Ibrahim [Abraham] told his son to do, to die as a good Muslim.

Atta then ticked off a list of instructions for his burial, assuming that his body would be treated with respect despite the atrocity of the crime he was about to commit. He wrote, in part:

- The people who will prepare my body should be good Muslims because this will remind me of God and his forgiveness.
- The people who are preparing my body should close my eyes and pray that I will go to heaven and to get me new clothes, not the ones I died in.
- I don't want anyone to weep and cry or to rip their clothes or slap their faces because this is an ignorant thing to do.
- I don't want anyone to visit me who didn't get along with me while I was alive or to kiss me or say good bye when I die.
- Those who will sit beside my body must remember Allah, God, and pray for me to be with the angels.
- I don't want any women to go to my grave at all during my funeral or on any occasion thereafter.
- During my funeral I want everyone to be quiet because God mentioned that he likes being quiet on occasions when you recite the

Koran, during the funeral, and when you are crawling. You must speed my funeral procession and I would like many people there to pray for me.

- When you bury me the people with whom I will be buried should be good Muslims. I want to face East toward Mecca.

- I should be laying on my right side. You should throw the dust on my body three times while saying from the dust, we created you dust and to dust you will return. From the dust a new person will be created. After that everyone should mention God's name and that I died as a Muslim which is God's religion. Everyone who attends my funeral should ask that I will be forgiven for what I have done in the past (not this action).

- The custom has been to memorialize the dead every forty days or once a year but I do not want this because it is not an Islamic custom.

- All the money I left must be divided according to the Muslim religion as almighty God has asked us to do. A third of my money should be spent on the poor and the needy. I want my books to go to any one of the Muslim mosques. I wanted the people who look at my will to be one of the heads of the Sunni religion. Whoever it is, I want that person to be from where I grew up or any person I used to follow in prayer. People will be held responsible for not following the Muslim religion. I wanted the people who I left behind to hear God and not to be deceived by what life has to offer and to pray more to God and to be good believers. Whoever neglects this will or does not follow the religion, that person will be held responsible in the end.[2]

In the video that U.S. authorities say they discovered in bombing raids of Afghanistan and that was broadcast around the world, Osama bin Laden clearly seemed to know Atta and referred to him as the leader of the operation.

But Atta probably was only one of many people whom bin Laden befriended and who may have come to him with some grand scheme to hit the United States.

This does not necessarily mean that the Saudi millionaire directed the operation, was involved in its planning, or even believed it could be carried out. It is likely that at some point bin Laden provided funding to Atta, or that he provided the men with training, equipment, or a haven in Afghanistan from which Atta could plan his operation. What is indisputable is that bin Laden and Atta shared a hatred of the United States and Israel and were dedicated to overthrowing governments in the Middle East that they considered corrupt and despotic.

Taher Masri, former prime minister of Jordan, said in an interview at his home in Amman in November 2001 that American support of governments in Egypt, Jordan, Saudi Arabia, and the Gulf states was directly connected to the attack. "Part of what happened September 11 was the feeling that America is supporting Israel and that Israel has been humiliating all Arabs. But there is an added element," he said, "in that those 19 people who were on the plane were not only protesting against the United States but against the internal situations in their own countries."

U.S. support for undemocratic regimes in the Middle East was at the root of much hostility directed toward Americans, he said. "The lack of democracy is the key word here," Masri said. "We suffer from so many things here because it is a one-man decision in most Arab countries. There is no collective decision making." Masri warned that the thirst for democracy that was evident throughout the region was helping to fuel support for extremists who advocated overthrowing Arab leaders and monarchs.

Extremists such as Atta believed they had a duty to right the evil they saw so prevalent in the Arab world, even if it meant carrying out operations that resulted in their own deaths. There are likely hundreds, if not thousands, of Attas around the world who look to bin Laden, and possibly even to Iraq or militants in Iran, for support in their schemes against governments in the Middle East or to attack American targets. In December 2001 Dr. Ayman Zawahri, leader of Egypt's militant al Jihad organization and a top official in al Qaeda, talked about the growing numbers of Muslim youths who had committed themselves to jihad:

> This age is witnessing a new phenomenon that continues to gain ground. It is the phenomenon of the *mujahid* [fighter] youths who have abandoned their families, country, wealth, studies, and jobs in search of jihad arenas for the sake of God . . .
>
> There is no solution without jihad: With the emergence of this new batch of Islamists, who have been missing from the nation for a long time, a new awareness is increasingly developing among the sons of Islam, who are eager to uphold it; namely, that there is no solution without jihad. The spread of this awareness has been augmented by the failure of all other methods that tried to evade assuming the burdens of jihad.[3]

What is clear is that dozens of people in many countries were involved in the September 11 attack, and American authorities believe they were part of an international network with connections to al Qaeda. Bin Laden and his colleagues issued a series of messages beginning in 1998 in which they laid out their platform and intentions.

"The war has just started," bin Laden said in a statement faxed around the world in August 1998 after the Clinton administration bombed Sudan and Afghanistan. "Americans should wait for the answer."[4]

Sheikh Omar Bakri, who until August 1998 described himself as bin Laden's spokesman in London, said bin Laden had emerged from the attacks unscathed and had issued the new communiqué calling on all Muslims to wage jihad against the United States and warning them to stay away from U.S. embassies and other buildings. Bakri is a leader of a radical group called al Muhajiroun ("the Immigrants") that was based in London but that had supporters throughout the United States and Europe. The group's name suggests that members see themselves in the role of the first Muslims who immigrated from Mecca to Medina, where they grew strong enough to conquer the entire Arabian peninsula.

Members of al Muhajiroun do not hide their goal of wanting to establish a new Islamic caliphate, which they believe is destined to rule the world. Their official web site is dedicated to promoting jihad against the United States. One statement reads:

> The USA are at war with Muslims. They have committed various atrocities against the Muslim Umma, ranging from killing, raping our honour and land, mass murders in Iraq, funding and assisting the establishment of Israel, violating the sanctity of Muslims in Iraq and controlling Muslim land, sea, and air space. The US are not only targeting the military but also civil areas in the Muslim land of Iraq.[5]

Al Muhajiroun officially labeled Pakistan's president Pervez Musharraf and several other Arab leaders as apostates for their support of Bush's war on terrorism. The organization reminded Muslims that the penalty for apostasy was death, and it offered verse V, chapter 33 of the Qur'an as justification: "The punishment of those who wage war against Allah and His apostle and strive to make mischief in the land is only this, that they should be murdered or crucified or their hands and their feet should be cut off on opposite sides or they should be imprisoned; this shall be as a disgrace for them in this world, and in the hereafter they shall have a grievous chastisement."[6]

In that same article, al Muhajiroun also detailed the punishments proscribed for an apostate:

1. He/She has no sanctity for his life and he must therefore be killed whether he asks for repentance or not.
2. Any marriage with a wife will become invalid, his children will no longer belong to him and all his blood relations must be cut.
3. His money becomes permissible, which will either go to the *Bait-al-Maal* [community treasury] . . . or it will be taken as booty by the *Mujahedeen* [holy fighters]. He will receive no inheritance nor will he pass any inheritance to others.
4. His body will not be buried with the Muslims.
5. He will be treated with animosity by all Muslims. . . . No Muslim sister will be allowed to marry him, and even people of the book will be stopped from marrying him. Anyone who gives his daughter to him will also become an apostate.
6. There is no distinction between a man or women with regarding this *Hukm* [law]. Therefore we ask Muslims with the capability, especially the army of Muslim countries to move quickly and capture those apostates and criminals involved in these crimes, especially the ruler of Pakistan, King Fahd of Saudi Arabia and [Burhanuddin] Rabbani of Afghanistan [whose Northern Alliance front opposed the Taliban] and his followers. . . . We call upon Muslims worldwide to support Muslims in Afghanistan, whoever cannot support them physically must do so, whosoever can support them financially must do so and whosoever can support them verbally must do so according to his capacity.

After the August 7, 1998 bombings of the American embassies in Africa and Britain's enactment of laws making it illegal to support terrorists, al Muhajiroun's al Bakri stopped calling himself a spokesman for bin Laden. Before then, however, he circulated bin Laden's edicts, including one in February 1998 in which the Saudi exile put the world on notice that he had teamed up with several other extremists groups and they were preparing for war.

Calling itself the World Islamic Front, the group's leaders were identified as bin Laden; Zawahri; Abu Yasir Rifa'i Ahmad Taha, a leader of al

Gamaa al Islamiyah; Sheikh Mir Hamzah, secretary of Jamiat-ul-Ulema-e-Pakistan, a Pakistani group; and Fazlul Rahman, leader of the Jihad Movement in Bangladesh. Bin Laden apparently merged his al Qaeda network with these groups to take on a larger mission against the United States. Before then, al Qaeda had been focused on trying to scare U.S. troops out of Saudi Arabia and trying to overthrow the House of Saud, the country's family of ruling princes.

Claiming to speak in defense of Islam and guided by the example of Muhammad and his earliest companions, bin Laden's newly formed group laid out grievances in a February 1998 fatwa that resonated with millions of Muslims from Mauritania to Indonesia, calling on them to fight and be prepared to die to redress those grievances: "First, for over seven years the United States has been occupying the lands of Islam in the holiest of places, the Arabian Peninsula, plundering its riches, dictating to its rulers, humiliating its people, terrorizing its neighbors, and turning its bases in the Peninsula into a spearhead through which to fight the neighboring Muslim peoples."[7]

The message spoke specifically of the campaign against Iraq, claiming that "despite the great devastation inflicted on the Iraqi people by the crusader-Zionist alliance, and despite the huge number of those killed, which has exceeded 1 million . . . despite all of this, the Americans are once again trying to repeat the horrific massacres, as though they are not content with the protracted blockage imposed after the ferocious war on the fragmentation and devastation."

In the message, bin Laden and his partners also railed against the Israeli-Palestinian conflict. They blamed the United States for what they saw as its supporting Israeli ruthlessness in occupying Arab land, demolishing Palestinian homes, preventing Muslim men from praying at Jerusalem's al-Aqsa mosque, and slaughtering hundreds of Palestinians:

If the Americans' aims behind these wars are religious and economic, the aim is also to serve the Jews' petty state and divert attention from its occupation of Jerusalem and murder of Muslims there. The best proof of this is their eagerness to destroy Iraq, the strongest neighboring Arab state, and their endeavor to fragment all the states of the region such as Iraq, Saudi Arabia, Egypt, and Sudan into paper statelets and through their disunion and weakness to guarantee Israel's survival and continuation of the brutal crusade occupation of the Peninsula.

All of these crimes and sins committed by the Americans are a clear declaration of war on God, his messenger [Muhammad] and Muslims. And throughout Islamic history, *ulema* [religious authorities] unanimously agreed that jihad is an individual duty if the enemy destroys the Muslim countries.

Bin Laden declared war on the United States because he believed Americans had declared war on God, and he believed all Americans were guilty because of their complicity in the war. This is evident in messages in which he repeatedly warns that even American civilians are not exempt from targeting. In the February 1998 message he said: "The ruling to kill the Americans and their allies—civilian and military—is an individual duty for every Muslim who can do it in any country in which it is possible to do it, in order to liberate the al-Aqsa Mosque and the holy mosque [Mecca] from their grip, and in order for their armies to move out of all the lands of Islam, defeated and unable to threaten any Muslims."[8]

Many Muslim scholars argue that bin Laden's call for jihadees to attack civilians goes against Muhammad's basic teachings about how Muslims should conduct themselves in war and who are just targets. They point to Surah 5:8 of the Qur'an: "O ye who believe! Be steadfast witnesses for Allah in equity, and let not hatred of any people seduce you that ye deal not justly. Deal justly, that is nearer to your duty. Observe your duty to Allah, Lo! Allah is informed of what ye do."

Less than a year after bin Laden's message was issued, bombs struck the U.S. embassies in Dar es Salaam, Tanzania, and Nairobi, Kenya, almost simultaneously, killing hundreds of innocent people, many of them Africans who just happened to be in the wrong place on that August day. Bin Laden denied he was responsible for the attacks, but praised them. The following year suicide bombers sailed a small boat next to the USS *Cole* docked in Yemen and blew themselves up, killing nineteen American soldiers. Again bin Laden denied responsibility but proclaimed that the men had joined the ranks of Islam's shuhada.

This form of jihad, in which the body is used as a weapon, is a recent development in the annals of Islamic warfare, even if the concept of holy war and martyrdom is as old as the religion itself. As with Jewish and Christian history, early Islamic history has more than a fair share of treachery and bloodshed, as Muslims were forced to defend their faith from powerful adversaries from the very start. Cain killed Abel, Judas kissed Jesus and then turned him over for crucifixion, and many of Muhammad's early companions died in wars with each other. It was Muhammad himself who first raised the banner of jihad as his new religion was besieged by hostile forces in the region.

In fact, from the very beginning, when Muhammad claimed to have received a new revelation from God, Mecca's powerful Quraysh tribe both feared and despised him. His message that there is only one God and that he was God's messenger made a mockery of their beliefs in many deities, all collected neatly inside a big, square block that later would be purified to become Islam's holiest site, the Kaaba. As more people became interested in Muhammad's teachings, the ruling elite grew even more afraid that he would usurp their authority and power, so they began plotting to kill him and his followers. Muhammad sent some followers to seek safe haven in Ethiopia under the Christian king Negus As'ha'mah, whom they considered both good and wise. The Prophet himself was forced to flee to Medina, miraculously escaping an assassination attempt. Muslims refer to Muhammad's flight to Medina in 622 C.E. as the *hijira*.

In the book *Jihad*, Saudi Sheikh Abdullah bin Muhammad bin Humaid explained that when the Prophet established the new religion, his teachings were closer to those of Jesus, admonishing his followers against fighting, even in self-defense. "And it is now obvious, at first 'the fighting' was forbidden, then it was permitted and after that it was made obligatory against them who start the fighting against you [Muslims] . . . and against those who worship others along with Allah."[9] Humaid refers to the following quotation from the Qur'an as the first order given to Muslims regarding fighting: "'Restrain your hands, and establish regular prayers and *zakat* (alms),'" demanded the early revelations of the Qur'an, which Muhammad received gradually beginning with the visit of the Angel Gabriel in about 610 C.E."

Humaid noted that Muhammad adhered to these guidelines even when he was being directly attacked. In Mecca, when his enemies stoned him and covered him with garbage while he was praying, Muhammad did not fight back.

Muslim scholars say it was only after repeated persecution in Mecca, including the slaughter of many of the early Muslims, and pressure from companions such as Abu Bakr that Muhammad changed his teaching and allowed them to defend themselves through military means. According to Surah 22:39–40: "Sanction is given unto those who fight because they have been wronged; and Allah is indeed able to give them victory. Those who have been driven from their homes unjustly only because they said: Our Lord is Allah."[10]

Finally, Humaid noted, in Surah 2:190–191 Muhammad made jihad obligatory: "Fight in the way of Allah those who fight against you, but begin not hostilities. Lo! Allah loveth not aggressors."

Most Islamic jurists contend that Muslims are required to seize the opportunity for a just peace whenever it is presented. According to Abu Dawud, who lived during the time of Muhammad and whose collection of his words and deeds is considered authentic, the Prophet is reported to have said: "Do not kill a decrepit old man, or a young infant, or a woman . . . do not be dishonest about spoils, but collect your spoils. Do right and act well, because Allah loves those who do well."[11]

Muslims scholars believe that Muhammad expressly forbade killing children and say he set down clear rules for warfare. In his book *The Prophets of Islam*, Syed Muhammad Hussain Shamsi, an Islamic authority who was born in India and spent many years working in Africa, listed the rules of warfare:

- Call Upon Allah for help when you mount for a battle in His name.
- Try and negotiate settlements with peace.
- If you have to draw arms in war, do not resort to devious means in your battles and avoid the tactics of ambush.
- Do not disfigure or dismember the fallen.
- Do not kill or harm the old, the sick or the infirm, women, and children.
- Leave the monks and ascetics alone.
- Do not cut or burn fruit trees.
- Do not destroy cultivations or other vegetation.
- Do not harm those who seek your protection. If they agree to pay the tithe for their safe conduct, accept it.
- Allow the besieged to come out for peace or safe conduct.[12]

Stretching the definition of defensive war, Muhammad's followers also undertook what they considered to be preemptive strikes against their enemies and pursued wars to expand their power and ensure the safety of Muslims in other lands.

But Sayyid Qutb, the Egyptian Islamic thinker, took the argument one step further. He contended that jihad is not just defensive but can be offensive, as well. And he explained Muhammad's gradual move toward making jihad obligatory in this way: "The command to refrain from fighting during the Makkan (Meccan) period was a temporary phase in a long journey. The same reason was operative during the early days of hijira, but after these early phases, the reason for jihad was not merely to defend Madinah [Medina]. Indeed, its defense was necessary, but this was not the ultimate aim. The aim was to protect the resources and the center of the movement—the movement to free mankind and demolish the obstacles that prevented mankind from attaining this freedom."[13]

In other words, Qutb interprets Muhammad's message to advocate preemptive military action to help propagate the faith and to ensure Muslims freedom of worship. This philosophy is not unlike that of President George W. Bush, who has refused to rule out preemptive action against those considered a threat to American security.

Before Muhammad died in A.D. 632, his power extended throughout the Arabian peninsula. And after his death, Islam became more than a religion; it became an empire, led by a series of men, some of whom have been described as brutal, corrupt, and bloodthirsty. They saw war as a way to expand not only Islam but their treasuries, as well. Under these treacherous rulers, Islam's rules on war were abused, leading to massacres not only of "infidels" but of fellow Muslims. Even some members of Muhammad's own family suffered the most brutal deaths at the hands of people who professed to be devoted to his teachings.

Hussein ibn Ali, Muhammad's grandson, is known as the Master of Martyrs, especially among the Shia. Hussein held firm, in the face of death, against a ruler whom he believed usurped authority, and was not righteously grounded in the fundamental precepts of Islam, and whom he felt would irreparably defile the religion if unchallenged. He also died while fighting, surrounded and outnumbered by a superior army.

Hussein's murder was a profound event in Islamic history that helps to explain the deep roots of martyrdom in the religion and how death on the battlefield has come to represent its highest ideals. It has taught Muslims that they should not always expect victory on this earth, even if they are fighting for a just cause.

Ayatullah Muhammad Husayn Fadlullah, perhaps the world's leading Shia scholar and considered by many to be the spiritual father of Hezbollah, strongly condemned the September 11 attack even as he supported Hezbollah's suicide bombers who fought Israeli targets in southern Lebanon. The United States and Israel consider Hezbollah a terrorist organization.

Hani Abdallah, Fadlullah's political and media advisor, took pains in an interview in November 2001 to distance the sheikh from Hezbollah and insists he now had "no connection whatsoever" to the group. Yet Jihad, a young man of about 19 who was a proud member of Hezbollah, consistently referred to him as the group's spiritual leader, explaining that even though there had been a difference of opinion over theological issues, it had nothing to do with such a major issue as martyrdom or jihad.

Being granted a meeting with Fadlullah is an occasion of great importance, especially for Shias and Hezbollah devotees. Just before our meeting, Fadlullah had received the male representatives of two families, who asked for him to bless the wedding of their children. Jihad greeted the sheikh by rushing to bow before him and kissing his hand, pressing it gently to his forehead, then retiring meekly to await his summons. Fadlullah seemed used to such greetings and accepted it with the same benevolence that the Pope receives his faithful. He smiled easily and maintained a fatherly demeanor of wisdom and calm. Dressed in a long gray robe, his head covered with a black turban, symbolizing descent from Muhammad, the sheikh stood to greet his visitors then retired to a seat behind a huge desk in the cavernous room. As is usual with Islamic scholars, the walls of Fadlullah's office were lined with bookcases and decorated with framed verses of the Qur'an. He is widely known as one of Islam's most learned men and he was eager to set the record straight on Islam's teachings about war.

Fadlullah explained that there are major differences between the attack on the United States and Hezbollah's war with Israel. Because Israeli troops were occupying Lebanon, attacking them fell within the limits of Islam's teachings on "just war." But Islam does not condone attacking civilians in a country that was not directly threatening Muslim land or its people, he said. "I'm against any attack that targets civilians of a country whose government policies we oppose," Fadlullah said.

"Just because we are against the policies of that government does not mean we should attack the people of that country," he said. "We consider such an act unjust and if the government is criminal in its policies, it does not mean that people of that country are also criminals."

But Fadlullah's opinion, however weighty, is just one among many within Islam. There is no one central religious authority in Islam, no Pope or even universally accepted high priest, a fact that provides an open field for people such as bin Laden to manipulate the precepts of the religion. While there are religious authorities whom many Muslims look to for guidance in interpretation of the Qur'an and the *hadith*, the record of Muhammad's words and deeds, there are sometimes contradictory fatawah from equally respected scholars and religious institutions.

"A fatwa is simply a scholar's opinion on Islamic law," Taha Jabir al Alwainy, a respected Islamic jurist with the Graduate School of Islamic and Social Sciences in Leesburg, Virginia, said in an interview in late September 2001. "It doesn't mean this is the one Islamic opinion."

Most leading Islamic authorities forthrightly condemned the September 11 attacks and did not call Atta and his band martyrs. But many of the same authorities support suicide bombings against Israel, if they are conducted against military or government targets. Others believe Islam supports such attacks against any Israeli, holding that none is innocent since all Israelis are occupying Muslim land.

That was clearly the opinion of Izzidene al Masri and many people in the West Bank town of Jenin. On the warm August day that al Masri blew himself up in Jerusalem's Sbarro Pizzeria, his neighbors danced in the streets and sang the praises of their latest and most deadly *istishhadi*, one who martyrs himself. Al Masri killed sixteen people, six of them children. Many more children were left motherless, fatherless, and forever scarred from having lived through those terror-filled minutes.

Yasser Arafat condemned the attack and called for a cease-fire. He also used the opportunity to call for international monitors, which Israel opposed, arguing that they would only provide cover for Palestinian militants to attack Israeli civilians.

"I denounce the bombing attack that took place in West Jerusalem and I denounce all acts that harm civilians," Arafat said, and canceled a meeting that had been scheduled with members of Hamas and Islamic Jihad.[14] Both groups had vowed to carry out more suicide attacks against Israelis, threatening to make them even more deadly than the Sbarro tragedy.

Hamas, which claimed responsibility for al Masri's bombing, had committed itself to war with Israel until it withdraws from the West Bank, Gaza, and East Jerusalem. Founded in December 1987 by a group of prominent Islamic clerics that included Sheikh Ahmed Yassin, Hamas started as a political wing of the Muslim Brotherhood in the West Bank and Gaza, attracting not only poor, angry youths but also middle-class professionals and intellectuals. By 2001, Hamas had grown so powerful that even Arafat loyalists were calling for the group to be included in the governing body of the Palestinian Authority. While Israel and the United States pressured Arafat to crush the group, Palestinians knew that any attempt to do so would risk civil war among them, and Arafat might not emerge victorious.

If the Palestinian Authority, established in 1994 to govern the Palestinians, were a democracy, Hamas certainly would seriously threaten Arafat and his Fatah colleagues. The Palestinian Authority was established in 1994 under guidelines set out in the 1993 Declaration of Principles on Interim Self-Government Arrangements, also known as the Oslo Agreement. But Arafat and his government are roundly criticized as corrupt while Hamas enjoys a stalwart reputation as one of the few places besieged Palestinians can turn for help.

While the West views Hamas as a terrorist organization, Palestinians see another side. Hamas acts as a Palestinian charity, disbursing money and free healthcare and other services to needy families, widows, and orphans. It receives money from Arab governments as well as from individual donors around the world, including Muslims in the United States. It is fair to say that many Muslims consider Hamas an Islamic charity and political organization that is challenging the ineptitude of the Palestinian Authority and doing worthwhile work helping Palestinians suffering under the Israeli occupation. Many Muslims consider Hamas's military wing, known as the Brigades of the Martyr Izzidene al Qassam, a resistance army, not terrorists. Hamas's disciplined and secretive military core actually operates independently of the charitable and political branches. It was named after a religious scholar who became one of the Palestinian's most heralded martyrs. Born in Syria, Izzidene al Qassam claimed direct descent from the Prophet Muhammad and studied for ten years at Egypt's Al Azhar University, the Islamic world's preeminent religious school. In the 1920s, Sheikh al Qassam began recruiting men to join his fighters from those he observed at the mosques in Haifa, where he regularly preached. He was most interested in men who were devout and who seemed to be sober and serious, believing that those who wage outer jihad must also be proficient at inner jihad, overcoming their own weaknesses and abiding by Islam's teachings.

According to Maryam Jameelah, a Jewish American convert to Islam who has written about al Qassam, he "insisted that righteous character was more important than military bravery."[15]

By the time he died in 1935, in a shootout with British soldiers, he had established throughout the Palestinian areas guerrilla cells, which had become proficient at attacking the British as well as Jewish settlers, who had been immigrating from Europe to Palestine since the nineteenth century. Al Qassam demanded that his fighters adhere to the Qur'an's injunction against excess in war. According to Jameelah, al Qassam "gave strict orders to the mujahedeen that if they captured any Jewish or British prisoners, they were not permitted to torture them. If there was a shortage of food, the prisoners must be fed first, even if it meant that the mujahedeen would have to go hungry. He also forbade his men to mutilate corpses of the fallen enemy."[16]

The al Qassam Brigades now fighting in the West Bank and Gaza are composed of two branches, secretive cells that gather information, and plan and organize attacks, and youths known as al Sawa'ed al Ramiyeh, (the Throwing Arm). The Throwing Arm is composed of young men in the streets who fuel the intifada and who so often are killed in clashes with Israeli troops. The al Qassam Brigades cells are known for their meticulous planning of attacks and for their efforts to stamp out criminal, immoral activity and thwart Palestinian collaborators. Before 1994 they primarily confined their operations to Israeli military and government targets in the region. But after the Jewish extremist Baruch Goldstein, a former Israeli soldier, gunned down 42 Muslims as they were praying in a crowded mosque in Hebron in March 1994, the al Qassam Brigades vowed to kill an equal number of Israelis, civilian or military, to atone for the massacre. Shortly thereafter, a man named Ra'ed Zakarneh drove a car fitted with explosives into an Israeli bus in the town of Afula, killing nine Israeli civilians and injuring 52. Four more Israelis were killed and 30 wounded in a subsequent attack in the town of Hadera.

Although Hamas's guerrillas are committed to armed struggle against Israel, its leadership has not claimed responsibility for any attacks outside of the region and has at times cooperated with Arafat's Palestinian Authority as he pursued peace efforts with the Israelis. In 2001 Hamas even declared several short-lived cease-fires and suspensions of suicide bombings as world pressure mounted on Arafat to stop Islamic militants. Hamas leaders vowed not to engage in internecine bloodletting as Arafat reeled under the weight of U.S. pressure to stop attacks against Israel, even as Palestinian leaders were being assassinated and Palestinian cities bombed.

On March 2, 2002, a suicide bomber waded into a crowd leaving a bar mitzvah celebration at a synagogue in an ultra-orthodox part of Jerusalem. Ten people were killed, including an 18-month-old Jewish girl. Fifty-seven people were injured in what Knight Ridder reporters Dan Rubin and Michael Matza described as an explosion that "touched off an enormous fireball that rose three stories."[17]

The suicide bomber was identified as Mohammed Ahmed Draghmeh, 19, a resident of the Dehaishe refugee camp near Bethlehem and a member of the al-Aqsa Martyrs Brigade, which was allied with Arafat's Fatah organization.

Marwan Barghouti, head of Fatah in the West Bank, said Sharon's tactics had forced all Palestinian factions to unite and the Palestinian Authority would not move against Hamas and Islamic Jihad, as Israel wanted. Israel had demanded that Arafat arrest militants within the organization, and he had gone so far as to put Sheikh Ahmed Yassin under house arrest. But it was clear that even within Arafat's cadres, there was sympathy for the groups and their tactics.

"They are a part of our national liberation movement," said Barghouti, interviewed in November 2001 in the West Bank town of Ramallah in an office he had commandeered for a few hours. Barghouti, believing Israel had targeted him for assassination, refused to give a location for the meeting until 15 minutes before it was to take place. Even then he came with several bodyguards.

"I will not accept—the Arabs will not accept—the description of the Americans for terrorism. If they did not describe the Israeli occupation as terrorism, nobody will believe them." Barghouti, a short, stocky, powder keg of a man known for his street smarts, was among those close to Arafat who were on a short list to succeed him as head of the Palestinian Authority, and Barghouti did not dissuade such speculation. He also did not flinch from stating his belief that there was little hope for peace negotiations under a Sharon government and that Palestinians were left only with the military option.

"We will continue," he said. "We have no alternative except to continue the intifada and the resistance against the Israeli occupation. I think it's legitimate."

Despite the growing toll of Palestinian deaths, Barghouti said the intifada had helped his people. "I think we have succeeded in sending a very clear message all over the world . . . that never will there be any kind of security in the Middle East . . . more than that, in the world, if they don't put a stop to the Israeli occupation . . ."

"I think what we succeeded in doing during this intifada is letting every settler understand that they have no future in this land. We have succeeded in making their lives very difficult in the West Bank and Gaza. And we will continue in this policy."

The intifada, including suicide bombings, had hurt Israelis in another important area, Barghouti said: in their pocketbooks. "Tourism decreased 64 percent . . . the rate of the unemployed people is very high. And there is emigration now instead of immigration. So not only the Palestinians will pay the price of this occupation, but also the Israelis. And we are not happy to see any Israeli who will be a victim, believe me. Prime Minister Sharon's terror policy, this fascist policy, this Nazi policy, is responsible for the victims on both sides. The Israeli victims are victims from his policy as well as the Palestinians victims."

Like almost every Palestinian leader, secular or religious, and many youths, Barghouti said he, too, was prepared to die for the cause of independence:

> I have been a target for the past three months. And one of my colleagues who was working with me was shot by three rockets. But I was not in the same car. In spite of that, after these huge number of people I see assassinated, I don't feel that death is a big deal anymore. After this experience. In spite of the fact, I feel very bad about my children, my wife, my people, I'm ready to sacrifice myself.

Sharon was convinced the only way to deal with the Palestinians was through the military, so he routinely sent assassins to hunt out Palestinian leaders such as Barghouti and tanks to bomb towns such as al Masri's Jenin.

Jenin, the town where al Masri, the Sbarro suicide bomber, grew up, is the picture of torment and brutality. It is a dismal town of cinder-block houses with blown-out windows, pockmarked roads, and dirt streets that turn muddy black when it rains. Even before the Israelis reduced much of Jenin to rubble in their April 2002 campaign to wipe out Palestinian militants, much of the town looked like a war zone and every youth said he was ready to die a shaheed.

Throughout the city, soot stains freshly bombed houses where the primary occupation of most young men like al Masri, and even some women, is fighting Israeli soldiers, often only a few blocks away. There are few jobs for smart, restless young men, and mothers are often too afraid of Israeli bombs to let their children go to school. In Gaza, five little Palestinian boys in Gaza were killed on their way to school one morning when they stepped on unexploded mines that Israeli soldiers left along the road. Their deaths also inflamed the townspeople.

As in much of the Palestinian areas, in Jenin guns are plentiful, including big American M-16s. And the threat of death is omnipresent.

In the fall of 2001, just reaching is a risky proposition. Israeli checkpoints are scattered along the road from Jerusalem, and Israeli soldiers are stationed behind sandbags and inside bunkers and towers just outside the town to seal it off and monitor traffic in and out. Israeli tanks seem to emerge from nowhere to block cars on the road, allowing only those deemed suitable to enter Jenin. And few are allowed to leave once they were inside.

The soldiers have to let journalists into Jenin, and they do so with intimidating smirks, suggesting that only fools willing to risk death or terrorists dare enter. They consider the town a virtual factory for suicide bombers.

The difficulty of getting to Jenin may have made it impossible for Arab leaders to get donations to the al Masri family. But many people also seem as ambivalent as al Masri's mother, Um Iyad, about whether he had actually done something worthy of praise.

"What prompts a 20-year-old to blow himself up and kill as many Israelis as he can, in the process?" asked Labib Kamhawi, a political analyst in Amman, Jordan, who has studied the phenomenon. "It definitely takes more than belief in God to turn a boy into a martyr. It takes desperation, anger, loss of hope. It's believing that your life is not worth living anymore."

To the people in Jenin, al Masri is not unlike the biblical Samson, who used his body as a powerful weapon to bring down the building in which he was chained to a post, killing himself as well as hundreds of his enemies. And there are dozens of young Samsons in Jenin alone, youths so angry they are willing to turn the Middle East into an inferno to strike at what they consider the source of their oppression, Israel.

There is little in Jenin to make life more attractive than death. There are no jobs, adults live in perpetual anger and depression, and their world is mired in humiliation. Young men in Jenin see no future outside of war. They spend their days and nights in the only activity that has any meaning—fighting the Israelis. By the time most young men in Jenin are 19 or 20, they are already war veterans, having seen young rock throwers killed, heard their mothers wail in grief, and listened as their fathers cursed the people they say stole their land.

Young men in Jenin grow up listening to the imams in the town's mosque rail against the bright new Israeli settlements perched near what once were Palestinian villages and olive groves. And they hear the singing and dancing that envelop the town when a young man such as al Masri dies in a battle or a suicide bombing against the Israelis. Many have watched their houses destroyed by Israeli bulldozers in retaliation for an attack on a Jewish settlement, and others have seen boys shot down by Israeli soldiers. Most have watched their fathers humiliated at Israeli checkpoints after waiting in lines hours long, trying to bring sick, crying babies to the hospital. It is hard to find a Palestinian youth who does not believe he has a duty to hate the Israelis and to fight them to regain Arab land.

"Do you know what it means to live under Israeli occupation?" asked Dr. Eyad Sarraj, founder and director of the Gaza Community Mental Health Programme in a commentary that was first published in August 1997 and again in August 2001. In "Why We Have Become Suicide Bombers?" Sarraj wrote:

> You are given an identity number and a permit to reside. If you leave the country for more than three years in succession, you lose that right to residence. When you leave the country on a trip, you are given a *laissez passer*, a traveling document, valid for one year and it tells you in its recording of your particulars that you are of undefined nationality.
>
> Israeli occupation means that you are called twice a year by the intelligence for routine interrogation and persuasion to work as an informer on your brothers and sisters. No one is spared. If you are known to be a member of a political organization, you will be sentenced to ten years. For a military action you will be sentenced to life.
>
> To survive under Israeli occupation, you are given the chance to work in jobs that Israelis do not like: sweeping the streets, building houses, collecting fruit or harvesting. You will have to leave your home in the refugee camp in Gaza at 3 A.M., go through the road blocks and check posts, spend your day under the sun and surveillance, returning home in the evening to collapse in bed for a few hours before the following day. We simply became the slaves of our enemy. . . .
>
> The struggle of Palestinians today is how not to become a bomb. . . . The amazing thing is not the occurrence of the suicide bombing but rather the rarity of them.[18]

And today suicide bombers are becoming more and more popular among Palestinians. The men who decide who will be allowed to become suicide bombers say they have no need to coerce or cajole anyone, that there is a ready cadre of young men, and increasingly of young women, who sign up for such operations. But it is not the leaders of their organizations who go on such missions; they are needed to train future istishhadis. It is young people such as al Masri who may be considered dispensable, who are allowed the privilege of killing themselves.

Yet al Masri seemed the most unlikely candidate for becoming a suicide bomber, his mother said. Izzidene al Masri was a mild-mannered youth who had never been in a fight, not even with his brothers. "He was a person who prayed and who fasted and who observed religion and who never hurt anyone," Um Iyad said. "I've never seen him hurt any person, and I never would have thought that he had the ability to do so."

That seems to be the profile of many Palestinian suicide bombers—often described as gentle beings who never gave any sign that they would be capable of undertaking such an act.

Al Masri had a lot of help to carry out his mission, even though none of his accomplices stayed in the pizzeria to die with him. His operation took special planning. Someone had to help him get into Jerusalem, prepare the explosives, and strap them onto his body. And probably people helped him prepare emotionally and spiritually for his expected passage into paradise.

Israeli authorities arrested two Palestinian students, a man and a woman, who attended Bir Zeit University near Ramallah and whom they believe helped al Masri. Mohammed Douglas, from Burka in the West Bank, was, according to authorities, a member of Force 17, Arafat's personal guard force. During questioning, Israelis said, Douglas said a student at Bir Zeit who was a member of Hamas recruited him for the mission. Douglas allegedly rented an apartment in Ramallah for al Masri and bought a guitar and case for him to hide the bomb.

The woman accomplice, Ahlan Timimi, was identified as a Jordanian citizen who for the past few years had lived in Nabi Salah. She allegedly accompanied al Masri from Ramallah to Jerusalem and hid the explosive device in the guitar case. Israeli authorities said Timimi had been responsible for a failed attack in which she planted a booby-trapped beer can in a Jerusalem supermarket. No one was injured in the explosion, but it was another example of an attack designed to target civilians.

Um Iyad seemed certain that someone convinced her son to become a suicide bomber. "I don't believe that my son went as an act of revenge because no one in our family was ever directly hurt through the occupation. But I think that someone put it into his head that this was a way to go to paradise. He wanted to go to paradise."

Al Masri believed in one God and the resurrection of the dead at a final Day of Judgment. He believed that martyrs were guaranteed a special place in heaven. "He was a very good boy. He was a pious person, not someone to be with gangs and to do bad deeds. He cared a lot about praying and fasting and being pious," his mother said. "His day was spent working in his father's restaurant in Jenin, going to the mosque and then home. Those were the three destinations he went every day. His life revolved around Palestine."

Al Masri was dedicated to doing something to help liberate Palestine from what he considered brutal Israeli oppression. And he believed that if he died a shaheed, he would be instantly transported to be with God in heaven. A family member said he thought it was God's will that he avenge the deaths of eight Palestinians, including two children, killed when Israeli soldiers shelled the headquarters of the Islamic group Hamas in the West Bank town of Nablus a few weeks earlier.

Um Iyad's words were unsettling. She did not reveal her suspicions until well into our interview in her comfortable home in Jenin, but she clearly believed that someone played on Izzidene's religious fervor and on his obsession with the afterlife to convince him to walk into the Sbarro Pizzeria and take his own life.

That is not to say that al Masri did not fully know what he was doing or that he was forced to do it. Before he set out, al Masri posed for a photo in which he was wearing a green Hamas headband and brandishing an assault rifle. He was ready for martyrdom. But Um Iyad's comments raised haunting questions about al Masri's mental capabilities, a young man whose neighbors thought he would never amount to much.

Was al Masri, whose only refuge outside of his home was the mosque, and who restricted himself to male friends, convinced by stronger minds to take the martyrdom path? There is nothing to prove this, of course, and his mother said he had long been obsessed with religion, but his interest in death and the afterlife became evident when he was around 16 years old. He thought deeply about God and longed to be with him, his mother said. Perhaps martyrdom was the inevitable path for a young, shy, religious boy surrounded by the kind of death, desperation, and anger that is so widespread in Jenin.

"The knowledge of the afterlife was a gift from God," Um Iyad said. "It wasn't from anyone. He would bring me cassettes to listen to, Qur'anic verses. I would listen to them and he would tell me it's the afterlife we should seek, not this life. He believed that we have another life waiting for us. . . . This came from God."

Al Masri went every day to pray at mosques where he heard imams lambasting the United States and Israel, whom they blamed for the despotism of Middle Eastern governments, for the lack of jobs, and for the overall misery so prevalent in the Arab world. Like al Masri, many young men join groups such as Hamas and Islamic Jihad, groups whose leaders believe that the United States and Israel are waging war not only against the Palestinians and the Arab world but against Islam itself.

Sheikh Ahmed Yassin, whom I interviewed in November 2001, was convinced that suicide bombers were the Palestinians' best weapons against the Israelis even as he insists that that Hamas only "targets" Israel's military. "In Islam, it's forbidden to hurt innocents," he said, covered in blankets in a wheelchair at his offices in Gaza.

Though in his early sixties, Yassin seems much older. He is gaunt and frail, nearly deaf, and speaks barely above a whisper. He had a stern demeanor, with a bony, sharp face dominated by a long, hooked nose. His supporters say his hearing deteriorated during the seven years he spent in an Israeli prison, from 1978–1985, but Yassin's health has been poor since he was paralyzed following a childhood swimming accident.

Any woman allowed to meet Yassin is required to dress in Islamic fashion; shaking his hand in greeting is out of the question. Should they be needed, an emergency supply of oversized coats and scarves for ladies are kept in a big box, not far from a stash of guns.

In his Gaza office, Yassin was surrounded by doting aides, who adjust his hearing aid and ensure that he is comfortable. Before Yasser Arafat placed him under house arrest, ostensibly to appease Israel, a month after a spate of suicide bombings killed more than two dozen people in Israel within 24 hours, Yassin was also protected by his own phalanx of armed guards who patrolled the busy, narrow streets and alleys around his offices in Gaza's Zeitoun neighborhood.

Red, green, and black Hamas flags fly from doorways throughout the area, and graffiti either honoring Hamas's shuhada, or else lampooning Prime Minister Sharon covered virtually every wall. Elsewhere in Gaza, clusters of children prowl the area, playing in the dirt, riding rusty tricycles, or pretending to be "black lion cubs," as Sheikh Yusef Qaradawi calls the Palestinian youth who throw stones and defy Israeli soldiers.

Despite his enfeebled body, Yassin's mind is still sharp and his words are like fire to the young men who fight under the Hamas banner against Israel. Yassin, a Sunni Muslim, spoke with a strained passion and commanded considerable respect among the young militants of Hamas.

"Everyone who dies in war or is killed by the enemy is considered a martyr," he said. He denounces the September 11 attack and rejects any parallel between Hamas and those responsible for hijacking planes and ramming them into buildings.

"We are here fighting occupation and settlements," he said. "The war against us is completely different. I reject any classification of us as terrorist. We consider the attack on America on September 11 a terrorist action mainly because it killed Americans. And the attack on Afghanistan by America is also a terrorist act because it hurt innocent people."

Yassin did not mask his disdain for the U.S. government and its actions around the globe:

First of all, the United States has always violated laws by supporting other people who violate laws. And the United States has taken by force other people's resources and has supported others who have hurt people and taken their land. It has supported the occupation policies of others against those who were trying to resist and fight for their rights. All of their policies have been unfair, whether they are economic or political.

Palestinians of all stripes have become so despairing of U.S. policies and the Bush Administration's apparent tolerance of the violence in the months following September 11 that almost all of the groups, religious as well as secular, see no option other than to continue fighting Israel, including with suicide bombers, which is proving so effective in terrorizing Israelis.

Yet Hamas spokesmen cling to the line that they target only Israel's military and not its civilians, saying Islam forbids any attacks that hurt the innocent. They maintain that their fighters never intend to harm the elderly and children, despite the long list of such casualties caused by their suicide bombers.

"In Islam, it's always a question of intention," Yassin said. "You can have the same actions but different intentions." So if a suicide bomber does not intend to hurt innocent people, according to Yassin's logic, he is blameless for their deaths.

But for many of people inside Hamas and other Islamic groups, there are no innocents in Israel anyway. "A number of people have argued that in the case of Israelis there are no civilians on the grounds that Israelis armed forces include both men and women and therefore any person of a certain age is eligible to be in the military," said John Kelsay, author of *Islam and War: A Study in Comparative Ethics,* in an interview in late 2001. "They are then excusing people who are under-aged who might be killed or hurt, or people who are too elderly or injured in some way. They are excusing the death or injuries to those as collateral damage. My own view of this is that it is quite problematic application of the Islamic view of war."

Many Muslims object to actions such as al Masri's for the very reason that he took little note of whether innocent children would be hurt.

"It's a very hard case to make if a person blows himself up outside of a disco or outside of a pizza restaurant that you are not targeting civilians," said Kelsay. "To my mind this really is the crux of the matter in evaluating suicide bombers. The actions of suicide bombers seem to be quite wrong, on grounds of Islamic law."

Despite such arguments even within Islamic circles, suicide bombers have expanded beyond the ranks of Hamas and Islamic Jihad to include even people allied with Arafat's secular Fatah movement. In his book *Introduction to Islam,* Muhammad Hamidullah, with the Cultural Islamic Center in Paris, argues against suicide bombings: "To commit suicide is religiously forbidden in Islam, for we do not belong to ourselves, but to God; and to destroy something before its full-fledged realization is to go against the will of God."[19] Hamidullah and those opposed to suicide bombers refer to two credible sources of Muhammad's words; the Muslim historians Sahih al Bukhari and Sahih Muslim, who recorded the prophet as saying:

> He who throws himself from a mountain and kills himself will be thrown down in the fire of hell and remain in it for ever; he who sips poison and kills himself will have his poison in his hand and sip it for ever in the fire of hell; and he who kills himself with a piece of iron will have his piece of iron in his hand and will be stabbed with it in his belly in the fire of hell forever.[20]

Abdulaziz bin Abdallah al Sheikh, the leading Islamic scholar in Saudi Arabia, site of Mecca and Medina, Islam's two holiest cities, also spoke out against suicide bombings even before September 11, saying that they violated

Islam's concept of "just war." Al Sheikh, asked by Arab reporters in April 2001 about whether Islam condones suicide bombings, said that Islam prohibits all forms of suicide for any reason, although he spoke in a way designed to be as least offensive as possible to those who would disagree passionately:

"Jihad for God's sake is one of the best acts [in Islam]," al Sheikh told the London-based newspaper *al Sharq al Awsat*, "but killing oneself in the midst of the enemy, or suicidal acts, I don't know whether this is endorsed by *Shari'a* [Islamic law] or whether it is considered Jihad for God. I'm afraid it could be suicide. Fighting to hurt the enemy is required but it should never violate Shari'a."

Al Sheikh continued: "Skyjacking and acts of terror against people contradict the Shari'a and are by no means acts of jihad. Muslims should abstain from such acts. . . . To my knowledge, suicide missions do not have any legal basis in Islam and do not constitute a form of jihad. I fear that they are nothing but a form of suicide, and suicide is also prohibited by Islam."[21]

Yassin dismissed the Saudi mufti's arguments without hesitation, exclaiming, "There is a world of difference between suicide and martyrdom. It's the same action but with different intent."

Yassin and supporters of suicide bombings against Israel acknowledge that Islam prohibits suicide, but they say it again boils down to a question of intention. Did the suicide bomber intend to kill himself, or was he merely prepared to die in a just war, using his body as his only available weapon?

Al Sheikh's critics say his opinion is self-serving and based on fear that such tactics could be used against the House of Saud, which bin Laden seeks to overthrow. Muntassir al-Zayat, a Cairo lawyer who has served as a spokesman for the two militant Egyptian groups al Gamaa al Islamiyah and al Jihad, said that al Sheikh's ruling "reminds us of the *fatawa*h issued by the Sultan in the old days. This fatwa wasn't issued on the basis of religious or legal evidence, but due to political inclination."[22]

The controversial Egyptian columnist Fahmy Howeidi, who often sympathizes with the Islamists, and Nabil Abdel-Fattah, chief editor of the *Report on the State of Religion in Egypt*, hurl similar criticisms. "The Saudi Mufti was playing a political game, but he went wrong," Howeidi said.[23]

"The Mufti's answer addressed a Saudi phenomenon, and is a message to the new American administration," Abdel-Fattah told *al Ahram* newspaper's *Weekly Magazine*. "Al Sheikh was addressing, and trying to prevent, the recurrence of the suicide bombings against American military targets in Saudi Arabia and the hijacking of Saudi planes." But his ruling should not be applied to the Israeli-Palestinian conflict, Abdel-Fattah said. Abdel-Aziz al-Rantisi, a leading Hamas figure in Gaza, also told *al Ahram* that suicide bombers don't kill themselves because they are bored with life or escaping problems on earth. They die to kill their enemy, even if means they will get killed in the process; but dying is not the sole purpose of their mission.[24]

Consider the story of Mohamed Rashed Daoud al Owhali, a young Saudi from a wealthy family who was supposed to become a shaheed after planting the bomb at the U.S. Embassy in Nairobi. Things did not quite work out this way; the main purpose of his mission was not to kill himself, he said, but to attack his perceived enemy. If he had to die in the process, he was prepared to do so. But since he found a way to complete his mission without killing himself, he did not.

Al Owhali was one of a two-member attack team that included another Saudi know as Azzam. Al Owhali had been to Afghanistan, met bin Laden, and was eventually sent on a "martyrdom operation." He was prepared to die to make sure the embassy guards opened the gate so that Azzam could drive the explosives-laden truck close to the compound. Then, if the explosives did not detonate once Azzam was close enough to the embassy, al Owhali was supposed to throw a grenade onto the truck. But he did not need to attack any guards to get the truck close enough, and it exploded without a hitch and with Azzam inside. Al Owhali ran away, injured. He was arrested and extradited to the United States, where he was found guilty of the murder of 213 people. But even his conviction did not bring him martyrdom. The jury sentenced him to life in prison without parole.

In addition to the theological question of whether suicide bombers violate Islamic laws against suicide, there is the fact that Islam prohibits attacks on innocents, which is why some of the most powerful Islamic jurists oppose it.

The Muslim World League, based in Mecca, Saudi Arabia, and one of the Islamic world's most influential organizations, issued a formal statement distributed around the world condemning the September 11 attack. Invitation to Islam, an Islamic education organization founded in 1993 by students at the University of Medina in Saudi Arabia, published an article on October 5, 1998 entitled "Islam, a Religion of Terror?" in which it flatly condemned suicide bombers:

> So what about suicide bombing, is this too a part of jihad in Allah's path?
> From what has already been stated above, it can be deduced that this is not

from the religion. However, unfortunately many Muslims have taken suicide bombing as being a virtuous act by which one receives reward. This could not be further from the truth. The Prophet said: "Those who go to extremes are destroyed." Suicide bombing is undoubtedly an extremity, which has reached the ranks of the Muslims. In the rules of warfare, we find no sanction for such an act from the behaviour and words of the Prophet Muhammad and his companions. Unfortunately, today [some misguided] Muslims believe that such acts are paving the way for an Islamic revival and a return to the rule of Islam's glorious law. However, we fail to bear in mind what the Prophet said.

So, for example, what is the end of a suicide bomber in Palestine? A leg here, an arm there. Massive retaliation by the Israeli's in the West Bank and Gaza. More Muslims killed and persecuted. How can we be delighted with such an end? What really hammers the final nail in the coffin of this act, is that it is suicide; something which is clearly forbidden in Islam.[25]

Mohamed Sayed Tantawi, the leading religious authority at Cairo's al Azhar University, and Sheikh Hamed al-Midawi, preacher at al Aqsa mosque and chairman of the Legal Appeals Court in Jerusalem, have decreed just the opposite. They believe Islamic teachings clearly support suicide bombings, but only against Israeli military targets. Suicide bombings are merely a form of jihad, one of the pillars of Islam, these jurists say. And they say Palestinian suicide bombers are helping to defend their land from Israeli aggression.

Yassin and Islamic fighters who target Israelis with suicide bombers use as their justification for their beliefs Surah 2:190–191 in the Qur'an: "Fight in the way of Allah against those who fight against you, but begin not hostilities. Lo! Allah loveth not aggressors. And slay them wherever ye find them and drive them out of the places when they drove you out, for persecution is worse than slaughter."

According to Yassin, "it is always our intent to target Israel's military, and it is that intent [to hit only military targets and not civilians] that is what is most important in Islam."

When pressed about al Masri's killing children in a pizzeria, Yassin dodged the issue and turned the tables to talk about Israel's behavior. "You should put this question to Israel," he said. "Israel has killed our children. Did anyone ask them about why they are killing children? When the Americans bombed Afghanistan, did they kill children? Our target is always the military."

But Yassin said Hamas fighters can attack soldiers wherever they are, "whether in a bus, in a car, or in a plane, they are justifiable targets."

In trying to gain public support for those who do die in martyrdom operations, on December 10, 2001, Hamas asked Muslim leaders meeting in the Persian Gulf state of Qatar to issue a declaration saying that suicide attacks against Israel are legitimate resistance against Israeli occupation of Arab land.

"The enemy will not recognize our people's right in his land unless forced to," said a one-page fax from Hamas to the fifty-seven-member Organization of the Islamic Conference. The conference did not respond to the request, apparently feeling that after September 11, such a stand could alienate the United States, even though many of the representatives probably agreed with Yassin.

Al Sheikh, Yassin, and Tantawi are all experts on Islamic law and qualified to interpret the Qur'an and the hadiths, but their competing rulings have thrown the Muslim world into intense debate over just what Islam says about martyrdom. Shortly after the attack on the United States, as President Bush prepared to go to war, Chaplain Abdul-Rashid Muhammad, the most senior Muslim chaplain in the U.S. military, asked leading Muslim jurists to rule on whether Islamic laws permitted U.S. Muslim servicemen to participate in the war effort in Afghanistan, given that the adversaries would be Muslim. Islam teaches that a Muslim should not wage war on fellow believers, even though Islamic history is replete with such wars. Some servicemen dreaded the prospect of facing their Muslim brothers in the mountains of Afghanistan. They were aware that Muslims throughout the world believed that President George W. Bush had declared war on Islam and had even dared to label the war against terrorism a "crusade," which made Muslims recall the brutal Christian crusades against Muslims and Jews in the Middle Ages in Jerusalem, which is an indelible part of their associations with the Western world.

Six respected Muslim jurists from Syria, Egypt, Qatar, and the United States signed a fatwa to resolve the issue. They ruled that American Muslims could and indeed should partake in the fight against terrorism as "all Muslims ought to be united against those who terrorize the innocents, and those who permit the killing of non-combatants without justifiable reason."[26]

The fatwa was written by Taha Jabir al Alwainy in his capacity as chairman of the North America Fiqh (Islamic legal) Council based in Sterling, Virginia; Mohammad al Hanouti, a member of the council; and Sheikh Yusef al Qaradawi, Grand Islamic Scholar and Chairman of the Sunna and Sira

Council, Qatar; and it was signed by Haytham al-Khayyat, a Syrian Islamic scholar; Muhammad Salim al-'Awa, an Egyptian professor of Comparative Law and Shari'a; Judge Tariq al-Bishri, retired First Deputy President of the Council d'etat of Egypt, and Fahmi Howeidi, Egyptian Islamic scholar and columnist. The ruling not only condemned the September 11 attack but encouraged American Muslim soldiers to support their government's efforts to find those responsible for the attacks who were "deserving of the appropriate punishment according to their offense and according to its consequences for destruction and mischief. . . . It's incumbent upon our military brothers in the American armed forces to make this stand and its religious reasoning well known to all their superiors, as well as to their peers, and to voice it and not to be silent." The fatwa stated:

> We find it necessary to apprehend the true perpetrators of these crimes, as well as those who aid and abet them through incitement, financing, or other support. They must be brought to justice in an impartial court of law and punish[ed] . . . appropriately, so that [this might] act as deterrent to them and to others like them who easily slay the lives of innocents, destroy propert[y] and terrorize people. Hence, it's a duty [of] Muslims to participate in this effort with all possible means, in accordance with God's (Most High) saying: "And help one another in virtue and righteousness, but do not help one another in sin and transgression. . . ."

The jurists held that in evaluating the actions of American Muslim soldiers, their intent "must be to fight for enjoining of the truth and defeating falsehood. It's to prevent aggression on the innocents, or to apprehend the perpetrators and bring them to justice." They also held that the American Muslim soldier has an obligation, as a member of a regular army, to obey orders, as "otherwise his allegiance and loyalty to his country could be in doubt. This would subject him to much harm since he would not enjoy the privileges of citizenship without performing its obligations." The jurists concluded that:

> To sum up, it's acceptable—God willing—for the Muslim American military personnel to partake in the fighting in the upcoming battles, against whomever their country decides has perpetrated terrorism against them, [k]eeping in mind to have the proper intention as explained earlier, [so that no doubts might] be cast about their loyalty to their country . . . [or about

preventing] harm to befall them as might be expected. This is in accordance with the Islamic jurisprudence rules which state that necessities dictate exceptions, as well as the rule that says one may endure a small harm to avoid a much greater harm.[27]

The courageous statement drew added respect because of Sheikh Qaradawi's association with it. Qaradawi, who counts among his publications such widely read tomes as *Islamic Awakening: Between Rejection and Extremism*, and *The Lawful and Prohibited in Islam*, is not known for mincing his words, even regarding criticism of the United States or Middle Eastern despots. Qaradawi had gone on the record as supporting suicide bombings against Israel, calling the youths who commit them "pioneer martyrs." The stand he took in the fatwa seemed to contradict some of his other rulings that forbade Muslims from joining nonbelievers to fight believers. The fatwa addressed that issue as well, saying that the prohibition was based on a hadith, but was specific to certain situations: "The noble hadith mentioned refers to the situation where the Muslim is in charge of his affairs. He is capable of fighting as well as capable of not fighting. This hadith does not address the situation where a Muslim is a citizen of a state and a member of a regular army."[28]

But their fatwa urging American Muslim soldiers to perform their military duty did not come without cost, especially for al Alwainy. Ensconced in his book-lined office within a modern office park in Leesburg, Virginia, which also houses his Islamic graduate school, al Alwainy said he had been harshly criticized by some Muslims for providing a religious cover for Muslim Americans to participate in the war against Afghanistan and to help stamp out Islamic movements that the United States considered terrorist. Months later he would find himself also the subject of an FBI raid, as agents searched his offices for any connections he might have to militants, despite his record of speaking out against them, as he did at a press conference at the National Press Center in Washington, D.C., to announce the fatwa. Al Alwainy and Hanouti fielded a deluge of questions from the press and Muslim activists about the Qur'anic prohibition against Muslims killing Muslims and whether the United States's bombing of Afghanistan was just. They effectively dodged questions about the justice of the American war on Afghanistan but stood by their assertion that Muslim-American soldiers who decided to participate in the war were not guilty of breaking any Islamic laws; they also ruled that those soldiers who felt they should not participate in the war had legal options at their disposal that they could use to keep them from serving on front lines.

But both al Alwainy and Hanouti condemned terrorism in the name of Islam and their fatwa contradicted the teachings of one of Islam's most provocative thinkers, Sayyid Qutb, who preached that Muslims should bow to no authority but God. Qutb also died a martyr, hanged in 1966 by Egypt's Gamal Abdel Nasser, who was attempting to unite the Arab world under a secular banner and thought Qutb's religious views dangerous and treasonous.

In the book *Milestones*, which cost him his life, Qutb offered guidance to what he called the Islamic "vanguard" as they sought to purify Islam of cultural corruption and establish its supremacy on earth: "Islam cannot fulfill its role except by providing the leadership for all of mankind, for which the Muslim community must be restored to its original form. That Muslim community is now buried under the debris of the man-made traditions of several generations and is crushed under the weight of those false laws and customs that are not even remotely related to the Islamic teachings."[29] Bin Laden and the September 11 hijackers believed they represented that vanguard. Like Qutb, they divided the world into two parts: true believers of Islam, and the *jahilliyah*, composed of those who are ignorant of or disobedient to God's law.

Most of the leaders of the Arab world were part of the jahilliyah, Qutb argued, urging Muslims to rise up against the region's governments that prevented them from following God's law and God's law alone.

"Islam does not force its beliefs on people, but Islam is not merely 'belief,'" Qutb wrote. "Islam is a declaration of the freedom of every man or woman from servitude to other humans. It seeks to abolish all those systems and governments that are based on the rule of some men over others, or the servitude of some to others."[30]

And Qutb, whom many believe laid the foundation for activist, radical Islamic movements, rejected the idea of jihad only in self-defense. According to Qutb, jihad was not only to be waged in self-defense, but against any power that oppresses people and tries to usurp God's authority over them:

> . . . Islam is not a 'defensive' movement in today's narrow technical sense of 'defensive war.' This narrow meaning is ascribed to it by those who are puzzled under the pressure of circumstances and are confused by the wily attacks of the Orientalists, who distort the concept of Islamic jihad. It is a movement to wipe out tyranny and to introduce true freedom to mankind . . .[31]

For people in the Middle East who are living under one-party states, such as Egypt, Libya, or Iraq, or under monarchies such as Jordan and much of the Gulf, any movement that promises to fight to wipe out tyranny is attractive, even if many suspect they will only be exchanging one form of tyranny for another.

"It's better to have one vote one time and then no vote at all," countered Anwar Haddam, the Algerian leader of the Islamic Salvation Front, in an interview in 1993. Haddam was responding to charges that if his party had been permitted to win the Algerian elections in 1992, it would have held on to power at any cost. Haddam, who came to the United States after the canceled elections to lobby on behalf of the front, ended up being held for years in a U.S. prison in Virginia on secret evidence, as Algeria's ruling generals and its Islamists outdid each other in brutality and bloodshed.

The Algeria fiasco convinced many Islamists that there was no point in trying to play by the rules and build political support in hopes of winning power at the ballot box, as the Islamic Salvation Front did. Algeria's civil war was an important milestone for Islamic movements because it convinced many of their supporters that war was inevitable under the jahilliyah governments of the Middle East, just as some thought it was inevitable with the superpower that supported them.

Dr. Ayman Zawahri wrote in his *Knights Under the Prophet's Banner:*

The Algerian experience has provided a harsh lesson. . . . It proved to Muslims that the West is not only an infidel but also a hypocrite and a liar. The principles that it brags about are exclusive to, and the personal property of, its people alone. They are not to be shared by the peoples of Islam, at least nothing more that what a master leaves his slave in terms of food crumbs. The Islamic Salvation Front in Algeria has overlooked the tenets of the creed, the facts of history and politics, the balance of power, and the laws of control. It rushed to the ballot boxes in a bid to reach the presidential palaces and the ministries, only to find at the gates tanks loaded with French ammunition, with their barrels pointing at the chests of those who forgot the rules of confrontation between justice and falsehood. The guns of the Francophile officers brought them down to the land of reality from the skies of illusions. The Islamic Salvation men thought that the gates of rule had been opened for them, but they were surprised to see themselves pushed toward the gates of detention camps and prisons and into the cells of the new world order.[32]

In fact, for many Islamic militants, war between Islam and the United States was well underway after Sept. 11—but a war the United State launched, not vice versa. And it is not just militant Islamists who hold this view; rather, people all over the Muslim world are expressing such thoughts. Laith Shubailat, one of Jordan's preeminent Islamists, has called the United States "an arrogant, imperialistic power" whose foreign policy is "based on carpet bombing. . . . And many of us would prefer to die under carpet bombing than as vassals of such a power." Shubailat, like many people in the Muslim world, including those who condemned the September 11 attack, hoped that the American people would begin to question if their government's policies around the world had made such an attack inevitable.

"If American people are feeling in their own homes what terror is, they should feel what other people are feeling. I see anger building everywhere," Shubailat said. "The youth especially are very angry."

Such sentiments were ominous for the future of U.S. relations with the Muslim world. Many members of radical movements had been long preparing for the kind of showdown that September 11 symbolized, one that would pit the military might of the United States against the Islamic world's young, angry, and desperate shuhada.

6

THE MOTHERS OF MARTYRS: MUNABRAHIM DAOUD AND UM IYAD

The tears of the mothers of our martyrs fill more space than Palestine will ever occupy.

—*Marwan Barghouti, Fatah commander, West Bank*

THE MOTHER OF IZZIDENE AL MASRI SAID SHE WOULD HAVE BOLTED every window and locked every door with a hundred locks to keep her son from walking into the Sbarro Pizzeria that warm August day in 2001. The mother of Mohammed al Daoud will not rest until her son's death is avenged. And the mother of Mohammed al Durrah was consumed with memories of her dead son even as she struggled to keep two others from joining him as shuhada. Only one, Um Iyad, the mother of the Sbarro suicide bomber, questioned whether her son deserved to be called a martyr. Although her neighbors assured her he was with God in paradise, Um Iyad was not so sure.

Each of these women commanded considerable prestige and respect in their community as the mothers of shuhada. Despite Islam's injunction that martyrs are not to be mourned, each mother desperately missed her son. And each managed her grief in a different way.

Neither of them had prepared her sons for martyrdom; Um Iyad insisted that she had no idea Izzidene was planning to become a suicide bomber. Yet the mothers of Palestinian youths killed in the conflict with Israel have something else in common: They were helpless to protect their children in a region consumed with hatred and violence.

The mother of Mohammed al Daoud, who was killed shortly after the second intifada broke out in the fall of 2000, was the angriest of the three. And she used that anger to help fuel the al-Aqsa intifada against the Israelis.

"There are two paths we can take—the intifada or peace," she said. "We had ten years of negotiations and what did they bring? In the end, we had negotiations over nothing. The other people were just biding their time. The intifada at least brought about the recognition that there should be a Palestinian state. We have rights and they have to give us our rights."

Munabrahim Daoud was consumed with a volatile combination of anger, grief, bitterness, and hunger for revenge. She was committed to making sure that her son had not died in vain and that a Palestinian state would eventually emerge from all of this suffering. As the mother of a martyr, her words had weight in her community and she was among those voices rallying Palestinians to keep fighting until they expelled the Israelis from the West Bank and Gaza and recaptured Muslim holy land in East Jerusalem. If the Israeli–Palestinian conflict were being fought on a traditional Arab battlefield, Munabrahim would be among the women on the sidelines ululating to spur the men into battle. And like the Prophet's favorite wife Aisha, who led an army against his cousin Ali to challenge Ali's leadership, Munabrahim seemed fully capable of mounting a camel and leading her own troops into battle.

"What if I took your scarf and took your shawl?" she asked. "This would not be right. What if someone took your land? They took our land, our wealth and even our children." Munabrahim's eyes narrowed and her hands tightened around the arms of the chair. "The intifada is not over yet," she vowed. "We've been suffering since 1948. Every time it calms down, we make sure the fire comes again because we are insisting on results."

"We have already recognized them and their state. What more do they want? How come UN resolutions get applied to Iraq and Afghanistan and not here? Are we not considered human beings? Are we from Mars? In Palestine, we are people with dreams, too. We have our own civilization, our own culture."

Munabrahim's son was shot running away from the Israelis as he tried to scale a fence. It is not clear if Daoud was involved in the stone-throwing against the soldiers or not. Munabrahim said he wasn't, his friends told reporters he was. Still, Munabrahim was outraged that no one had prosecuted the Israeli soldiers or even answered her questions about why they fired on a boy who was trying to run away from a confrontation.

"The soldiers that were there that day are savages," she said, her voice cracking with rage. "They came to kill. They thought that by killing a lot of people they would end it [the intifada] quickly. He wasn't a kid who had a death wish.

"The human rights organizations came and talked to us and took our statements, but they haven't done anything. The soldiers that killed Mohammed and the others, they have never gone to trial. They were never punished. They were never brought before the law. It was all talk. The army knows who the people are and where each soldier is stationed each day. Israel has said nothing to me."

Yet Munabrahim said her suffering had not led her to question her faith or to question God, only to despise the Israelis.

"I am a believer," she said. "I believe God wanted him to die in this way. We believe in fate. It was written that Mohammed should die young. But I wish I could have made the sacrifice instead of him."

"I believe in sacrifice," she said, "but sacrifice must bring results. We're sacrificing every day. And we go from one funeral to the next. It's like a soap opera on television. People have forgotten this is real. These martyrs have mothers and sisters and families and wives."

In November 2001 Munabrahim was aware that Americans were still reeling from the September 11 attack and that there were concerns that someone had begun spreading anthrax through the mail.

"Anthrax killed one person in America," she said, "and the whole country is in a panic. Here people get killed with bullets in their faces and it's the status quo."

As Munabrahim saw it, nothing would change until Israel changed its leaders and the United States stopped "blindly supporting Israel." And she said that was a large part of what made the United States a target for the September 11 terrorism.

"We believe in God," she said. "But as long as Sharon is in power and Bush is in America, nothing will get better for us. Only God can change that."

Palestinian mothers, especially those whose sons are out in the streets throwing rocks at Israeli soldiers, have been accused of sacrificing their sons for a few thousand dollars. While it is true that Hamas and the Palestine Authority often offered financial assistance to the families of people who were killed in clashes with Israelis, especially if they are male heads of families, Palestinians vehemently deny that martyrs are being bought. They especially deny that boys are being paid to throw stones at Israeli soldiers. Munabrahim was outraged at the suggestion that the mothers of Palestinian martyrs profited from their children's death.

"Some people say people want to drive nice cars and go on vacation on the money they get from the death of their children. There is no point in our young people dying. And it's nothing but young people. The most precious thing I have in the world are my children," she said. "It would be suicidal of me to say I want my child to die."

Munabrahim said her family did receive cash donations from friends, Palestinian organizations, and from Arab leaders and sympathizers throughout the region. She ticked off a list of gifts, including $2,000 from the Palestinian Authority, which she initially refused.

"It came too soon. It was only three days after he died. Later people told me I should have taken the money, so I took it and gave it to the poor."

Munabrahim said she received $10,000 from Saddam Hussein, $3,000 from the United Arab Emirates, and a few thousand more from Saudi Arabia and other Gulf states. But she made a point to note that nothing came from the United States.

"American sent F-16s," she said with undisguised bitterness. "And the English sent settlers to take the land and cut down the trees."

Unlike Amal Zaki Ahmad, the mother of Mohammed al Durrah, Munabrahim's husband could work to support the family, and they had no money problems. And many Palestinian parents had faced the horror of learning that their son had joined the ranks of the shuhada, but few had watched it on television as Ahmad had.

Ahmad had received substantial donations after her son's death but her husband was partially paralyzed and more than a year after that fateful Saturday, still faced serious physical and psychiatric problems. The outpouring of sympathy from around the world did help, as did the money that initially flowed to the family.

"The Jordanian ambassador came to see us and had him [her husband] taken to Jordan for free medical care," Ahmad said. "King Abdullah gave us $10,000 and Saddam sent $5,000 and we got $5,000 from the Women's Social Welfare Fund. What we got doesn't amount to very much when a man can't work and has six children."

The Palestinian Authority was virtually bankrupt, and she could not count on money from it to support her family. Somehow, only organizations such as Hamas continued to receive money from international supporters that they dutifully distributed to needy Palestinian families. It was clear that Ahmad was willing to accept help wherever she could find it.

More than a year after the incident, she still seemed numb with grief, as her young children scampered about her house. Even when her youngest son took a piece of wood and began attacking the wall with it, Ahmad was too deep in her thoughts of Mohammed to notice. Like other Palestinian parents, Ahmed was so overwhelmed with her own suffering that her children lacked supervision and discipline. Palestinian psychologists such as Dr. Eyad Sarraj were concerned that Palestinian children were being irreparably harmed by living under Israeli occupation.

"Do you know what it means for a child to see his father spat at and beaten before his eyes by an Israeli soldier?" he asked. "Nobody knows what happened to our children. We don't know ourselves except we observe that they lose respect for their fathers. So they, our children, 'the children of the stone,' as they became known, tried the intifada, the uprising."[1]

Dr. Sarraj, who, besides being in charge of the local mental health program is also commissioner-general of the Palestinian Independent Commission for Citizens' Rights, expressed the despair that so many Palestinian parents feel, realizing that their children risk death every day and that they can not protect them, even inside their own homes. "Seven long years our children were throwing stones and being killed daily. Nearly all of our young men were arrested, the majority were tortured. All had to confess. The result was every one suspected that all people were spies. So, we are exhausted, tormented and brutalized."[2]

Such conditions mean that children often do not confide in their parents or tell them about activities outside of the home, a situation not uncommon in many western homes. Um Iyad said she knew nothing about her son's involvement with Hamas, and she certainly did not know he was planning to become a suicide bomber, but it seems there was a lot Um Iyad did not know about her son.

Many Palestinian mothers and fathers say they did not know that their teenage sons were out flinging stones at Israeli tanks. Like Um Iyad, they certainly did not know that they were preparing for martyrdom. It seems Palestinian sons do not ask their mothers for permission before they go to their deaths, even if many Muslim scholars insist that parents must approve of their son's participation in jihad.

"You think I would have let him go if I had known? I would have closed the house with a hundred locks before I would have let him go. What is Palestine going to give to me? He's gone . . ."

"Nobody wants to lose a son in this world," Um Iyad cried. "Palestine is eating its children." While Palestinian leaders such as Sheikh Yassin were calling for more martyrs, Um Iyad was calling for it all to end. She said too many Palestinian children had died and too many mothers were suffering unbearable grief just as she was.

"There was a woman in Nablus who lost her two boys who were standing near a building that was hit in an Israeli raid," Um Iyad said. "She lost her only children. Many people have lost children in different ways." And all too many had lost sons and daughters, as suicide bombers like al Masri.

There are indications that some Palestinian parents are so alarmed at the growing numbers of youngsters who are choosing martyrdom that they have begun looking for early warning signs in their own children. In an article published on May 26, 2002, Knight Ridder Newspapers correspondent Alfonso Chardy interviewed Palestinian psychologists who said parents are increasingly coming to them asking for help.

"This has been happening more and more often in the last few months as the Palestinian resistance has deepened," said Dr. Mahmud Sehwail, general director of the Treatment and Rehabilitation Center for Victims of Torture in Ramallah. "The parents say they have detected a significant change in the behavior of their children, and they desperately want to know if their children are candidates to become human bombs."[3]

Palestinian mental health authorities told Chardy that many Palestinian parents were shocked when young women started becoming suicide bombers in 2002 and they were doubly alarmed in late April when three Gaza teenagers—Yusef Zaqout, 14; Ishmael Abu Naji, 15; and Anwar Hamdonah, 15, took it upon themselves to stage a suicide mission on an Israeli settlement. The youths, who were not sent by any of the major Palestinian groups, were armed with knives and makeshift bombs. Israeli soldiers guarding the settlement shot and killed them.

The article tells the story of a 17-year-old Palestinian girl whose parents prevented her from becoming another female suicide bomber. She had run away and left a note saying that she was going to blow herself up in Israel, but Dr. Sehwail said her father took quick action.

"The father called the Palestinian security officials and the Israeli security officials, and just a few days ago the girl was found safe and sound and her suicide was averted," the psychologist said. But the girl's parents went even further: they put their daughter under psychiatric care to deal with her depression and anger, an option other parents have taken. She wanted to become a suicide bomber, Dr. Sehwail said, because "a cousin had recently been killed by Israel soldiers, and she wanted revenge."

Dr. Sehwail and other Palestinian psychologists said they expected the trend to continue, potentially pitting militants against parents in a battle over Palestinian children. Um Iyad wished she could have battled the militants for her son's life. "What can I tell you?" Um Iyad sighed, clasping her gnarled hands with a grimace. "I have to say it was not a good thing that he did. There were many innocents there. So many children. We don't support it when the Israelis kill our people, so we can't support when their innocent people are killed. We just can't condone that kind of martyrdom."

The eve of his death, Izzidene left home with his father and brothers to head to work in their restaurant. "In the evening, when he didn't come home, I was wondering what happened to him. But then he called me and said, "I'm staying with a friend in Ramallah; don't worry about me, I'll be back by morning. I'll go directly from here to the restaurant. . . ."

"Now, I should point out that he's never slept outside the home. He's never slept at a friend's place. And actually, we didn't know who his friends were. We didn't know who his group was or who he socialized with. Because he was always here. Either he was in the restaurant or he was praying. So we didn't know of any group he was into. We didn't know any of this."

Um Iyad did not begin to worry until al Masri did not come home the next day. "That day I made bread, took my shower. It was day like any other day, a Thursday," she said. "I called the restaurant to asked if he had come and they said no, no. I kept on calling the restaurant and they said, "There are checkpoints, there are roadblocks. He must be held up." So, I waited until 7:30 in the evening. I was with my sister and I was sitting outside and I was waiting. I had been sitting there all afternoon waiting for everyone to come home, for him to come home."

Then the phone rang, Um Iyad said, and her life was forever changed. "It was from my nephew who spoke to his mother, who is my sister. He said to her to say '*Illahee lil Allah*' [There is no God but God]. So she said that. Then she said, 'But why am I saying this?'

"And he said, 'Because it was my cousin who did the operation today.' Of course I didn't hear all of this because I was outside," Um Iyad said. Then, suddenly, there was pandemonium. "I heard screams from inside the house and the next thing I knew people were all over me. My cousins and my sister and my daughters-in-law and everybody just sort of enveloped me with screams and hugs and cheers."

Months later Um Iyad sat wondering what she could have done to prevent her son from walking into Sbarro. "I would never have allowed him to go," she said. "I would have tied him down somewhere. I would have locked the house up. I would have chained him to the bed. . . ."

At the very least, Um Iyad said she would have tried to give him a reason to go on living. And she is haunted by the prospect that she missed one major opportunity.

Although al Masri, who was twenty-three, did not have any girlfriends and did not appear interested in girls, something strange happened a few months before his death, she said. "He told me, maybe it's time now that I should get married. And he said, 'Why don't you find me a bride.'"

It makes sense that a devout Muslim man would seek his parents' permission and help in finding a wife, since Islam frowns on the kind of dating common in the West. Young men and women can meet with chaperones but al Masri shunned even those kinds of opportunities. He was painfully shy and seemed afraid of women, even his mother's friends.

"He didn't really socialize with people, even among the neighbors. He was the only one of my sons who would never talk to any of the women. He would just say from afar '*Salamu aleikum*' (peace be upon you) and that would be it. He wouldn't even look at people, he wouldn't interact with people." And Izzidene was not above chastising his mother for improper behavior with her friends, she said. "He would get upset if he heard people gossiping or talking about others. He would fuss at me if he heard me say something that was not appropriate." So his mother was understandably surprised by his sudden interest in marriage. She asked him to put it off for a while. "I told him it's a little bit early for you. . . . it's not time yet. But when the time comes, I said there are many girls that are potential brides for you."

Um Iyad explained, rather plaintively, that one of Izzidene's brothers had married the year before and she wanted things to quiet down a bit before another wedding. "You know, the situation with the intifada is not so conducive for weddings and so we said we'd wait another year. I also didn't take it very seriously. I think he partly said that because he wanted to make me happy. He was trying to find something that he could busy me with so I would stop thinking about the son I lost three years ago in the car accident. He would always try to cheer me up."

That's what she missed most about he son, his attentiveness. "He always was very worried about me, especially my health," she said. "I had just found out that I had diabetes and he would always eat with me to make sure I was eating the right things."

Um Iyad was the only one not dancing with joy when they got the news about her son. She stood in dazed and confused silence, unable to believe that her quiet, shy Izzidene, the boy who made sure she ate well to contain her diabetes, had killed 16 people and himself.

"I didn't realize at first that he had committed suicide," she said. "I thought that he had been killed at a roadblock or something. I realized that he was dead, but I thought he was martyred by having been shot, because such a thing would not be part of his character."

Um Iyad made it clear that Izzidene was not the brightest of her children, although he was considerate and kind. But "he never failed a grade," she said, adding; "Somehow, he got through it." But what was even more telling was how Um Iyad described the surprise of her neighbors at her son's actions. "They all thought he was a simpleton who could never succeed at doing anything. They thought he was the least likely person to succeed at hitting the Israelis where it hurt."

He may have hurt the Israelis, but al Masri also clearly hurt his mother, who said his death has brought her nothing but bitterness. If he thought she would revel in being the mother of a martyr, he was woefully mistaken. And if he thought his name would be praised around the world as a soldier of Islam, even that is debatable. Outside of Jenin, the Sbarro bombing brought shame not only to the Palestinian cause but to Muslims as well. Yet Um Iyad said her neighbors treat her with the respect due the mother of a martyr. "It's been three months and fifteen days. People come and visit every day. The people in our town are good to each other. People who go through tragedies have full support from the community. Of course people who come and give condolences say my son died a hero and not a useless person or a bad person. They say he went to paradise and did a heroic act. I'm not sure I agree with that."

"But you have to consider what's happening. You see how much we're under siege and the Israelis are making our lives miserable. You've seen the roads, you've seen the conditions under which people live. Our leaders and what the Israelis are doing—do you think this is right?"

Um Iyad blames Israeli prime minister Ariel Sharon for the outbreak of violence and the second intifada that led to her son's death; he enraged Muslims by setting foot on the sacred al Aqsa mosque complex, she says. "We were okay before Sharon went to Jerusalem and did that terrible thing . . . before the intifada. We weren't in this situation before. We were living a normal life together, but when Sharon went to Jerusalem he made the Arabs burn. He stepped on the holy ground."

Al Masri's mother said she could not talk about what was in her son's heart the day the walked into the pizzeria. She only could talk about the boy she thought she knew well but really knew so very little.

With eleven other children, Um Iyad left it to the older ones to look after themselves and had no time to pry into their comings and goings. She was more than busy enough caring for the younger children. But al Masri never required much taking care of, she said. He was a devoted, caring, and obedient son who had always been a strong support for a mother besieged with the demands of a huge family.

Um Iyad was fifteen when she married her first cousin and had her first child. She gave birth to fourteen children but had already lost two boys before Izzidene died. "I lost one in a car accident and one was stillborn," Um Iyad said. "I had a total of ten boys and four girls." Al Masri's remaining seven brothers are also devout and observe Islam's ritual prayers, "but they're not like him," she said. "They're just religious and they fast, like normal people."

Um Iyad looked at least ten years older than her 46 years, and al Masri's death seems to have stripped her of any remaining pretext of youth or joy. The room where Um Iyad sat remembering her son was clearly a memorial for a shaheed. Red, the color of martyrs, was the color of all of the sofas as well as the carpet stretched across the tile floor. Gold-framed verses from the Qur'an decorated the walls along with a portrait of al Masri, painted by "some boys from the village," Um Iyad said. In the picture, al Masri is staring purposefully ahead, clutching a gun in one hand and the red, white, and green Palestinian flag in the other.

Despite Islam's injunction not to mourn martyrs but to rejoice at their burial, Um Iyad said she had cried many times for her son. She seemed tormented by very real doubts that his death did not bring him what he wanted most, to be with God in paradise.

"He always told me that the life we are living is not the permanent life. It's temporary," said Um Iyad, sinking into the red velvet sofa and looking sadly around her living room. "Even when we built this sitting room, he said these were all superficial things. He worshipped the afterlife. He wanted to be there." Um Iyad said as far back as she can remember, her son was religious but his interest in death and the afterlife became evident when he was around sixteen years old.

"The knowledge of the afterlife was a gift from God," she said. "It wasn't from anyone. He would bring me cassettes to listen to, Qur'anic verses. I would listen to them and he would tell me it's the afterlife we should seek, not this life. He believed that we have another life waiting for us. . . . This came from God."

Yet many Arabs caution that Palestinian martyrdom is not just about religion, although religion is used, or misused, to justify it. It is also about what Palestinians say is the daily misery that has made fanatics of young men such as al Masri.

Um Iyad insisted that neither she nor her husband taught her son to hate Israelis and that no one in his immediate family had been killed in clashes with Israeli soldiers.

"On the contrary, there were many Israelis who came to my husband's restaurant in Jenin," she said, tucking a few stray hairs back beneath her flowered scarf. "Sometimes they were soldiers and they would put their guns down while they were eating in our restaurant. . . . My husband frequently visited people in Israel. So we had social contact. And there was never any animosity."

But Shaheel al Masri, Izzidene's father, gave reporters a different story at his son's wake, saying that he was proud of Izzidene and that he supported his suicide attack. Shaheel al Masri, in his fifties, was a striking figure in a red and white *kuffiyeh* (the traditional headdress worn by many Arab men) and a thick black beard. He told reporters after his son's death that Israeli Prime Minister Ariel Sharon was responsible for such attacks. "He is continuing the policy of killing our people, and my son succeeded in carrying out a suitable response," he said, to the praise of friends and relatives.[4]

Shaheel al Masri said Izzidene was a devout Muslim who had participated in Hamas rallies and funeral marches during the ten months of Israeli-Palestinian fighting, the elder Shaheel learned after his son's death. And Shaheel said that his son had hinted that he was going to die an istishhadi. At the funeral, Shaheel and his remaining sons seemed proud of Izzidene. They said they were rejoicing at his death. As the Qur'an states, they said, Izzidene is not dead but "with God in heaven."[5] But months later, as his wife spoke of her regrets, Shaheel simply shook his head and walked away. It was clear that he and his wife did not see Izzidene's actions the same way.

This attitude of pride among the male relatives of shuhada was also evident during U.S. bombing of Afghanistan in late 2001 to root out Taliban and al Qaeda fighters. Knight Ridder reporter Barry Shlachter visited the families of two Taliban fighters who had been killed in the bombing near the northern city of Mazar-e-Sharif and found the family celebrating.

"We handed out sweets in the neighborhood," the father of one of the men identified only as Hayatullah, believed to be 22 years old, told Shlachter. He had received word of his son's death only days before and was basking in the congratulations from his friends and relatives.

"As a Muslim martyred in jihad against unbelievers, his death is a great source of pride," said the father, who said he goes by only the name Jhrafunuddin. "He died for Allah." Jhrafunuddin, a teacher of the Qur'an in his village, knew well the prohibition against mourning for martyrs, and he was doing his best to abide by it.

A sign was strung up in the neighborhood proclaiming the street where Hayatullah and another dead Taliban solider, Mohamed Umar Khan, lived. It boasted "Street of the Martyrs."

Jhrafunuddin conceded that there had been some tears from his wife. It was only natural. But even Hayatullah's mother reminded herself that he was far better off in paradise than in the misery that was his lot on this war-torn earth.

"His mother expected him to become martyred," Shlachter quoted the brother, Hidayat-ullah Serdehri, 28, a real estate broker, as saying. "A family member might be momentarily sad, but everyone dies eventually. His mother is thankful he died in a good place, in a good way. There is a sense of satisfaction in this. A shaheed's death is the best death."

This glorification of martyrdom is common throughout the Islamic world, but when some Palestinian students at al Najah University in the West Bank town of Nablus decided to create an exhibit to honor suicide bombers, Arafat shut it down, and one of his aides issued a public statement saying Arafat was "gravely disturbed and offended" by it. The exhibit, designed to mark the first anniversary of the Palestinian intifada, featured a recreation of the Sbarro bombing scene. Some students associated with Hamas even went so far as to splatter fake blood and body parts around the room. It was too much for Arafat to ignore, especially after Israeli officials pointed to the exhibit as another sign that the Palestinian leader was doing nothing to try to abate extremism.

But there were even clearer signs about the ambivalence Arabs felt about suicide bombers like al Masri. Arab leaders and Muslim charities around the world often send money to the families of Palestinian martyrs, but Um Iyad said her family received nothing.

"We got nothing from the Palestinian Authority or from anyone," she said. "Many people said, oh, you must have received some money for Izzidene and my husband got very upset. He said I don't want to be accused of taking something I never got. He didn't want people to say he was paid for his son's death."

Um Iyad could not mask her bitterness in criticizing Yasser Arafat's Palestinian Authority for offering her family no support, only condolences, even though, she said, her husband was suffering with a heart condition, his restaurant was closed, and they had no other source of income. "Of course I'm angry. I'm upset that no one has asked after us. My husband is not well and I've got many young children. One is in second grade, another is in third grade. We've put one of the boys in private school and that costs money. Of course money would help. I'm angry no one cares."

"We got some phone calls of condolences from Jordan, people who know my family," she said, but Arab leaders such as Iraqi president Saddam Hussein and Jordan's King Abdullah had not called or sent gifts, as they usually do for the families of martyrs.

Yet from the looks of the al Masri home, they were not destitute. Many of the suicide bombers recruited and trained by Hamas and Islamic Jihad came from middle-class families and were well educated, which made them even more bitter about their bleak prospects under Israeli occupation. Sitting with Um Iyad in the comfortable house that al Masri shared with his eleven brothers and sisters, it would appear that he has been better off than most young people in Jenin. His home sat behind a rocky garden atop one of Jenin's most dramatic hills, with large porch that offered a sweeping view of the countryside. It was a virtual palace in the war rubble of Jenin.

These days Um Iyad watches her remaining sons carefully, looking for the signs that she missed in Izzidene. "Of course, one is always afraid for their children," she confided, conceding that there was nothing she could do if one of her children wanted to become an istishhadi. But it is a little granddaughter who seems obsessed with al Masri's picture in the living room who worries her the most. Young women increasingly were joining men as suicide bomber. In the first four months of 2002, there already had been four.

"She looks at the picture all the time and says, look, look, this is my uncle who went to paradise. He's a shaheed. She's always talking about him." Um Iyad says all of this with the resignation of someone who's been crushed by too many tragedies. Most of all, she has resigned herself to the fact that her most caring son was no longer there to make sure she ate her vegetables.

"He left this life in this world so I hope he gets to have his paradise in the next," Um Iyad said, straightening his picture on her living room wall. "If that's the way he chose, and he's happy being with God, then who am I to say that he has chosen the wrong way?"

7

THE TRAINERS:
ABU MUHAMMAD AND
MUNIR AL MAKDAH

*They shall be a target for all of our freedom fighters. . . . They are
not allowed to walk in the streets in peace. They are not allowed to
eat pizza.*

—*Munir al Makdah*

RUSHING IN FROM THE MUDDY STREETS OF JENIN RECENTLY,
Abu Muhammad looked like he had just returned from a battle. His left hand
was bandaged and fresh blood oozed from beneath the dingy white gauze. But
he would not say how he was injured, where or when, only that he was shot.

Just getting into Jenin to meet Abu Muhammad was a feat that meant
driving past roadblocks, tall barbed wire fences, and Israeli tanks and Israeli
troops stationed in towers overlooking the city. Gun battles with Israeli soldiers and nearby settlers were common in the hills around Jenin.

"I was hit here and here," Abu Muhammad said, gesturing to both his
wrapped hand and his thigh.

Abu Muhammad is not the real name of the military chief of Islamic
Jihad, one of the most militant Palestinian Islamic guerrilla groups. But he
proclaimed it "good enough," picking the name out of thin air and plopping
down a plastic chair just inside the doorway of a home deep inside the
bombed-out town. Abu Muhammad had selected the house for the meeting
as randomly and as impulsively as he had selected his pseudonym.

A squat elderly lady in a faded flowered dress sidled into the room and seemed amused that her home had been expropriated by men with guns and an American reporter, but she was neither alarmed nor offended. Her curiosity satisfied, she deemed it best to retire back to the kitchen.

"I'm a wanted man," Abu Muhammad said without taking notice of the woman. But his eyes immediately latched onto the tape recorder positioned in front of him and he motioned abruptly to turn it off. "I don't want anyone to know what my voice sounds like," he said. "They could use this recording to identify me."

"They" were the Israeli government of Prime Minister Sharon, which was determined to kill men like Abu Muhammad who are responsible for much of the violence of the second intifada. On April 2, 2001, only months before, an Israeli helicopter bombed the pickup truck of Mohammed Abdel Al, a senior member of Islamic Jihad. Al was driving his car in Rafah in Gaza when it was hit by four missiles. Israeli officials said Al's killing was in retaliation for an Islamic Jihad bomb attack on a shopping center in Jerusalem that killed six people the week before.

But closer to Abu Muhammad, on April 5, Israelis had killed Iyad Hardan, a member of Islamic jihad's military wing in Jenin. Hardan, who was 30 years old, had gone into a phone booth outside the governor's office. When he answered the phone, it exploded.

Although Abu Muhammad knew the Israelis probably would kill him, as well, he was not interested in becoming a shaheed anytime soon—at least not before he killed a few more Israelis. But soon he would wind up in an Israeli jail, a prize captive of Israelis troops who stormed into Jenin in April 2002 to hunt down those responsible for the increasing number of suicide bombings. Palestinians accused Israel of massacring hundreds of civilians in the Jenin assault, which was part of a military campaign that included incursions into other Palestinian cities. Israel denied the charges, but Sharon refused to allow a UN fact-finding team to investigate the allegations. However, in August, the UN General Assembly issued a report acknowledging that "it is impossible to determine with precision how many civilians were among the Palestinian dead." But from information gathered from several sources, including from Israelis, Palestinians, journalists, and human rights organizations, the report concluded:

> By the time of the IDF [Israel Defense Forces] withdrawal and the lifting of the curfew on 18 April, at least 52 Palestinians, of whom up to half may have been civilians, and 23 Israeli soldiers were dead. Many more were injured.

Approximately 150 buildings had been destroyed and many others were rendered structurally unsound. Four hundred and fifty families were rendered
homeless. The cost of the destruction of property is estimated at approximately $27 million.[1]

It is surprising that the Israelis did not kill Abu Muhammad then. But he
was probably more valuable alive since he held valuable information about
his network of shuhada.

Abu Muhammad is a big, bearded, middle-age man, dressed at the time
of our interview in dusty green fatigues. Despite his advancing years, he had
so much nervous energy that he could barely contain his hulking body on the
edge of the chair. Just before Abu Muhammad's dramatic entrance, word had
filtered through Jenin that two Israelis from a nearby settlement had been
shot while driving on the road to Jerusalem. "One is seriously hurt," a young
man whispered into a cell phone.

Abu Muhammad heard the news without expression.

Abu Muhammad probably knew about the attack, and maybe even
planned it or carried it out. But he would not talk about it. He did talk about
why he was sending young men to carry out such missions and what it took
to become a shaheed. In Jenin, Abu Muhammad decided which of Islamic
Jihad's young men were ready to undertake specific operations, such as attacks on Israeli settlers, spraying gunfire on marketplaces in the nearby Israeli town of Netanya, and suicide bombings as far away as Tel Aviv and
Jerusalem.

"The martyr is not someone who commits suicide, as people always
think he is," Abu Muhammad said. "And people who commit acts of martyrdom by using their bodies are not stars in the organization. They are people
seeking revenge for acts done against us. There have been, all along, assassination attempts on people through the use of helicopters and planes and
using car explosives. Recently two Fatah people were killed, and the retaliation came from our organization."

The Islamic Jihad group that operated in Jenin was part of the main
branch of a guerrilla organization with affiliates in Jordan and Lebanon,
where it cooperated with Hezbollah when Israeli troops occupied the southern part of the country from 1982 to 2000. Fathi Shqaqi, founder of the main
Palestinian Islamic Jihad group known as the Fathi Shqaqi faction, was once
affiliated with Egypt's Muslim Brotherhood, but became disillusioned with
its growing moderation. Shqaqi, who was born in Gaza, left the group in

1974. In 1980 he collaborated with Abd al Aziz Odah and Bashir Musa to form Islamic Jihad in Gaza, made up mostly of Egyptians who had fled or been expelled from their country for their militant connections. Although he was a Sunni Muslim, Shqaqi was enamored with Ayatullah Khomeini and the Shia revolution he led in Iran and was greatly inspired by its success.

It is believed that Israeli agents killed Shqaqi in October 1995 in Malta. Dr. Ramadan Abdallah Shalah, who once lived in Florida but moved to Damascus in 1996, took over leadership of the group after Shqaqi's death. The U.S. State Department believes that Iran provided the main support for Islamic Jihad in the West Bank and Gaza.

Islamic Jihad's Shqaqi faction is considered one of the most dangerous in the region. Interviews with several of its top leaders in the West Bank during the fall of 2001 confirm that they are uncompromising about their commitment to armed struggle to regain land lost to Israel. And while Hamas is primarily concerned with Palestinian land and has no interest in fighting anyone but Israeli targets in the region, it is not hard to envision Islamic Jihad taking its battle outside the Middle East, especially if it feels threatened.

Islamic Jihad boasts of having inspired, by its bold attacks against Israel, the intifada that broke out in 1987. Ahmad Rashad, a researcher with the United Association for Studies and Research, a Muslim think tank in Annandale, Virginia, agreed. Rashad contends in the book *Hamas, Palestinian Politics with an Islamic Hue:* "It was Jihad's spectacular acts of daring and courage throughout the 80s that lent credence to the Islamist movement as a whole in the occupied territories. The Jihad's attacks on Israeli military targets peaked during the mid-80s and set the stage for the intifada, the Palestinian uprising."[2]

Islamic Jihad's actions to spark the first intifada embarrassed Arafat's secular Palestine Liberation Organization as well as Hamas, which was still then in planning mode. But its brazen attacks increased the popularity of Islamic guerrilla groups in the West Bank and Gaza. According to Rashad. "The intifada, the drive to 'shake off' Israeli rule, is widely believed to have been spontaneous. It spread rapidly due, in part, to the pride that Palestinians had begun to feel in the Jihad's actions."[3]

For Islamic Jihad, liberation of Palestine from Israeli occupation is not a nationalist cause but a religious one. The group believes that should be the paramount goal for Muslims around the world, as it involves returning the holy city of Jerusalem to Muslim control. Islamic Jihad was once a rival of the larger and more popular Hamas, but since Ariel Sharon was elected Israel's prime minister in February 2001, the Palestinian groups, secular and religious, had begun cooperating in towns such as Jenin, which faced Israeli blockades as well as bombing. Islamic Jihad and Hamas had decided it was in their best interests to work together, even though there were differences in their approaches and philosophies.

According to Abdel Hakim Masalma, Islamic Jihad's spokesman in the West Bank, his group was even more hard-line than Hamas and was opposed to attempting peace talks with Israel. In his offices in the Palestinian town of Ramallah, Masalma explained: "The difference between Hamas and Islamic Jihad is that for Hamas, the occupation created the resistance. But for Islamic Jihad, the resistance always existed. Jihad started the struggle against the occupation. Hamas didn't really start with the armed struggle until 1988. Before that, Hamas didn't do anything against the occupation. They didn't resist.

"Hamas is the child of the Muslim Brotherhood in Egypt, and the Brotherhood accommodated the powers that be at different periods. When we were founded, this was a time when Hamas and the leadership of the Brotherhood had decided they were in a period when they would wait it out instead of continuing the armed struggle."

In fact, by the 1990s Egypt's Muslim Brotherhood had mellowed into a moderate political and religious activist group, controlling trade unions and much of civil society in Egypt, while being careful not to threaten President Mubarak's regime. Islamists such as Masalma considered them sell outs. "We believe in continued struggle and that there aren't times when we sit back and go to the movies. No, the struggle is a continuous thing. It's not in stages."

According to Boaz Ganor, executive director of Israel's counter-terrorism institute, there once were clear differences between Hamas and Islamic Jihad:

> Until 1987, the differences between Hamas and the Islamic Jihad could have been summarized in three points: Hamas claimed that a solution to the Palestinian problem might come about only after an Islamic state was established outside Palestine; the Islamic Jihad insisted that the order should be reversed. Hamas and the Islamic Jihad were at odds with respect to the importance and centrality of the Islamic revolution in Iran. The third point of discord was the major one: had the time come to launch a Jihad against the Jews? The Muslim Brotherhood and Hamas argued that they had to develop their infrastructure in the Gaza Strip and the West Bank by means of Islamic

indoctrination, and that a changeover to armed struggle at that stage could diminish the relative freedom of activity afforded them by the Israeli security forces. The Islamic Jihad counter argued that armed struggle was a divine obligation that had to be effected immediately.[4]

Islamic Jihad initially claimed responsibility for the Sbarro bombing, believing one of their suicide bombers had gone out that day. Hamas later set the record straight, praising al Masri as its own istishhadi.

Masalma refrained from criticizing Hamas too stridently, even though that organization had agreed to a cease-fire, which eventually failed dismally. But Masalma said Islamic Jihad would never give up its war against Israel until its objectives were met. "Each group has their own way of doing things and their own reasons for doing things. We believe that all of Palestine belongs not just to us as Palestinians, but to all Muslims, including Muslims in America. So we will not back off from fighting for all of it."

And Islamic Jihad would not abandon its tactics of sending suicide bombers to terrorize Israelis. "We believe that Israel actually forces us to have the kind of strategies we have. We're not going to sit and be spectators to what Sharon and his government are doing here and not answer them in their own language. We do not follow the teaching of Christ when he said if someone hits you on one cheek, turn the other cheek. We will not initiate that slap, but if we are slapped, we will slap back."

It was a refrain heard again and again among Islamic guerrillas. Islam called on them to fight to defend themselves and their religion. They were not called on to be pacifists but activists in fighting evil in the world. Jihad was their duty. "There are five obligations in Islam and there's a sixth one, which is the invisible one, which is jihad," Masalma explained.

"Jihad is until Armageddon. There are also Surah [verses] in the Qur'an on jihad. It says if 10 of you die then 200 of the others must die. But there is no measurement of too little or too much in warfare. Only God will decide what is too little or too much."

Yet Masalma, just like Hamas's Sheikh Yassin and Hezbollah's Sheikh Fadlullah, contends that Muslim fighters are bound by Islam's strict code of conduct in war. He insists that they are defending themselves from Israeli aggression, backed by the United States.

Of course, we differentiate between innocent and between government and people. And we felt very bad about what happened in the United States, but

we also felt that this was a result of American policies. In our initial operations we always targeted soldiers. But when we saw that Sharon was not
being careful in his targeting as we were, we opened the door to other operations, which would include civilians. We believe in do unto others as they
do unto you.

Masalma was pleased at this distortion and had a ready answer when
asked if he agreed with the true meaning of Christ's teachings: Do unto others as you would *have* them do unto you. "In a normal situation, yes," he
replied. "We have to do this because although in a normal situation we would
act differently, this is not a normal situation. And when we're dealing with
something as serious as life, which is God given and only God should take,
then our relationship with the other becomes different."

Author John Kelsay has attempted to explain the Muslim fighters' attitudes
toward war, noting that many believe there are two kinds of war in Islam—regular jihad and irregular jihad. In regular jihad, which is to expand Muslim territory, Islam's strict rules of war must be followed. But the rules can be stretched
in irregular jihad, which is a rebellion, revolution, or uprising against an alien
authority, like the Palestinian intifada against the Israelis. According to Kelsay:

> From the perspective of groups like Hamas and Islamic Jihad, irregular war
> is a fact of life. The necessity to struggle against injustice is an obligation
> that Muslims cannot ignore . . . assassinations, deception, kidnappings—
> these are acts which are either justified or excused by the realities of the
> struggle that contemporary Muslims are commanded to undertake. Or so ir-
> regulars argue.[5]

Yet many Islamic scholars hold firmly to the argument that Islam does
not allow its devout to behave like nonbelievers, even in the most egregious
circumstances, and that Muslims are called to higher standards, especially in
times of war. Masalma claimed to hold to that argument, as well, even if he
did not apply such teachings in the conflict with Israel. "In our morality, we
differentiate between right and wrong, in times of peace and in times of war.
We differentiate between *haram* and *halal* [the forbidden and the permitted].
We're not drinkers of blood. But if war is imposed on us, we're ready. We
don't have any problems. We trust in God and in the afterlife."

Muslims have always been called to make the supreme sacrifice of martyrdom, Masalma said, from the founding of their religion in a cave in Mecca

until the present day. At its inception, the religion was under threat from the powerful Quraysh tribe but today, Islam has to defend itself against the one remaining superpower. "All of this has been explained by Omar Abdel Rahman, who declared [that] jihad against Egypt was an obligation." Omar Abdel Rahman is infamous in the United States; he is the sheikh convicted and imprisoned in New York for ordering or approving of the February 1993 bombing of the World Trade Center that killed 6 and wounded 1,000 others. But he was esteemed among jihadees such as Masalma. Abdel Rahman was spiritual leader of the radical Egyptian group al Jihad, led by Ayman Zawahri, one of Osama bin Laden's lieutenant's in Afghanistan. Bin Laden himself vowed to free the sheikh.

In fact, many believe that the September 11 attack was also meant to avenge Abdel Rahman's imprisonment. People like Masalma saw the sheikh's imprisonment as one of the clearest signs that the United States is waging war on Islam and its leaders. He also pointed to the terrorism list that the Bush administration had drawn up. "There is not a single name on the list that is not Muslim," said Masalma. "None of the other groups around the world are on the list. I watched for this carefully. Any names that come out are always Muslim names." While it is true that the terrorism lists that the Bush administration put out shortly after September 11, 2001, included only Muslim organizations, in December other groups were added to the list, including several Irish groups.[6]

Masalma also warned that the United States was risking even more attacks if it continued to target Islamic groups as terrorists and threaten them with military action, as Israeli officials were encouraging the Bush Administration to do.

"If I'm attacked by America, all of America becomes a target for me," he said. But he did not appear too worried about becoming embroiled in war with the United States. "We're not a state or a government or a military base that can be hit." He expected that the United States and Israel would pressure Arafat to try to crush the Islamic movements.

"Everything is in God's hands," he said. "We'll shuffle the cards. We will have to be careful and stay awake and be aware of what could happen. But everything in life has limits. We know that God whenever he wants us will take us."

As Islam triumphed over the great Quraysh who persecuted the Prophet Muhammad and his early followers, it would triumph over Israel and the

United States, he said. And it would do so through its martyrs, as it has done throughout Islamic history:

> In Islam's early days and in the battle for Constantinople, there were operations when people would blow themselves up in battle. In the early days the kind of warfare needed was different from what's needed now. In this world of modern warfare, we need methods that will have a real effect. To fight the jets and the bombs, we have something called human bombs. It's a different kind of balance of power.

As political leader of Islamic Jihad in Jenin, Abdel Halim Izzidene also knew he was a prime target for Israeli assassination. And, like Abu Muhammad, the Israelis had captured him during their April 2002 siege.

"We are fighting for both religion and country," Izzidene said in November 2001, seated in a building in an area that already had been damaged in Israel's bombing. "We work in defense of Palestine. Our jihad is defensive, to defend Palestine, Arab, and Muslim land."

Izzidene maintained the studied emotional control that is typical of Islamic jihadees as he explained why Islamic Jihad would not back down from its vow to wage war against Israel until its soldiers withdrew from all of the West Bank and Gaza and took the estimated 200,000 Jewish settlers with them. Like many Arabs, Izzidene blames the United States for supporting Israel and believes that no one in the West is interested in brokering a fair settlement to the Israeli-Palestinian conflict. "We don't expect much good from the United States because they always are supporting Israel. Always, from 1948 until now. The United States gives Israel weapons to kill us and to destroy our land. But we hope and dream that the Americans will be more balanced in their relations with the Palestinians and Israelis."

His office was part of an apartment that also was his home and one of his sons ran in and out at will. A child wailed from another room but none of it seemed to bother Izzidene, who was intent on detailing Islamic Jihad's grievances with both Israel and the United States. "The United States says it supports a Palestinian state, but it's not enough. It doesn't say what will be the boundaries of that state. It just wants to stop the intifada and divide the Palestinians. But we will not stop it and the jihad will continue even greater."

Like many people who had dedicated themselves to jihad, Izzidene was convinced that they would ultimately win the struggle with Israel, even if it meant defying the United States. "I think the United States is against Muslims. It is against our life and freedom," he said. "America wants to dominate people. America is against Muslims, against Islam. It only likes Muslims who take the American way . . . without prayer, without fasting. . . . Muslims it can control. But true Islam struggles against evil. Jihad is a part of Islam."

Izzidene's walls were covered with photos and posters of men who had died as shuhada, in gun battles with Israelis, or as istishhadis in suicide bombings. He pointed to each photo with pride, saying that all of the men had died to fulfill the inevitable dream of an independent Palestinian state, with Jerusalem as its capital. Izzidene believed that even before September 11, the United States had declared war on Islam to ensure Israel's survival and its dominance of the region.

Abu Muhammad definitely thought so. "Unfortunately, American policy and Israeli policy are one in the same. And unfortunately the U.S. policy is with Israel, right or wrong. I have no confidence in the United States."

While Masalma and Izzidene represented Islamic Jihad's brain, explaining its philosophies and rationale for using suicide bombers against Israel, Abu Muhammad was its brawn. He was there in the thick of battle on a daily basis, planning attacks, organizing them, and sending young men to carry them out, even if it meant their deaths.

"You have to understand that in Islam, the martyr holds a very special place," Abu Muhammad said, cradling his wounded hand but showing no sign of pain. "He holds a place above all others, and this has been clearly written about in the Qur'an. Hopefully God will lead to the way to many more."

About a dozen young men surrounded Abu Muhammad. They hovered around the doorway outside and several stood silently near him inside the dark room. One, a somber young man about 20 years old, who picked the name Ali out of thin air, said that he was dedicated to jihad and was prepared to become a shaheed.

"I am willing to die to fight the Israelis and to defend Palestine," Ali said with quiet determination. "I'm only waiting for the right time."

The other young men nodded as if taking the same oath; doubtless, many of them will have the opportunity to fulfill their oaths of martyrdom, whether willingly or from Israeli bombing raids, which are becoming more frequent in Palestinian cities such as Jenin.

It was impossible to tell whether all of the young men there actually were prepared to die, or if they were simply adolescents full of bravado. Abu

Muhammad must have known which of the youths were serious enough, controlled enough, and angry enough to become a shaheed or an istishhadi. He had known most of them since they were babies, and he knew their families. This is what makes it so difficult for outsiders to infiltrate such groups and why Israelis try to pressure Palestinians to collaborate. People within the cells of militant organizations usually are related and know they can trust each other. Commanders like Abu Muhammad have seen the youths in their cadres grow up, but they know the ancient histories of their families, as well as their extended families and even their tribal affiliations.

Anyone who becomes a suicide bomber is of a special breed, he said, since he must be utterly self-controlled, convinced of the holiness of his mission, and determined to carry it through. Abu Muhammad must have known that al Masri, the Sbarro suicide bomber, was a devout and serious youth, who kept to himself and could guard a secret, even from his mother. And foremost, like al Masri, the istishhadi must be spiritual enough to yearn for union with God.

"This has to be a person who believes in God and believes in his book and has gotten very far in his belief that he is on the right path," he said. "He follows the right path because his rights are legitimate and he is fighting for those rights." The young men in the room again nodded in silence.

"I know this is something that Europeans and Americans will not understand because they don't believe in the Qur'an," he said. "But it is something that is honored in our religion, to be a martyr and a martyr for God."

Abu Muhammad insisted that he did not have to go out looking for suicide bombers. Young men such those in the room come to him begging to be trained, to be allowed to strap on explosives and detonate themselves in an Israeli marketplace or spray machine gun fire at Israeli soldiers. And Israel's assassination of Palestinian leaders had only increased the number of young men willing to die as istishhadis.

Abu Muhammad has a simple philosophy in life. Power is everything. "What you need to know is that journalists and simple people, they don't really make a difference. It's the Zionist lobby in America that makes a difference. It's people with power that make a difference. It's the powerful that rule the world not those who are interested in justice. And so, if tomorrow, the Arabs were powerful, they would rule, right or wrong. It's always about the powerful. But what we're saying is, don't look at the powerful, look at right and wrong."

Abu Muhammad clearly has little admiration or respect for Westerners. He said that the United States was guilty of only looking after its own power in the region, to the detriment of the Palestinian people and the Arab world in general. "The problem is that America doesn't want to understand what the problem is here. It is only concerned about supporting Israel. Look, [Secretary of State Colin] Powell has spoken a lot and Bush, the father and the son, have spoken a lot. It was all words. The only thing that really makes a difference is power. This land was taken through power and violence and it will be gotten back through violence. There is only one way, either us or them."

Abu Muhammad and his young men believe they were guided by God to throw off what they saw as Israeli oppression. "I want you to know that we want justice and what we're looking for is justice. We're not looking for war, we're looking for peace. But our enemies, whether it's Sharon, or [Israeli defense minister Benjamin] Ben-Eliezer or [Israeli minister of foreign affairs Shimon] Peres are not looking for peace. We gave them a golden opportunity and they failed to take it," he said, referring to the Oslo Accords, which were supposed to pave the way toward eventual peace between Israelis and Arabs. "If they had really intended to make peace, all they had to do was abide by the agreements and give us what was rightly ours by those agreements. But they think they're superior and better than other people. But they're not, they're worse than other people."

Maybe it was because he had been in the thick of so many battles or maybe it's because he had just come from one, but Abu Muhammad lacked the practiced self-control that was common among jihadees. He showed his anger and his impatience at what he saw as the injustice in the world. "This is a very long battle," he said. "It's not about one shaheed or two shuhada; or one battle here or one battle there. This is a long war. This involves people getting killed and houses getting blown up. As even if there is one Palestinian, we will continue on the path of jihad."

Abu Muhammad made it clear that he did not ask the young men around him to do anything more than he was willing to do himself. Even his family was constantly exposed to danger from potential Israeli assassins, he said. He knew that the families of Hamas and Islamic Jihad leaders had been killed and wounded in Israeli attacks, if not actually targeted. In March 2002, the wife and children of Hamas activist Hussein Abu Kweik were killed when an Israeli tank fired on their car in West Bank town of Ramallah, about 10 miles from Jerusalem. Bushra Hafez Nimer Abu Kweik, 36, had just picked up her children, ages 8, 14, and 17, from school. Two children, ages 4 and 16, riding in a second car also were killed in the incident.

Israeli Defense Minister Binyamin Ben-Eliezer expressed "regret at the loss of life of Palestinian civilians" and said the killing was an accident.[7] But many Palestinians believed the killing was deliberate and intended to send a clear message to Palestinian militants that even their families would be subject to assassinations. Such tactics only seemed to reinforce Palestinian resolve. At the funerals of his wife and children, Abu Kweik vowed revenge.

"I swear to God they (the Israelis) will pay a very high price for this crime," he said. "We will continue our resistance until it's the end of the last soldier on our lands."

"Yes, I have daughters and sons," said Abu Muhammad. "But I'm not worried about them. God will take care of them." With that, Abu Muhammad had had enough of talk and was ready to head back out onto the battlefield. He refused to allow me to photograph him, and he was too impatient to suffer through the usual departing niceties, even to thank the old lady for the use of her house.

"I am willing to die for my country," he said, tossing aside the flimsy chair that had barely contained his weight and heading for the door. "I haven't been fighting just since yesterday. I've been fighting since 1975, and I am willing to keep on fighting for another twenty years or another hundred years if necessary. And I hope that I will die a shaheed in this land." With that Abu Muhammad disappeared from the room as abruptly as he had entered, leaving his young entourage of hopeful shuhada racing to catch up.

A few hundred miles away, in the teeming Ain al Helwah refugee camp, Abu Muhammad's counterpart in the Bekaa Valley strutted through his domain of hodge-podge, cinder-block buildings, dirt streets, and rusting cars like a prince surveying his kingdom. He moved in step with two tall steely-faced young men at his side, each brandishing an M-18 that looked as if it could shoot a rocket through a brick wall. The guards held the guns upright in front of them, their dark eyes like incessantly scanning the alleys that served as playgrounds for children, scrawny dogs, and chickens. The men often turned in dramatic sweeps, guns held high, scouting for potential trouble in their flank.

Munir al Makdah, a tall, lean man in his mid-30s, with large, soft-brown eyes and a thick black beard speckled with gray, took no note of any danger himself. He wore no visible gun and was so at ease, he paused to caress the face of a young child scooting by on a rusty tricycle, as if posing for a publicity

shot. He seemed far slicker than Abu Muhammad, the rough and gruff guerrilla. Al Makdah seemed more like the godfather, albeit a young one, of a
Mafia dynasty.

He was once military chief of Yasser Arafat's Fatah forces in southern
Lebanon. Although al Makdah is not an Islamic fighter seeking to unite Muslims in an Islamic state, he had worked closely with those in Hezbollah to
push Israeli troops out of southern Lebanon. His mission is to retake Arab
land and create a secular Palestinian state, not an Islamic one, as the Islamic
jihadees wanted. Yet, like the Islamic groups, al Makdah had a powerful
weapon to help achieve his goal: suicide bombers whom he had trained.

"Children train for such missions from 5 to 15 years of age," al Makdah
said, providing them a sense of camaraderie and purpose that boys crave at that
age. In Ain al Helwah, there are no Boy Scout camps, sports clubs, or video ar-
cades to command the attention of growing boys; so al Makdah's jihad camps
fill the gap. Boys here learn early that they live in a war zone; and their families
believe they have no other options but to teach them how to shoot Kalashnikovs and explode hand grenades. Al Makdah's camps are meant to begin
preparing the boys mentally and physically for the rough life they will face
under Israeli occupation, but they are not the immediate staging grounds for
suicide missions. "Children of that age are not sent off to suicide missions," al
Makdah said. "They are not aware at that age. There has to be awareness to go
out on a suicide mission. They can go out when they are at least fifteen."

Al Makdah said he had trained martyrs of all ages, from "16 to 65 years
old. The last martyr I sent out was 55 years old." No one is forced to go on a
suicide mission, he emphasized. They willingly undertake such missions in
full knowledge that they will die. Yet al Makdah says there is never a shortage
of young men—and there had been women, as well—willing to become istishhadis to strike at Israel.

Al Makdah was known throughout Lebanon's largest refugee camp, near
the southern port of Sidon, and although he was leader of one of the most
powerful Palestinian groups associated with Arafat's Fatah faction, he had
plenty of competition from Islamic militant cells operating in the camp. He
left his post as chief of all Fatah forces in southern Lebanon when Yasser
Arafat signed the Oslo Accords in 1993. In fact, al Makdah had vowed to kill
Arafat for what he considered a betrayal of the Palestinian people, since the
Oslo Accords did not return all of the land Israel had seized since 1948. And
Oslo offered nothing to Palestinian refugees such as al Makdah, whose family

home was inside what is now Israel, and who were demanding the right to return to their homes. This issue was one of the toughest for Israeli and Palestinian negotiators to resolve because allowing Palestinian refugees the right to return and reclaim their property would seriously threaten the Jewish state by changing the demographic balance. Arabs would quickly outnumber Jews. Yet by ignoring their loss Arafat would risk the wrath of an estimated 4.5 million Palestinian refugees scattered around the globe. After the question of who would control the Muslim holy places in East Jerusalem, the right of return was the most explosive issue for him and his negotiators.

At one point in Israeli-Palestinian negotiations under the Clinton administration, it had seemed that the issue of Jerusalem's holy places might even be settled. One proposal that both sides had at least discussed involved a shared control, in which Palestinians would control the buildings and the surface land of the Haram al Sharif, and Israelis would be given control of the area underneath, which is believed to hold the remains of Solomon's Temple.

In a similar effort at compromise in the last-gasp peace efforts of the Clinton administration, proposals also had been floated that would have had Israel acknowledging the "right" of Palestinians to return in exchange for Palestinians not exercising that right and accepting financial compensation for their lost property. But even that compromise was not acceptable to radicals such as al Makdah, whose grandfather, more than 100 years old, still held fast to the dream of going home to his land that is now a part of Jewish Haifa.

Al Makdah had reconciled with Arafat, but the issue of peace with Israel and the "right of return" still divided them. Arafat had sent more loyal Fatah commanders into southern Lebanon to ensure his control of the area, but al Makdah was still the best known and probably the most powerful commander in Ain al Helwah, and he was absolutely opposed to peace negotiations with Israel, although he had no choice but to hold off any attacks until his main supporters in Syria permitted them. But Syria, which shares al Makdah's disdain for Israel, did not want to incite Israeli attacks on Beirut or, worse, Damascus.

Al Makdah argued that he had sent too many people to die as suicide bombers and in other operations against Israeli soldiers to accept a peace that did not win back all of the land he believed Israel had stolen from the Arabs. Often, he said, he had personally trained the people he had sent to die.

"We had training camps and from these training camps all kinds of fighters used to come," he said. "We were able to recruit a lot of people because the Palestinian people are a wounded race, suffering from Israeli oppression in the West Bank and other places on a daily basis."

But even though Israel has withdrawn from southern Lebanon, al Makdah still maintained a cadre of what he called "human bombs," young men who were ready to die in attacks against Israel and even the United States, should he call them to action. And he is convinced that Lebanon and Syria would untie his hands and allow his martyr brigades to liberate Palestine through jihad. "Jihad and the resistance begins with the word, then with the sword, then with the stone, then with the gun, then with planting bombs and then with transforming bodies into human bombs," al Makdah said. "The last weapon is a weapon the Israelis can never have: suicide bombers."

Al Makdah was the epitome of calm and control as he explained what it takes to become an istishhadi. He spoke slowly with a disturbing smile, even when he talked about war and sending children to their deaths. He had walked deep into Ain al Helwah, past a courtyard of clucking chickens, to reach a small, tile-floored room, freshly painted in turquoise and pink. A large television and VCR commanded one wall, not far from a fax machine that was positioned under a picture of Jerusalem's al-Aqsa mosque.

The Palestinian commando said he had been sentenced to death in Jordan, where authorities maintained he was part of Osama bin Laden's al Qaeda network and had been actively involved in planning attacks against Israel and the United States. Al Makdah refused to say directly if he was allied with bin Laden, but his answers indicated that they once had worked together, that he had received support from bin Laden, and that he was still willing to accept his assistance. Al Makdah complained that bin Laden and his organization had expanded their mission beyond the Palestinian cause to take on other issues. "I would have liked that bin Laden's work would be continually against Israel. And were it such, I would have worked hand in hand with him. I'm sorry that is not the case and that is not the path that he has chosen. Their strategy is completely different. And we have no details about his ideas or his program or anything like that. Our goal is the struggle and resistance against the Israeli occupation, and we thank whoever contributes to the struggle no matter where he is from or who he is."

Although Lebanese authorities knew that al Makdah was only 30 minutes away from Beirut in the squalid, teeming refugee camp that was home to thousands of Palestinian refugees, they could not go inside Ain al Helwah to bring him out. Lebanese forces are stationed just outside the country's twelve Palestinian refugee camps that house an estimated 360,000 people, but they are forbidden from entering, even to track down someone like al Makdah.

It would take an army to capture al Makdah in Ain al Helwah's maze of cinder-block squares, and even then there would be a bloodbath that would wash over the innocent as well as his regiments of jihadees. And in Ain al Helwah, it was hard to tell who is innocent and who is not.

Al Makdah provided photos of his training camps for both men and boys. In one, the men were dressed in camouflage uniforms and some had their faces covered in black masks, some in green masks. Another photo showed al Makdah supervising a training session in which an instructor shows a young man how to load a machine gun. Still another showed young men learning how to shoot rocket launchers.

He also had dozens of photographs of young boys marching in step in what looks like a sport stadium. They were draped in white capes and white masks that revealed only their eyes and mouths. Each mask was adorned with green [the color of Islam] head-bands proclaiming "In the Name of God, the Compassionate, the Merciful." The boys carried machine guns in one hand, and they wore black aprons fitted with red blocks of dynamite. They were only in training, so the dynamite, adorned with realistic looking pins and wires, was not real. The exercise was just to get them used to the feel of explosives strapped around their bodies, to help them become comfortable with the idea of martyrdom. The children received sobering lessons about warfare at these camps, including how to shoot and how to kill.

"I held my first rifle when I was ten years old. And I had my first fight when I was ten years old," al Makdah said. "But Ali there," he said, pointing to a young man of about eighteen sitting near what appeared to be a collection of hand-held rocket launchers, "he was eight years old when he entered the movement."

"When I was very young, my mother put me with what is known as the Ashvel. . . . It's the children's group. We were trained with weapons, small weapons," Ali explained.

Ali is a slender, quiet youth who stayed in al Makdah's shadow, watching him respectfully, waiting for any order he might give. He had grown up looking to al Makdah as a mentor, and he awaited the day when he might be trusted to become one of his bodyguards or even sent out on a martyrdom mission against the Israelis.

"When I was eight years old," Ali said, "I learned how to use light weapons, Kalashnikovs. And when I grew older I discovered that I liked it, and I continued my training to join the struggle."

Now a young man, Ali had committed himself to jihad and to liberating Arab land from Israel. He made it clear he was willing to die when the time came. Life inside Ain al Helwah was like a living death. Except for joining one of the myriad of guerrilla groups inside the camp, there is no employment for smart young men such as Ali. And Palestinians faced severe discrimination in trying to find jobs within Lebanon and are prohibited from pursuing many professions, especially those in the public sector.

"Discriminatory labour laws mean that Palestinian workers here experience higher un- and underemployment rates than elsewhere, and more families live in a state of 'ultra-poverty'," author Rosemary Sayigh wrote in an article entitled "No Work, No Space, No Future: Palestinian Refugees in Lebanon."[8] "A diminished Palestinian professional and trading stratum survives through sharing with a Lebanese 'partner', accepting lower wages, or staying within camp boundaries."

Even after the civil war of 1975 to 1990, which many Lebanese blame on Palestinian intrigue, there were serious tensions between Palestinians and Lebanese. The powerful Maronite Christians feared that allowing the estimated 360,000 Palestinian refugees in the camps to become Lebanese citizens would upset the delicate balance of power that kept them at the top of the sectarian heap. And in a country whose economy is already reeling, Palestinian refugees represent a drain on scarce jobs and resources. So while the Lebanese claim to support the intifada in the West Bank and Gaza and push for a Palestinian state, they are less than hospitable to the Palestinian refugees in their own midst, deliberately keeping them out of mainstream politics and society, and denying them not only the right to work but even to own property.

In 2001 the Lebanese parliament revised its property laws to prohibit anyone without citizenship in a recognized state from owning property in the country. This was a blatant attempt to prevent Palestinians from settling permanently in the country. The revisions mainly affected poor, stateless Palestinians forced to live in the camps. Even if they were able to acquire enough money to buy an apartment outside the camps, the law would prohibit them from doing so. It did not affect wealthier Palestinians who were able to pay bribes for Lebanese or foreign passports.

Lebanese who support such measures argue that they are in the long-term best interests of the Palestinians. They say making it comfortable for Palestinians to settle in other Arab countries would take the pressure off of Israel to address the issue of the refugees who fled in the wars. If Palestinians settled in other countries, their arguments for the "right of return" to their homes inside what is now Israel would be weakened, they say. This issue al Makdah and other Palestinian fighters insist must be resolved before there can be peace.

Permanently settling Palestinian refugees would please Israelis such as Sharon, who long ago declared that Jordan was the Palestinian state. But living conditions inside Lebanon's refugee camps also feed the anger of young men such as Ali, whose only outlet and identity come from affiliation with militant groups.

Al Makdah is actively preparing for the prospect of returning to war against Israel, and he is counting on young shuhada in waiting such as Ali.

"The training goes on all the time," Ali said. "I'm always developing my skills and practicing. There is always something more to learn."

Al Makdah was willing to provide as much information as anyone might want about his operations inside Ain al Helwah. He went into elaborate detail about the organization structure of his forces, explaining the branches dedicated to education, training, even public relations. But he would not tell exactly when or where the training camps are held. "The Israelis are always listening," he said. "We have to be careful." Apparently there is no set calendar for the training camps for children or men, but they are called as needed.

Ali said as a boy and as a teenager, he spent several weeks each year in basic military training, learning about discipline and self-control, how to march, sing patriotic songs, and shoot Kalashnikovs. There were regular sessions in which the boys learned about the land their parents lost to Israel, about the duty of each Arab youth to fight until it is regained and about Islam's teachings about the joys of martyrdom. The religious teachers were people who shared al Makdah's interpretation of Islam, which many Islamic scholars would refute. Mainstream Islamic scholars would point out Islam's prohibition against targeting the weak, and emphasize its code of proper conduct in war, and the Prophet's instruction that Muslims should always be willing to negotiate peace with the enemy.

Ali and other boys did not need to be motivated to fight for their people, Al Makdah said. The misery of life in the camps, the visibility of their parents' suffering, and the presence of Israeli troops in their villages do a good job of that before they arrive. Most Palestinian youths have heard their mothers cry over lost homes and have watched Israeli troops carting off their fathers and brothers to jail. Many even have seen boys like themselves killed by Israelis. And some mothers, such as Munabrahim Daoud, are vocal and persistent reminders of the duty Palestinians have to avenge martyrs such as her son.

"Much of the work is already done by the suffering these people have been subject to," al Makdah said. "Only 10 percent comes from me. The suffering and living in exile away from their land has given the person 90 percent of what he needs to become a martyr. All we do is provide guidance and help strengthen his faith and help set the objectives for him."

When Makdah decides it is time for a young man to go on a martyrdom mission, he decides where the young man should strike, provides help with transportation, assigns people to aid in the mission, and helps the prospective martyr prepare a last message to his family. "Here's an example of a video that we also do, if they want that," al Makdah said, presenting an unmarked black video cassette done to commemorate one of his istishhadis. On the film, a young man of about 20 stands facing the camera, his forehead covered with a green headband with Qur'anic script dedicating himself to God. With triumphant music in the background, he declared his intention to die as a shaheed and asked for God's blessings that his mission be successful. The youth appeared calm and resolute, and his final words were interspersed with pictures of Palestinians in battle scenes, firing rockets from barren hilltops, apparently at Israeli soldiers below. There was not the slightest hint of hesitancy to go to his death. That is why al Makdah says his job is really not very hard. He does not have to be a good salesman, an outstanding motivational speaker or a good spiritual guide. Al Makdah's job is little more than that of a traffic cop, giving the green light to young men who are intent on dying to avenge families, the Palestinian people, and God.

"The Palestinian youth comes from his parents' house already imbued with a certain sense of wanting to fight, wanting to defend himself and wanting to be trained," he said. All of them have been raised singing the praises of martyrs and believing there is no nobler act than to die fighting. Shuhada are convinced they will go immediately to heaven on death, that they will experience no pain, and that they will become heroes to their families.

Many also believe that their sins are forgiven and that they will be able to intercede with God for seventy family members. But while much has been made in the West of reports that young men are hoping to enjoy "seventy virgins" in heaven as a reward for killing themselves, this is not based on true teachings of Islam, according to Muslim scholars such as Dr. Maher Hatout, an official with the Muslim Public Affairs Council and imam of the Islamic Center of Southern California. According to Dr. Hatout, such myths are not based on the Qur'an or Islamic teachings. "There is nothing in the Qur'an or in Islamic teachings about seventy virgins or sex in paradise."

Palestinians jihadees like al Makdah said Palestinian shuhada do not undertake their missions expecting to have a reward of sex in heaven. There are other motivations far more compelling. Palestinian youth live constantly with the threat of death from Israelis soldiers, al Makdah said. And they tell themselves, "'You are going to die anyway, so it is better to die as a shaheed.'"

Here al Makdah became virtually poetic, closing his eyes as if reciting from a holy text: "There is but one death, so let it be for God and for the land. I leave the world and what is within it and I go toward death as a martyr with this saying in my mind," he said, quoting Surah 3:185: "'Every soul shall taste death. And ye will be paid on the Day of Resurrection only that which ye have fairly earned. Whoso is removed from the Fire and is made to enter Paradise, he indeed is triumphant. The life of this world is but comfort of illusion.' The noblest sons of the human race are the martyrs."

As al Makdah waxed on about the spiritual dimensions of martyrdom, he emphasized that it was the experience of living in war that molded the Palestinian child into a shaheed and that nurtured his hatred of Israel.

"If you ask my children who their enemy is they're going to say Israel, because they occupied the land. In 1996 the Israelis bombed my house, and one of my children was wounded," al Makdah said. "Israeli planes frequently frighten the children so they come to their own conclusions and make their own decisions about Israel."

Al Makdah himself has known only war. He grew up in Ain al Helwah and admitted he has never even seen the land his family lost in what is now Israel. He rushed into an adjoining room and came back with a photograph of an old man with a long gray beard, sitting on a bed surrounded by children holding big, yellowing sheets of paper. One of the boys was al Makdah when he was about eight years old.

"This is my grandfather," he said. "Here he's showing me the deeds to our land in Palestine. My grandfather is 110 years old. The very act of the grandfather showing the child the leases makes the child feel that there is really land that he owns and he wants to take it back. He grows up with this thought. There are five generations in my family. My grandfather is still alive, his son, myself, my son, and my grandson."

Yet it was doubtful that al Makdah would live to be as old as his grandfather. Israeli officials had targeted him for assassination, he said. But he has vowed to kill Sharon first. "Sharon is a target for all the freedom fighters of the Palestinian people. His personal history is full of ugly massacres, and he will pay the price of the massacres that he has committed from 1948 until today," al Makdah said softly, smiling ever so sweetly.

People such as al Makdah say they will not rest until Sharon is punished for the deaths of an estimated 800 people killed in the Sabra and Shatilla refugee camps. Sharon was forced to resign amid international outrage, even as he maintained he could not foresee the disaster. Yet even in Israel, thousands of people took to the streets to protest the massacre, and many insisted that Sharon should have known what would result in allowing the Lebanese Christian militiamen, Israel's allies, into the camps. Palestinians believed Sharon was a racist and that his actions were a deliberate attempt at ethnic cleansing.

In June 2001, Human Rights Watch, an international organization, called for a criminal investigation into Sharon's role in the massacre, just as the Israeli prime minister was visiting the United States. There were similar calls in Europe after a BBC documentary aired that same year on the event. According to Hanny Megally, executive director of the Middle East and North Africa division of Human Rights Watch, "There is abundant evidence that war crimes and crimes against humanity were committed on a wide scale in the Sabra and Shatilla massacre, but to date, not a single individual has been brought to justice. President Bush should urge Prime Minister Sharon to cooperate with any investigation. As defense minister, Ariel Sharon had overall responsibility over the Israeli Defense Forces and allowed Phalangist militias to enter the camps where they terrorized the residents for three days."[9]

The organization noted that the Kahan Commission in Israel, which was named after the president of its Supreme Court, investigated the incident in 1983 and concluded that "Minister of Defense [Sharon] bears personal responsibility" and Israeli authorities should "draw the appropriate personal conclusions arising out of the defects revealed with regard to the manner in which he discharged the duties of his office."

Although Sharon resigned in disgrace, he continued to hold government posts in subsequent years. The Arab world was outraged when Israelis, after the outbreak of the second intifada, elected him prime minister in February 2001.

"He has massacred Palestinian people and the Lebanese and Arabs and my people will kill him sooner or later," al Makdah said. "He will forever be a target for the freedom fighters, as will his government and the settlers, as long as there is one grain of Palestinian land under occupation."

Al Makdah said he was training the youth for the day when Lebanon and Syria, which exerts considerable influence with its smaller neighbor, would once again call for war against Israel. Although Israeli troops withdrew from most of southern Lebanon in May 2000, Israel still occupies a small strip of land called Shebaa Farms, which Lebanon considered its territory. But Syria had not given the green light for action against Israel yet, he said.

Peace talks were useless with the Israelis, and certainly not with Sharon, al Makdah insisted. The Israelis had taken Arab land by force and the only way to get it back, "all of it back," was through jihad and martyrdom.

"The Israelis did not withdraw from the south out of their own goodwill or around a negotiation table," said al Makdah. "The Israelis withdrew because they were under attack by the resistance. This gave the Palestinian people great will to pursue the same resistance in Palestine itself."

Al Makdah was uncompromising in what he wanted from Israel: full withdrawal from the West Bank and Gaza, including all settlements, and permission for Arabs to return to the homes they fled in 1948, homes that are now owned by Israelis in Haifa, Tel Aviv, and West Jerusalem. He does not see this as an impossible dream, even though he accepts that it will probably take generations to achieve. "I swear that the Israeli state will sooner or later disappear from Palestinian land. That is my oath . . . and that is not a dream. It is an oath. Palestine is ours and not theirs. And the Jews that have come from all over the world to Palestine, they should go back to where they've come from before they are killed and they begin to regret what they have done."

Palestinian militants such as al Makdah especially despise Jewish immigrants from Europe and other parts of the world, many of whom have become settlers in the West Bank and Gaza. They maintain that Jews have always been a part of the Middle East and that they are not antagonistic toward the Jewish religion, from which they acknowledge their own religion had flowered. But Western Jews are aliens to the region, they believe, and represent another form of colonization, taking land that once belonged to Arabs and creating Western-style communities, complete with swimming pools. Al Makdah and other militants do not exempt women or even children from their attacks, especially if they live in the settlements. Unlike leaders of Hamas and Islamic Jihad, who concede that Islam does not allow them to target women and children, al Makdah did not even pretend to obey that injunction.

"Everyone in Israel is a fair target," he said.

> They are all occupying Palestinian land. . . . We as a Muslim race are against the killing of women and older people, against the killing of innocent people. But I'd like to make one thing clear. Anyone who occupies one piece of land in Palestine is worthy of being killed by us. We have the right to kill anyone who occupies our land. We believe in an eye for an eye and a tooth for a tooth. He who begins the aggression is the unjust one. When the Jews return to their original country, where they came from, America, Poland, or any other place in Europe, then maybe we will consider they are forgiven and we will not kill them anymore. But as long as they are in our country, we have a right to kill them."

Like Sheikh Yassin of Hamas, al Makdah preferred to talk about the Palestinian children who have been killed in Israeli attacks, not the Israeli children who have been killed in Palestinian attacks. "Imam Hajji was six months old. She is a martyr, isn't she?" he asked. "The Israelis killed her intentionally. Farah Audi was nine years old and he attacked an Israeli tank with a stone. He was shot three times and every time he would go back and fight. And on the third time, he died. This was during the last intifada. This summer. Six months ago." Farah Audi was the ideal martyr, al Makdah said. "He treaded where even men would not tread."

Al Makdah pointed to what he called one of his most important operations, which involved a woman, Bilal Mugrabi, who hijacked a bus in the Nahariya area of the Galilee.

"She entered the Nahariya from the Lebanese side, and she took control of a bus that contained Israelis settlers and soldiers and then she negotiated for the release of certain Palestinian prisoners for the return of these people," he said. "The Israelis refused and they boarded the bus. She exploded the bus and she died with everybody else on the bus. This was in 1979. She was 19 years old."

"There's definitely a role for women," said al Makdah, and in an unexpected touch of humor, he asked, "Would you like to train?"

Unlike many Islamic religious leaders, al Makdah did not condemn the September 11 attack on the United States. In fact, he used poetic language to describe the men who hijacked the planes and flew them into the symbols of American power and wealth.

"I call them eagles, not suicide bombers or martyrs," he said, refusing to accept U.S. contentions that they were members of bin Laden's group. "These eagles could even have been Americans. They could be Arabs. They could be Japanese. Until now the American administration has not shown any proof to the American people or to the Islamic world about the identity of these people. But even if they are [associated with] bin Laden, I call them eagles because of their bravery, and I hope that all of our armies become eagles against the Israeli occupation."

Al Makdah echoed the sentiments of many Arabs and many people around the world, including those who condemned the September 11 attacks in blaming American foreign policy for inciting such hatred. "What you received was the result of your actions," he said. "As a Palestinian, I speak for myself and for my people. That is what interests me. We are not going to condemn the attacks on the United States as terrorism before America itself condemns what Israel does to my people as terrorism.

"I believe the American government is a terrorist government, has terrorist policies because it supports Israeli terrorism in killing the Palestinian people on a daily basis, killing children and women, and old and senior citizens. It supports the destruction of homes, cutting down trees, and all form of persecution and torture are being practices on our people."

Suddenly, al Makdah seemed to feel a tinge of compassion, however slight and misplaced. "I know that you are a reporter and an American and that might make you feel bad because I call your government a terrorist government," he said, in a soft voice. "But we are suffering very greatly from the results of American foreign policy. Every time the UN Security Council considers an Israeli act terrorism and tries to condemn Israel, America uses its veto to cripple all action against Israel. Every single resolution for the benefit of the Palestinians is being crippled because of American intervention."

But his compassion did not extend much further:

> I believe that September 11 was a lesson to the American people. The majority of Americans don't care about anything that has to do with foreign policy. I believe that after September 11, newspapers in America are sold out very early in the morning. Sooner or later the American people are going to say to the American government, "Where are you going in your absolute

support of Israel?" And this support of Israel and its policies is going to bring evil upon the American people. I believe the American government will more or less rectify its foreign policy. Definitely the American people should know so they can find a way to stop their government's direct support for Israeli terrorism.

Al Makdah said he was asked once to meet with American officials, who were sent to Lebanon to try to locate Ron Arad, the Israeli soldier who has been missing in action in Lebanon since October 1986. He had nothing but disdain for their attempts to find the Israeli navigator. "This man was here on a mission to look for one Israeli whose plane was missing in Lebanon. How am I supposed to meet with a man who comes looking for one Israeli when there are 4 million Palestinians in the diaspora all over the world? Why doesn't he look for them? No meeting with the American administration could ever benefit the Palestinian people. And so we have no interest in meeting with them even if they ask for it."

Al Makdah said he believed his work and his views were fully sanctioned by Islam:

We as Muslim Palestinians, our religious guidance is that we should liberate Palestine. The bride is the liberation of Palestine and the dowry of that bride is that we be religious, with faces bent toward prayer, hands washed for prayer, and hearts that are surrendered to God. These are the three elements that constitute the basic guidance and what we teach our people. It is through these three things that we will liberate our country. The Qur'an teaches, "Kill them where you find them and expel them from where they expelled you. . . ." This verse inspires us because the Israelis took our land and we will make them leave our land.

Al Makdah warned that Palestinians are developing new tactics against the Israelis, which suggests the possibility that the explosives might be filled with a different kind of material, possibly chemical or biological agents. Officials with Islamic Jihad in the West Bank have indicated that they, too, are working on more deadly kinds of attacks, including spraying public places and government buildings with gunfire. "Hopefully the coming days will witness a new kind of suicide bomber against the Israeli occupation of our land," al Makdah said. "And hopefully, if God helps us, you will hear such news in the near future." Before he headed back out into the thick of Ain al Helwah, al Makdah took time to emphasize one point:

Martyrs are the most noble of people, that's what I want you to remember. Israelis always seem to come up with news ways of aggression and new ways to persecute our people. It's only normal that we come up with new ways to defend ourselves . . .

As long as there is one occupier on Palestinian land, there should not be any security for this occupation and for the Israeli people in their houses, not even in their bedrooms. They shall be a target for all of our freedom fighters no matter where they are on Palestinian land. They are not allowed to walk in the streets in peace. They are not allowed to eat pizza. . . .

And they shall be a target for all of our freedom fighters, our muja-hedeen, no matter where they are on Palestinian land. And they shall face the mujahedeen and the mujahedeen shall hunt them from where they think that they shall come and where they don't think that they shall come.

8

CAN THEY BE STOPPED?

If I die in the battle to defend Islam, my son will rise to avenge me.

—*Ayman Zawahri, leader, al Jihad*

EGYPT AND ISRAEL ARE THE TWO STATES THAT HAVE THE MOST experience battling Islamic militants and martyrdom. Osama bin Laden's al Qaeda network despised the leaders of both countries as much as their perceived benefactor, the United States. And the successes and failures of both countries in fighting their own wars against terrorism offer valuable lessons for the United States as it attempts to protect Americans from another attack.

Egypt has waged a decade-long struggle against al Gamaa al Islamiyah and al Jihad, the two groups that killed President Anwar Sadat in 1981 and that had combined their forces to keep the country in a state of siege during the 1990s. In fact, the atmosphere in Cairo, Luxor, and Aswan, Egypt's major cities, was in many ways more terrifying than what Americans faced after September 11 since at times it was a nearly daily assault.

Banks and public buildings were frequently bombed during the 1990s; tourists were repeatedly attacked, including a particularly gruesome massacre at Luxor in 1997; and government officials lived with the threat of assassination. Even artists and writers, such as Nobel laureate Naguib Mahfouz, whom Islamic militants stabbed in 1994 with a kitchen knife, continues to live under a death threat. Islamic radicals killed the secular commentator Farag Foda in 1992 and they tried to assassinate President Mubarak in June 1995. Al Gamaa and al Jihad effectively spread fear throughout the country, from Cairo to Upper Egypt, to try to force Mubarak from power and establish their dream of an Islamic state.

Mubarak fought back with a brutality that only an authoritarian regime could tolerate. His agents rounded up scores of militants and terrorized their families. Many of the militants were tried in open court and executed. International human rights groups roundly condemned Egypt for sending security agents to conduct massive arrests and the violent raids in search of Islamic militants that killed many innocent people. In July 1993 Human Rights Watch issued a report sharply critical of Mubarak's tactics:

> In a major shift of policy, the Egyptian government in October 1992 began to try in military courts civilians accused of "terrorism" offenses, bypassing the security-court system staffed by civilian judges that has been in place under Egypt's long-standing emergency law. President Hosni Mubarak said that he would use military courts "in cases that require quick measures." Since the trials started last year, the proceedings have been conducted swiftly by Supreme Military Courts sitting in Alexandria and Cairo. Sentences have been harsh. The death penalty has been imposed on a total of twenty-three men, and executions by hanging began last month. As of the date of publication of this newsletter, nine of the condemned men have been executed, including seven who were hanged on July 8, 1993.[1]

Human Rights Watch also documented cases in which Egyptian authorities tortured and abused prisoners, and intimidated and threatened family members. In its 1993 report it detailed cases of reported torture and abuse, including the arrest of Mustafa al-Sayyid, who said he had been held for 25 days at the Cairo headquarters of Egypt's State Security Investigation (SSI). His lawyer said: "He was blindfolded the entire time and tortured. They threatened to rape his wife. He was interrogated for sixteen hours a day. They took turns. He was naked and was forced to stand, while blindfolded. He was electric-shocked and beaten."[2]

Human Rights Watch also noted that the Egyptian bar association accused the Egyptian government of killing one of its members, Abdel Harith Madani. Reports were that Madani died after state security investigators gave him electric shocks, burned his body, and whipped him.

Yet the Egyptian government believed that such tactics were necessary in dealing with the likes of al Jihad and al Gamaa. Intellectuals such as Said Ashmawy, former chief justice of the Egyptian Supreme Court and an Islamic scholar, were convinced that the government had to deal strongly with the militants who had placed officials on a hit list for their arguments against Islamic extremism. Ashmawy had no doubt that Islamic militants, which he said also included Egypt's Muslim Brotherhood, were bent on killing him as an example to other Egyptian intellectuals. Egypt's militants had declared Ashmawy an apostate, worthy of death, for his theories that some of the Qur'an's teachings were not applicable in modern societies and were intended for specific periods of the past. "The secretary general of the Muslim Brotherhood wrote an article in their magazine, which is called Dawa in Arabic. He said, Judge Ashmawy should stop talking by any means. It was a sign for the militants to murder me," Ashmawy said in an interview in his Cairo apartment in February 1994.

Many argued that Egypt's politically repressive government fueled the kind of anger that fed Islamic militancy. Ashmawy himself argued against democracy in Egypt, saying the people could not be trusted with the ballot since they might vote for Islamic parties. "If you are offering now democracy in Egypt, it will be used by the fascists, by the militants," to enable them to come to power.

Ashmawy feared that most Egyptians were close-minded and that they would need to become more "liberal" and tolerant before true democracy could be instituted. "The Muslim Brotherhood is always attacking anyone who is offering any idea that is different from their own . . . accusing anyone either directly or indirectly of being secular, which means atheist in Egypt, which means pro-Western . . . which is [to say] a heretic."

Egypt's moderate Muslim Brotherhood is not allowed to organize as a political party, but Mubarak had also kept his secular political opponents weak and unable to challenge the existing power structure. This lack of true political participation which was at the root of the unrest. Power remains in the hands of an elite that long ago stopped being representative of the learned classes. Today, increasing numbers of Egyptians are literate and there is a growing professional class of engineers, doctors, and lawyers who are excluded from political power.

Many of this educated elite are members of the Muslim Brotherhood and exert considerable influence in civil society as heads of professional unions even if the Brotherhood is banned as a political party. They are staunch critics of Mubarak, who has ruled as Egypt's president since Sadat's assassination, winning every election that Egyptians knew were mere shams of democracy. And although the Muslim Brotherhood officially and publicly renounced violence, Egyptians such as Ashmawy did not believe them and suspected they were secretly helping al Gamaa and al Jihad perpetuate violence against the regime.

Mubarak succeeded in ending the reign of terror that had consumed Egypt, but he also forced the most hard-line militants and their leaders out of the country and into the world at large, setting the stage for the tragedy of September 11.

Dr. Ayman Zawahri, leader of al Jihad; Abu Yasir Rifa'i Ahmad Taha, leader of Egypt's al Gamaa al Islamiyah, and many other Egyptian militants ended up joining forces with Osama bin Laden in Afghanistan and expanding their holy war to encompass not only Arab leaders such as Mubarak but their benefactor, the United States.

Zawahri found safe haven in Afghanistan with bin Laden and is believed to be the brains of al Qaeda. Apparently during the U.S. bombing of Afghanistan, Zawahri wrote what he called *Knights Under the Prophet's Banner*, excerpts of which were published on December 2 in Arabic by the newspaper Al Sharq al Awsat. In the article, he discussed his thoughts on jihad and on the future of radical Islamic movements:

> The Islamic movement and its jihad vanguards, and actually the entire Islamic nation, must involve the major criminals—the United States, Russia, and Israel—in the battle and do not let them run the battle between the jihad movement and our governments in safety. They must pay the price, and pay dearly for that matter.
>
> The masters in Washington and Tel Aviv are using the regimes to protect their interests and to fight the battle against the Muslims on their behalf. If the shrapnel from the battle reach their homes and bodies, they will trade accusations with their agents about who is responsible for this. In that case, they will face one of two bitter choices: Either personally wage the battle against the Muslims, which means that the battle will turn into clear-cut jihad against infidels, or they reconsider their plans after acknowledging the failure of the brute and violent confrontation against Muslims.
>
> "Therefore, we must move the battle to the enemy's grounds to burn the hands of those who ignite fire in our countries."[3]

Zawahri believes engaging a superpower like the United States is fully within the power of the Islamic cadres that would exist even after the bombing of Afghanistan had ceased: "Tracking down the Americans and the Jews is not impossible. Killing them with a single bullet, a stab, or a device made up of a popular mix of explosives or hitting them with an iron rod is not impossible. Burning down their property with Molotov Cocktails is not difficult. With the available means, small groups could prove to be a frightening horror for the Americans and the Jews."[4]

Israel's prime minister is less worried about al Qaeda's cells than he is about the lone suicide bomber that Palestinians were sending to strike deep within the Jewish state. Elected on a security platform, Israeli Prime Minister Ariel Sharon, like Egyptian president Mubarak, believes in fighting fire with fire and he had tried almost everything to stop the attacks. Under Sharon's government, Israeli soldiers had bombed Palestinian cities, sent tanks into Palestinian villages, assassinated Palestinian leaders, killed Palestinian youths, as well as the wives and children of Palestinian militants, demolished Palestinian homes, blockaded Palestinian towns, planted mines in Palestinian fields, and even made Palestinian leader Yasser Arafat a virtual hostage in the West Bank. But the suicide bombers kept coming. A few Israeli settlers came up with a creative idea that they hoped might be a disincentive to suicide bombers: They smeared the body of one Palestinian shaheed with pig grease, declaring his body too unclean for paradise. Both Muslims and Jews consider the pig a filthy animal.[5]

It is clear that the Israeli government, like leaders of Islamic Jihad and Hamas, believes there is little to be gained from diplomacy and negotiations, and that the military option is the only effective response. The Bush administration seemed to agree with that.

In a March 20, 2002 address to the Foreign Policy Association, Henry Siegman, senior fellow and director of the U.S./ Middle East Project at the Council on Foreign Relations, said the United States "had given the Israeli government a green light to deal with the Palestinians in their own way." And Prime Minister Sharon had left no doubt about how he planned to use that green light.[6]

"He said that we have to beat and kill enough Palestinians so that they know they are beaten, and then when they know they're beaten we'll sit down at the table and we'll tell them what we're prepared to do."

Siegman also contended Sharon's tactics have not ended the violence against Israelis and are actually "a recipe for creating lots more cadres of terrorists." In fact, as Sharon pursued his assassinations, bombings, and demolitions, the Israeli government had done nothing to stop the suicide bombings and drive-by shootings. On the contrary, Sharon's tactics had only created more reasons for Palestinian extremists to attack Israel. According to Palestinian officials, Sharon had actually prevented Arafat from stopping the militants.

"Sharon is trying to undermine Arafat's legitimacy. He wants to weaken him so that he can negotiate on Sharon's terms," said Ziad Abu Amr, chairman of the political committee of Palestinian Legislative Council, during a November 2001 interview in Gaza's Palestinian Authority offices. Yet Sharon was making a big mistake that would not stop the suicide bombings, he said.

> Arafat should be empowered politically, not undermined. Only then can he move against the militants. Arafat was the only man who signed an agreement with Israel, and he is the only one who can. But Arafat is losing his popularity to suicide attacks. If there's nothing for him to brag about . . . nothing that he has accomplished . . . he has no standing. It all boils down to politics, power, and interests.

It is clear that Sharon wants to crush Arafat as well as the Palestinian leadership. And he has gotten George W. Bush to agree with him. In the summer of 2002, Bush severed ties with Arafat after a spate of suicide bombings and called for new Palestinian leaders, accusing Arafat of encouraging terrorism. Bush and Sharon may have expected new leaders to be more moderate, but not everyone is convinced that would be the case, considering the anger within the Palestinian areas and the popularity of Hamas.

The truth is, Arafat has no love for Islamic militants in Hamas and Islamic Jihad. He is definitely opposed to any idea of creating an Islamic state in Palestine and he resents the threat to his absolute power that Hamas and Islamic Jihad represent. Even during our interview in Tunisia in 1989, Arafat had stressed that his vision of Palestine was as a secular democracy. Still, that did not mean, he said, that he was any less devout than leaders of Hamas or Islamic Jihad.

Bush and Sharon want Arafat to crush Hamas and Islamic Jihad, but to do so would require serious bloodletting within Palestinian ranks. Before he can count on the Palestinian people to stand with him and not with Hamas, Arafat has to convince them that he can improve their lives through peace with Israel, said Abu Amr.

"When there was an ongoing peace process, the Palestinian Authority was empowered enough to exercise its control over all the citizens . . . to persuade Palestinians to go along with the peace process," he said. "But after ten years of negotiations, Jewish settlements have doubled since the signing of the Oslo agreement. Palestinians are not a bunch of fools."

The Islamic groups enjoy more respect among Palestinians than the Palestinian Authority, which has little to show for its years of negotiating with the Israelis and is widely criticized as being corrupt and ineffective. Arafat cannot move against them and end the suicide bombings as long as the groups are so popular among Palestinians, without risking full-scale civil war, from which he might not emerge victorious. And many of Arafat's closest advisors believe that Sharon's tactics have actually forced Arafat to join forces with the very people he despises.

"Hamas and Islamic Jihad are political organizations that have substantial standing in the street," Abu Amr said. "We risk internal civil strife."

Arafat would have to completely dismantle Hamas and Islamic Jihad to stop the suicide bombings, said Siegman, "because if he does not destroy them, there is no way he can prevent that violence from continuing. As long as those groups have the capacity to inflict damage on Israel, they'll continue doing it."[7] To go against the Islamic militants, Arafat has to be assured that he could promise his people a state free from Israeli domination.

"It is not a war he will undertake, I guarantee you, it is not a cost he is prepared to pay or risk that he will assume unless he knows that if he does that, he can say to Palestinians that he has done this, inflicted this damage, risked a war of brothers, because he knows it will produce x, y, and z," Siegman said. "It will produce a viable Palestinian state, and it will produce that state in real time—one year, two years, three years, but not ten or twenty years down the road."

But that is also not a promise Israel's hard-line government, under perpetual siege from suicide bombers, is willing to make to Arafat. His own inner circle also is growing more militant and it appears as though he is unable to control the al-Aqsa Martyrs Brigades, which also is responsible for several suicide bombings.

Arafat's advisors are growing desperate. Abu Amr and others are pushing for the Islamic militants to have an official voice in the Palestinian Authority as a way to try to control them. "I don't think Mr. Arafat can turn against the Palestinian organizations," warned Abu Amr:

We are asked to observe pluralism. I can't punish anyone because of their colors, politics, or religion. We need to respect the principle of broader political participation. We need to include more people in the decision making process. People should encourage Arafat to bring them [Hamas and Islamic Jihad] into the fold. Including them means they would become equally responsible. We don't bring them in by alienating them.

Abu Amr believes that only Islamic militants can stop the suicide bombings against Israel. Hamas was too powerful for the Palestinian Authority to crush, but Hamas could be convinced to cooperate with peace efforts if it becomes part of the decision-making process. And it is better to have them involved in the peace process than criticizing and sabotaging it from the outside.

Abu Amr pointed to Jordan's example. The Islamic Action Front is Jordan's most powerful political party and represents a peaceful, loyal opposition to monarchy. "Look at the Jordanian regime," he said. "You have to allow their real participation. It would be easy to convince them to stop suicide bombings. But the Israelis are asking Arafat to hit them. Bloodshed is not the solution."

Jordan has taken a different approach in trying to ward off Islamic militancy within the kingdom and it has experienced far less religiously motivated violence than Egypt, despite large numbers of disgruntled Palestinian and Iraqi refugees. Instead of stifling Islamic parties, Jordan has allowed Islamists a voice in its government as the loyal opposition. In fact, the powerful Islamic Action Front has helped the monarchy maintain stability in the country.

"One of the lessons we should have learned from September 11 was that you can't just use repression" to battle militants, Abdul Latif Arabiyat, secretary general of Jordan's Islamic Action Front, said during our interview in Amman in late 2001. "Societies which are closed and nondemocratic are going to fuel extremism."

And if the United States is perceived as supporting nondemocratic regimes, extremists will target American interests, he warned. "The United States must be seen encouraging democracy in the Middle East and supporting moderate Islamists in society as a counterweight to the militants." But the regimes of the Middle East have "atomized" the moderates, who could have worked within society against the radicals, as they do in Jordan. "We are Islamic but moderate," Arabiyat explained. "Our people are well educated with good political experience. We have learned from the mistakes of other parties and we are people who offer hope. People trust us."

Like Islamic groups in other parts of the world, the Islamic Action Front offers free and low-cost medical care, and legal and other social services to Jordan's poor, which have won them a loyal following. And although they frequently criticize the government, they did so to improve it, not to over-throw it. "Our methods are for gradual reform," Arabiyat said, "evolution, not revolution." As a result, Jordan's Hashemites, who have the added benefit of being direct descendants of the Prophet Muhammad, has suffered little re-ligiously motivated violence.

The question is, can Hamas be controlled if it is permitted a voice in Palestinian government? Hamas has proven it could moderate its position, restrain its shuhada, and cooperate with Arafat, Abu Amr said. On several oc-casions Arafat has been able to convince Hamas leaders to honor cease fires, however short-lived, and allow him to pursue peace negotiations with the Is-raelis. Arafat also persuaded Hamas leaders to stop attacks against Israel shortly after September 11, according to Abu Amr, who quoted Arafat as say-ing, "'It would provoke Israel to attack us and the world is busy and will not notice.'" Hamas agreed to a cease fire provided Israel stop the assassinations, but "unfortunately, Israel did not stop."

Hamas also was on the verge of declaring a suspension of suicide bomb-ings in July 2002, but then Sharon sent an F-16 to bomb the home of Sheikh Salah Shehada, leader of the Izzidene al Qassam Brigade, killing Shehada, his wife, and his three children. The strike on Shehada's apartment building also killed fourteen Palestinians, nine of them children, and caused Hamas to re-scind its proposal to suspend its suicide bombings and to vow to retaliate.

Islamic Jihad is far less compromising than Hamas, however, and often criticizes Hamas leaders for cooperating with Arafat. As Abu Amr sees it, once Hamas is on the bandwagon, the Palestinian Authority can move with greater surety against the weaker but more strident Islamic Jihad. It seems as if leaders of the Palestinian Authority have no problem killing Jihad's fight-ers, but Hamas is too large and has too much popular support.

Palestinians like Abu Amr believe that Sharon's hard-line policies have sabotaged their plan to divide and conquer the Islamists and the prime minis-ter has strengthened them and weakened the Palestinian Authority.

In a January 4, 2002, article entitled "Is Israel More Secure Now?" Palestinian intellectual Edward Said, one of Arafat's staunchest critics, lam-basted Sharon's reoccupation of Palestinian towns in the West Bank and his policy of assassinating Palestinian leaders:

> Since last May Israeli F-16s (generously supplied by the U.S.) have regularly
> bombed and strafed Palestinian towns and villages, Guernica style, destroy-
> ing property and killing civilians and security officials (there is no Palestinian

army, navy or air force to protect the people); Apache attack helicopters (again supplied by the U.S.) have used their missiles to murder 77 Palestinian leaders, for alleged terrorist offences, past or future. A group of unknown Israeli intelligence operatives have the authority to decide on these assassinations, presumably with the approval on each occasion of the Israeli Cabinet and, more generally, that of the U.S. The helicopters have also done an efficient job of bombing Palestinian Authority installations, police as well as civilian. . . . [8]

But Said questioned whether all of that had brought security to Israel. "Every official Israeli policy thus far has made things worse, rather than better, for Israel. Ask yourself: Is Israel more secure and more accepted now than it was ten years ago? Can its current war of attrition be any more successful than the one it lost in Lebanon?"[9]

The truth is, the same argument could be used against the Palestinians. Have the suicide bombings dried the tears of Palestinian mothers or made it easier for Palestinian fathers to protect their children either from Israeli soldiers or from their own militants who are luring them into the paths of martyrdom? Have the martyrdom operations brought fewer Israeli troops into their towns and villages or increased their numbers?

Yet both the Palestinian militants and Sharon seem doggedly committed to the military option. Sharon even has convinced Bush that he was fighting the same battle against terrorism as the United States. The Israeli prime minister is pursuing another option. He has started building a gigantic fence to separate Israelis from the Palestinians. Many critics say a fence will not keep Palestinian attackers out of Israel, but terrorism expert Barry Rubin is convinced it would reduce the number that were able to get through.

"It's not all or nothing," said Rubin in an interview in the summer of 2002. "I'm very strongly for the wall because it will make it harder for terrorists to do their work. If you're able to cut attacks by 60 or 80 percent, it's a victory. You can't stop everything but you can reduce the risks."

In fact, neither Israel nor Egypt can claim victory in dealing with their terrorist threats, and both countries' inability to solve the problem has made the world considerably more unsafe for Americans. Israelis are still dying from Palestinian attacks, and much of the Muslim world is seething over Bush's apparent decision to stand with Sharon. And while Egyptian militants inside al Qaeda are on the run, thanks to the United States' bombing of

Afghanistan, they still represent a serious threat not only to Egypt and other Arab governments but to the world at large.

Yet like the Israelis and the Egyptians, the Bush administration is determined to use its military might as the central focus of its campaign against al Qaeda and Islamic militants. And like the Israelis and Egyptians, the U.S. military campaign in Afghanistan has not done what Americans wanted most: ended the threat of terrorism. After months of bombing and searching for al Qaeda's remnants in the rubble of Afghanistan's mountain caves, American defense officials can not guarantee that they have vanquished their enemy. They are still warning that another attack is not only possible but inevitable.

In short, Americans are facing the same bleak prospects for stopping suicide attacks in the United States as the Sharon government faces in battling Hamas and Islamic Jihad. But unlike Egypt, the United States is prepared to pursue militants around the globe in its all-out war on terrorism.

At the time of this writing, al Qaeda's forces were on the run but not annihilated. The FBI is issuing regular warnings about new threats of terrorist attacks in the United States, and few people believe that al Qaeda will be easily defeated. Ayman Zawahri's *Knights Under the Banner of the Prophet* showed that they have a plan to ensure the survival of at least some of their members who would continue their jihad:

> An extremely important and serious question arises here; namely, what if the movement's members or plans are uncovered, if its members are arrested, the movement's survival is at risk, and a campaign of arrests and storming operations targets its members, funds, resources, and leaders? In this case, the movement must ask itself a specific question and give a clear answer. Could it disperse in the face of the storm and pull out of the field with the least possible casualties? Or is patience not feasible and means total defeat and there is no room for withdrawal? Or perhaps the answer could be a combination of the two aforesaid scenarios, meaning that it could pull out some of its leaders and members safely, leaving some others to face the risk of captivity and brutality. In my opinion, the answer is that the movement must pull out as many personnel as possible to the safety of a shelter without hesitation, reluctance, or reliance on illusions. The most serious decision facing someone under siege is the escape decision."[10]

Terrorism experts in Israel as well as in the United States fear that Zawahri, and bin Laden and many of their supporters have escaped the bombing of Afghanistan and are scattered around the globe.

Many experts, such as Daniel Pipes, director of the Philadelphia-based Middle East Forum, criticized the United States for not seeing the signs of danger long before September 11. In an article written hours after the attack and published in the *Wall Street Journal* the next day, Pipes wrote:

> Two parties are responsible for this sequence of atrocities. The moral blame falls exclusively on the perpetrators, who as of this writing remain unknown. The tactical blame falls on the U.S. government, which has grievously failed in its topmost duty to protect American citizens from harm. Specialists on terrorism have been aware for years of this dereliction of duty; now the whole world knows it. Despite a steady beat of major, organized terrorist incidents over eighteen years (since the car bombing of the U.S. embassy in Beirut in 1983), Washington has not taken the issue seriously.[11]

Israeli experts believe that the only effective counterterrorism strategy is one that is comprehensive. The Bush administration needs to launch a full-scale international war on all organizations that it believes are engaged in terrorism including groups such as Hamas, Hezbollah, and Islamic Jihad, says Boaz Ganor, director of The International Policy Institute for Counter-Terrorism in Israel. The United States also has to go to war with Iraq, Iran and probably even Lebanon and Syria, he argues, and it has to be done all at once. "The problem is the American administration believes they can do it one after the other and not simultaneously," says Ganor. "It has to be done simultaneously. It has to be launched immediately. . . . The U.S. has to launch a comprehensive campaign against radical Islamic organizations."

Ganor warns that United States' bombing of Afghanistan would increase the motivation of militant groups to attack again, perhaps with even deadlier results, unless they are severely crippled. "The main question we should ask is, is there any way the attack will limit the ability of the organization to carry out terrorist activity even when the motivation is increased? Even if Afghanistan is very successful, capturing bin Laden, demolishing al Qaeda's network, stopping Taliban, even if we achieve all of this militarily, I believe the operational capability would not be reduced. We're talking about an ideology. We're talking about a network worldwide . . . it is definitely all over the Arab states."

Ganor's multi-pronged approach includes unseating the Taliban and al Qaeda from Afghanistan, a military campaign against militant Arab or Islamic organizations around the world, a military campaign against states that sponsor terrorism, and a direct campaign against persons or groups that fund these organizations, many of whom he believes are in the West. "On 9/11 terrorism crossed the Rubicon," Ganor said. "It has become a real and present danger. You have to adapt the counterterrorism measures to the level of the threat. It's going to take drastic measures. You have to put counterterrorism at a higher stage than political and economic interests."

Ganor is not calling on the United States to go to war alone against all radical groups in every part of the world, however. He believes European countries as well as America's Arab allies have to commit to the all-out war effort led by the United States. Only a unified effort can subdue Islamic militants. "Everybody has his own mission here," he said. "Everyone has his role to play." Ganor is critical of European efforts to counter terrorism, believing that not enough had been done to go after militants in Britain, France, and Germany. He insists that in addition to contributing troops to a worldwide military campaign against terrorism, European governments need to arrest, deport, or imprison militants in their midst and stop the flow of cash from Europe to terrorist groups.

"The British have a lot to do in their own house. People who didn't have permission to get into Egypt got political asylum in Britain," he said. "This is ridiculous."

Many members of the Egyptian Jihad and al Gamaa al Islamiyah had fled to Europe during Mubarak's crackdown in the 1990s, and many were granted political asylum. Great Britain was home to some of the most radical Islamic groups in the world, including al Muhajiroun (the Immigrants), whose leader, Sheikh Omar Bakri, once identified himself as bin Laden's spokesman, distributing his edicts around the globe.

"The problem is that al Qaeda is not just an organization but an umbrella ideology for a number of groups," said Reuven Paz, an Israeli terrorism expert. "Most of the foundation, recruitment, and support for Islamist terrorist groups was coming from youngsters in the Muslim communities in Europe. The September 11 attack was planned in Hamburg, and London may be biggest Islamic center in the world." Yet European governments are reluctant to pass laws that would infringe on freedom of speech and political activity or even to move against organizations that provide financial support for militant groups in the Middle East.

"There is a problem," said Paz. "There are sometimes big differences between the United States and its allies in Europe. . . . I paid two visits to London in 1999 and 2000. They claim that as long as those people are not working directly against the U.K., it was okay. They can be left alone. I don't know if they realize there's a threat even now. As far as I know, there were no plans to attack British targets, not in the U.K. and not outside of the U.K. There were several plans to carry out attacks in Italy and France. In my view, the next phase of such Islamic terrorism might be in Europe."

Yet even with European help, it can be argued that Ganor's ambitious war plan might be too much for the United States to manage all at once, and it would alarm Arab leaders whom the United States needs in its coalition against terrorism. However, the Bush administration is intent on unseating Iraqi President Saddam Hussein, even if Arab governments have little stomach for helping the United States attack yet another Muslim country. There is only so much Arab leaders can do to contain the anger of their people. Arabs already are seething over reports of the deaths of hundreds of innocent civilians during U.S. bombing of Afghanistan and over the continued clashes between Israelis and Palestinians, which the Bush administration seems helpless to contain. And then there is the threat that the United States is preparing to attack Iraq to unseat Saddam Hussein. That would be acceptable, except Arabs do not think the United States has the best interests of the Iraqi people in mind. And they fear the United States has no viable plan to establish a stable government to replace Saddam's regime.

Moderate voices warn that the Bush administration needs to proceed carefully in its war on terrorism to avoid causing more turmoil to countries such as Jordan, which border Iraq and which already are hosting thousands of Iraqi refugees as well as thousands of angry Palestinian refugees from the wars with Israel.

"I believe the slightest spark could set things off," said Arabiyat, the Jordanian analyst, warning that the anger in the Arab world is the biggest threat to the security of the United States and world stability. "The rage that was engendered because of the al-Aqsa intifada is real," he said. "People felt the death of Mohammed al Dirrah" and the other Palestinians youths who were killed in the clashes with Israelis. Arabiyat said that in the months leading up to September 11, he expected something big to happen. He had warned that "sooner or later, you're going to see an explosion somewhere. But I thought it would be the overthrow of a regime."

Arabiyat and others think Islamic militants would succeed in launching another Islamic revolution like the one in Iran. And that scenario remains a real possibility, especially if the United States fuels the anger already in the region by attacking Iraq or another Arab country.

Jordan's King Abdullah told President Bush during a visit to Washington in early 2002 that a war to unseat Iraqi President Saddam Hussein could unleash mayhem in his country and have dire economic consequences. While Jordan receives more than $270 million each year in U.S. aid, making it one of the largest recipients of such aid, it also receives a substantial amount of oil from Iraq at greatly reduced prices, which its feeble economy desperately needs. And Jordan cannot bear the burden of another onslaught of Iraqi refugees.

Other Arab leaders also can not predict the impact such a war would have on their countries. But the bottom line is that no one has produced any proof that Iraq was involved in the events of September 11 or that it is a threat to U.S. security.

Gareth Evans, president of the International Crisis Group and former foreign minister of Australia, wrote in the *Georgetown Journal* that while the United States has both the "moral and legal right" to move against those responsible for September 11, it could not do so without constraints. A democratic superpower can not proceed as ruthlessly as Egypt did, either in dealing with threats inside the country or outside, he said. "First, the targets of the action must be credibly identified. The stronger the response, the stronger the evidentiary foundations has to be if the support of friends and allies is not to fall away, and even more importantly, if a generally cooperative international enforcement front against terrorism is to be maintainable in the future."[12]

Evans wrote that allies of the United States believed bin Laden was involved in the September 11 attacks, even if he did not directly orchestrate them. And they were convinced that he provided financial support for a variety of militant groups who were determined to attack targets throughout the West. But Europeans, and certainly not U.S. Arab allies, were not as convinced as Israeli experts about the guilt of Iraq, Iran, Lebanon, and other countries in sponsoring terrorism against the United States. And there is less support among European and Arab governments for targeting Hamas, Hezbollah, and Islamic Jihad as terrorist organizations with an international agenda.

"The second constraint is that the action must be proportionate," Evans continued. "In particular, killing and maiming the innocent has to be avoided at almost all costs. If it is not, not only will the present coalition of the willing—still extremely fragile at its Islamic edges—collapse, but the West will just create a whole new generation of people hating it."[13]

That would mean that our children and grandchildren will be fighting their own wars on terrorism.

What the United States is learning, and what is evident from Israel's experience, is that bombing alone will not end the threat of terrorism. Even protecting the country from within is proving an overwhelming challenge. Authorities thought they had given considerable attention to making airports safe and preventing another hijacking until July 4, 2002, when a gunman who must have known that he would be killed, walked into the Los Angeles airport and shot up Israel's El Al ticket counter, killing two people before security agents killed him. The United States is too big, open, and free a country to protect every door of every airport, government building, or shopping mall, especially from those willing to martyr themselves.

"There is no way of countering suicide bombings," Paz concluded. "You see what's happening in Israel. We can not thwart such terrorist attacks. The only way to try to fight it is with good intelligence or if the other side makes mistakes. But even then, you can try to minimize the damage but you won't stop it."

Israel has tried many ways to gather "good intelligence." It has tried forcing Palestinians to spy on each other, but such information is unreliable and even when Israel gets advance warning of a potential suicide bombing, it doesn't do much good, Paz said. "We still couldn't stop the act." He continued:

We've had cases when the guy who was planning an attack was arrested and he blows himself up when they go to arrest him. It's very dangerous. Then there were cases in which someone tried to get on a bus, for example. He was prevented from getting on the bus so he blew himself up outside the bus. There were only light injuries in one case, but he did it. He succeeded. No one could prevent it.

Worse, some of their collaborators became double agents, even suicide bombers, turning on their Israeli contacts. All of this meant that the Israelis, who have failed utterly at stopping the martyrs from using their bodies as weapons, can provide little help to the United States as it tries to prevent another attack like September 11. Yet the United States is even less prepared than the Israelis to deal with martyrdom as a security issue.

"The Americans don't have the kind of intelligence that the Israelis have. And the intelligence community in the United States doesn't understand Islamic culture so they cannot interpret the information they have," said Paz. "This was a big problem with September 11. They had information but they didn't understand it.

> They don't have enough Arabic-speaking people, and much more than Arabic-speaking, they don't have enough Arabic-reading people. If you just start to surf the web, there is so much information in Arabic, so many extremist websites, so many Islamist groups. And in many cases, you have to understand the codes. It doesn't mean they are talking in codes, but the use of certain verses of the Qur'an, the use of certain historical models, these are the codes. They are very well-known messages to their public, but they are not necessarily known to the Western security or intelligence people.

The United States lacks the human intelligence both inside the country and in the Arab world. In an article he wrote for the *Wall Street Journal* on September 12, Daniel Pipes raised the same issue: "It's a lot easier to place an oversized ear in the sky than to place agents in the inner circle of a terrorist group.... That the U.S. government did not have a clue points to nearly criminal ignorance."[14]

But there have been people trying to alert Americans about the danger. In January 1999, Sufi Sheikh Muhammad Hisham Kabbani, chair of the Islamic Supreme Council of America, warned that Osama bin Laden was planning a major operation in the United States. Kabbani's group is composed of 157 Muslim scholars from around the world who condemn extremism. He said his organization had received information that bin Laden had been able to purchase nuclear warheads from the ex-Soviet Union and was working on ways to use them against the United States.

> We want to tell people to be careful, that something major might hit quickly because they were able to buy more than twenty atomic nuclear heads from some of the mafia in the ex-Soviet Union, in the republics of the ex-Soviet Union ... they traded it for $30 million and two tons of opium that has been shipped to the Caucasus and now is being distributed through all the Caucasus and the ex-Soviet republics," Kabbani said in an address he gave at the U.S. State Department's Open Forum.[15]

"They were able to get more than twenty nuclear warheads and now they are hiring thousands of scientists from the ex-Soviet Union who have no jobs," Kabbani said. "They are giving them salaries of $2,000 a month, in order to try to build an atomic reactor in Khost [Afghanistan], underground," he warned. Bin Laden's scientists were feverishly working, he said, "to break these atomic warheads into smaller partitions, like small chips, to be put in any suitcase, even in a handbag, and be shipped anywhere in the world."

"This might affect the whole stability of peace around the world," Kabbani warned. "This has to be very well monitored, and very well looked upon, because it is a danger for all humanity." Kabbani said he was privy to such information because his supporters, Sufi Muslims who are known for their focus on their relationship with God and their abhorrence of violence, were inside Muslim communities in the United States and around the world.

Nuclear weapons experts did not take Kabbani's threat seriously, nor did American intelligence agents. Scott Parrish, a senior research associate with the Center for Nonproliferation Studies at the Monterey Institute of International Studies, acknowledged in our interview shortly after Kabbani's speech that he had heard the reports but said that creating such a weapon "would require facilities as well as people. I'm not saying it's impossible, but it would be a pretty sophisticated operation."

Some U.S. intelligence officials interviewed before September 11 dismissed the idea, saying "bin Laden's operations have not been very sophisticated." Yet these same people now believe bin Laden was capable of bringing down a symbol of American economic power and seriously damage a symbol of its military might. Americans can only hope that bin Laden had not been able to acquire nuclear weapons because if he had, he would certainly find a way to use them against the United States.

People in the Arab world also were warning Americans about the danger of bin Laden's network and trying to prevent a catastrophe. A few weeks before September 11, Hosni Mubarak allegedly warned the United States that a major attack was planned. After the attack, the Jordanian government offered to use its powerful intelligence agencies to infiltrate groups in the Middle East and provide information to the United States.

Some Americans, such as former U.S. Representative Lee Hamilton (a Democrat from Indiana), director of the Woodrow Wilson International Center for Scholars, saw some merit in the United States' working with the Jordanians. "We're going to need them," he said at a Washington, D.C. forum on terrorism sponsored by the United States Institute of Peace in late 2001. "A lot of work needs to be done in intelligence and we have a real limitation on how we can infiltrate Osama bin Laden's network. It's the toughest intelligence target there is." Paz, like Hamilton, believed Jordanian intelligence could be a valuable aid to American intelligence agents. "If the Jordanians would assist the United States, of course it's a very good direction," Paz said, because they can do what the Israelis cannot, infiltrate militant groups. Another high-ranking Israeli government intelligence official who asked not to be identified strongly encouraged U.S.-Jordanian cooperation. "We think U.S. cooperation with Jordanian intelligence is good," he said during an interview in Israel in late 2001. "Jordan has the ability to get inside these organizations perhaps more than anyone else. And I think they're trustworthy." Jordan also could help monitor extremist activities in other parts of the Arab world, the official said. "Jordan also still has connections with Iraq. These connections could prove useful. They border Syria and while there isn't a lot of contact. . . . They could be useful vis a vis Syria."

Yet many argued that there can be no substitute for strengthening U.S. intelligence and that Americans cannot rely on the goodwill of countries like Jordan, whose interests frequently diverge from that of the United States.

"We never want to be in a position to depend on a foreign government's intelligence," said Richard Solomon, president of the United States Institute of Peace and former assistant secretary of state for East Asia affairs, who spoke at the same forum as Hamilton. "We need to rebuild our own intelligence. It's a tough challenge, but it has got to be done." Yet, as Paz noted, even greater intelligence cannot guarantee an end to martyrdom being used as a weapon against the United States.

Arab analysts argue that effectively countering terrorism, especially when religious martyrdom is involved, requires a combination of military, political, and diplomatic initiatives. The causes of the hatred fueling the attacks must be understood, especially since such feelings are widespread, making the militants heroes instead of villains to millions. Countering the terrorist threat requires enlisting the help of not only America's Arab allies, many contend, but Islamic religious leaders around the world who can offer the masses a less militant interpretation of Islam's teachings and undermine the religious standing of the radicals. Finally, many Arab analysts insist that for the United States to deal effectively with the terrorism threat, it should re-examine its foreign policy.

"A change of policy in the Middle East is in the long-term best interests of the United States," said Arabiyat. "It is not good to have 200 million angry Arabs running around."

Arab leaders contend that the United States needs to push for a resolution to the Israeli-Palestinian conflict and to take a more even-handed approach to the parties. Solving the Palestinian-Israeli problem would go a long way toward ending terrorism in the region and against the United States, they said.

"Allowing the Palestinians to declare a state would help; it would definitely help," said Labib Kamhawi, a Jordanian analyst, in an interview in Jordan in late 2001. "If Bush is smart, he would try to introduce and implement policies that would be fair and equitable for the Palestinians."

As Kamhawi noted, the greatest threat to the United States was the widespread hostility that is shared by people across classes in the Middle East, even among those who should have been its biggest supporters—the educated elite.

"The people who might attack America, who might lead an anti-American campaign will be part of the enlightened, educated class," Kamhawi said, as were the leaders of al Qaeda and those who led the September 11 attack. "They will not be peasants. Here are the days when the middle class, the upper middle class unite with the peasants. When the Christian minority unites with the Muslims."

Kamhawi said changing its policies to reflect more balance between Israelis and Palestinians would be in the best interests of the United States since "during the last two major crises, Israeli proved to be a burden." In both Operation Desert Storm, fought to oust Iraq from Kuwait, and in the war on Afghanistan, Israel provided no help, and its actions against the Palestinians actually worked against U.S. efforts to form a strong Arab alliance. "The old fallacious concept that Israel is America's best friend in the area has proved to be wrong, so why should America invest so much?" Kamhawi argued.

Yet Kamhawi and others believe that merely resolving the Palestinian problem will not by itself end hostility toward the United States in the region. The Arab masses want something more than peace between Israel and the Palestinians. They want freedom like Americans. They want to be able to vote people into and out of office. They want to be able to criticize their leaders without risking prison. They want to know that their sons and daughters can get good educations and go on to meaningful jobs in a free society. They want the United States to push for democracy in Jordan, Egypt, and Saudi Arabia, countries that are American allies and where people believe the United States is really pulling the strings of government anyway.

"We are all vassals of the United States," railed Laith Shubailat, Jordan's former member of parliament and an independent Islamist political analyst, interviewed in Amman in the winter of 2001. "The responsibility of America now is to lead the world to peace. Instead, its policy is leading to turbulence everywhere in the world, from Latin America to Southeast Asia."

Shubailat was one of the region's loudest voices calling for democratic reform, and for that he was ostracized by Jordan's ruling elite, the country's television stations were forbidden to allow him on the air, and newspaper editors were afraid to quote him when he criticized the king, a fate faced by outspoken advocates of democracy all over the Middle East.

"I am considered to be a very big nuisance to the regime," Shubailat said with a grin. "My colleagues think that I am too hot. I am not allowed on local TV and yet I am the most popular person in Jordan. I am asking for a constitutional monarchy, that's all."

Although they might not be as outspoken as Shubailat, people throughout the region are asking for the same thing—democracy. And they blame the United States for providing the military and financial backing that allowed the regimes to crush all opposition, except that coming from the most radical of the radicals—the Islamic martyrs, who are destined to strike again and again at the regions monarchs and despots. But in Jordan, a pivotal state for Israel and the United States because of its proximity to Iraq and its sheltering of thousands of Palestinian refugees, the issue of democracy is especially acute.

The late King Hussein, who was widely respected and loved even though he also was no democrat, was replaced in February 1999 by his son Abdullah. For a time there had been hope that Abdullah, western educated and apparently enlightened, would steer the nation toward democracy, but the opposite had happened, whether by his own will or by the international crisis that made stability a higher priority than democracy. King Abdullah clamped down on dissent, strengthened the intelligence agents monitoring the Iraqi and Palestinian refugees, and even began to try to intimidate Jordanian opposition figures such as Shubailat. Jordan's youth are sullen and angry, complaining that there are no opportunities to pursue meaningful professions. They envy the freedom that American youth take for granted. And Palestinians, who make up the majority of the population in Jordan, complain that they are being denied any semblance of equal civil and political rights in the country. Jordan has long been a country on the brink of economic, political, and social disaster. Abdullah knew that another crisis in Iraq might easily set the dominoes falling and ignite a revolution in his own country against the Hashemite monarchy.

The United States has to step carefully in the quagmire of the Middle East. President Bush's cowboy tactics and inflammatory rhetoric are unsettling to the nation's friends and enemies alike in the region. The American war on terrorism needs the support of Arab and Muslim masses if it is to succeed and not cause more instability in countries around the world. Yet the United States has done poorly in the public relations battle, with missteps at home and abroad. President Bush's pronouncement that bin Laden is wanted "dead or alive" sounded like cowboy bullying to the Arab world. His retracted statement about launching a "crusade" against terrorism, saying it was absolutely the wrong message to send. And the tape of bin Laden that aired in the United States in late 2001 and that authorities said was found in Afghanistan did not convince Arab skeptics that bin Laden was responsible for the September 11 attack. To them, the Saudi millionaire was doing nothing more than lauding Atta and his cohorts for a deed he thought well done. The fact that that bin Laden was filmed saying that he had tried to figure out the number of people who would be killed meant nothing even if Americans believe it is clear evidence of his involvement: "We calculated in advance the number of . . . enemy who would be killed," bin Laden said in the tape, adding he had expected the plane crashes and the fires from the jet fuel to destroy only the top floors of the 110-story towers. "This is all that we had hoped for."

People around the globe, even in the United States, questioned whether the tape was authentic or somehow doctored. Seth Borenstein, a Washington-based correspondent for Knight Ridder wrote:

> If computer-generated graphics can fake Forrest Gump shaking President John F. Kennedy's hand and the late John Wayne hawking beer, how can viewers be sure that a videotape of Osama bin Laden bragging about the September 11 attacks is real?
>
> Special-effects wizards, who agree that such a tape could be faked, said they believe the one that aired Thursday is the real thing. Political and propaganda experts said the same, largely on grounds that it would be foolhardy, unnecessary and illegal for the Bush administration to engage in what one called "a Stalinesque doctoring of images."

Their assurances—even Defense Secretary Donald H. Rumsfeld's word that U.S. analysts had thoroughly tested the tape "to make sure that it was authentic . . . to see if it had been tinkered with"—are unlikely to change the minds of America's foes.[16]

Heba Raouf Ezzat, a well-known Egyptian academic and analyst I contacted in Cairo shortly after the tape was aired, summed up what many Muslims thought: "People just don't trust the USA. Most people will think it's a hoax or a lie. . . . Whether this tape is bin Laden or is not bin Laden is not the point. We don't believe the United States anymore."

Such attitudes toward the United States do not bode well for efforts to enlist world support in the war on terrorism. Ezzat warned that the Arab streets were boiling over U.S. actions against Afghanistan and threats to Iraq. Such anger could be turned against Arab governments that were U.S. allies, launching yet another wave of terrorism.

Analysts such as Abdullah Hassanat, editor of the *Jordan Times* newspaper, warned that many of the sentiments motivating Islamic militants were shared by millions of ordinary Muslims, who nevertheless are repulsed by the violence advocated by bin Laden and his supporters. Thousands of people in Egypt and Jordan are without jobs, living in poverty, and unable to see the fruits of their countries' peace treaties with Israel and the United States.

"These people are basically expressing in many ways a contention in the Arab and Muslim world that the deal we are having with the West in the region is not a fair deal," said Hassanat. "Our oil is now worth nothing, and most of it goes back to the West to buy weapons. "The economy is bad everywhere in the region . . . the Saudis are even talking about imposing taxes for the first time in history. These are very stringent measures," he said, measures that are likely to increase the unpopularity of the Saudi regime and increase tensions.

Yet if economics is at the root of much of the tension between the United States and the Muslim world, it can also provide a solution to help counter terrorism, according to Mohammad Sid-Ahmad, an Egyptian political analyst. "These people say they hate America, but if you give them schools, they will come to America. Deny them any course of civilized living, and you will be sowing the seeds of desperation and revenge. I believe what we are seeing is the politics of impotence . . . not just a clash of Islamic terrorism and the world, but the dispossessed against the mighty."

Aware that it needs to change the tide of public opinion in the Arab world, the Bush administration launched a radio initiative in the spring of 2002 through the Voice of America to try to win over Arab youths with news, provocative talk shows, and music. But there also are serious issues involving the Arab American community within the United States, which complained of being subject to racial profiling when they trying to board planes, and discrimination in daily life. The FBI, especially, is trying to ferret out Muslim groups that are supporting Islamic militants. Few who follow these issues can deny that many Muslims around the world, including many in the United States, look upon Hamas and Hezbollah as freedom fighters. Many Muslims in Europe and the United States also have contributed to organizations such as Hamas that also provide charitable and relief services for the Palestinians, which they contend are not contributing to terrorism.

In a commentary published by the Interdisciplinary Center in Herzliya, Israel, in October 2000, Paz noted:

> Hamas activists continue to feign innocence in regard to their activity in the U.S. They refuse to admit that their activity there is a combination of political and cultural activity, which creates not only a social infrastructure but a framework for terrorism as well. They, and other groups, act on the ground that there is no Islamic radical political or social activity without the element of the "armed struggle," which is expressed in terrorist activities—Jihad as a outgrowth of the various dimensions of their activity: social, cultural, political, military, economic etc.
>
> This point of view is not unique to Hamas. On November 1995, after the assassination of Dr. Fathi Shqaqi, the General Secretary of the Palestinian Islamic Jihad, his appointed successor was Dr. Ramadan Abdallah Shalah, a scholar who had operated for a few years in Miami in various Islamic activities.[17]

According to Paz, it is questionable whether the tactics of the FBI and other federal agencies will achieve even their goal of gathering information to prevent another attack on U.S. soil. Paz said it is essential for U.S. authorities to learn to discriminate between moderate Muslims and their groups and direct their efforts only "against the type of radical Islamist who used the democratic hospitality of Western countries to promote issues that ultimately serve terrorism."

The only way to glean information about radical Islamists was to have infiltrators inside the groups, Paz argued during an interview in late 2002, and for that, American Muslims are essential.

The U.S. intelligence community still does not have that kind of information because they have not made the kind of connections with American Muslims that would provide that information. Many American Muslims are suspicious of the American intelligence community and many American Muslims were arrested or interviewed by the FBI, which was very hostile. The FBI still is very hostile to most of the Muslims in the United States . . . including American citizens. Also, Immigration has been pushing and encouraging the administration in its hostile attitude. . . . It is a problem since the fact is that, for example, those suicide bombers in September . . . at least for a year or two, were part of Muslim communities in the United States.

The FBI's strong-arm tactics had thoroughly alienated the Muslim communities in the United States. While the Muslim American community could be a line of first defense against Islamic militants, the FBI seemed to be working against its own best interests. In March 2002 it launched what it called Operation Green Quest and raided the homes and offices of Islamic leaders in Virginia, outraging American Muslim organizations. Federal agents targeted officials with the International Institute of Islamic Thought in Herndon and the Graduate School of Islamic and Social Sciences and the Fiqh (Legal) Council of North America in Leesburg, Virginia.

At a press conference of leading Muslim organizations called after the raids, the American Muslim Council (AMC) expressed its "dismay and concern" at FBI conduct. The organization said FBI agents entered the homes of law-abiding citizens, "brandishing guns" and shouting at women and children. "In some raids, the ladies were photographed while handcuffed and without a headscarf that the ladies wear," the organization said. Muslim Americans said some of their most respected colleagues had been "humiliated."

The law enforcement agencies, which included the Customs; the Secret Service; the Bureau of Alcohol, Tobacco and Firearms; the FBI, the Immigration and Naturalization Service, confiscated personal items from the homes of American citizens—American Muslim citizens—without a proper cause. They took with them the baby pictures, passports, driver licenses, computers, and in one case, the wedding card of a Muslim girl who got married last week.

They described the raids as "inhumane and un-American." Leaders of the Muslim groups accused the Justice Department of using tactics reminiscent of the McCarthy era, in which many innocent families and individuals were devastated under the scare of communism. Worse, the raids succeeded in reinforcing the idea that the United States has declared war on all Muslims, no matter how moderate or law-abiding.

"It seems like the government is declaring open season on Muslim American groups," said Abdulwahab Alkebsi, executive director of the Islamic Institute.

"These raids and the manner in which they were conducted are un-American and hurt our image in the world as a nation with rules, and respect for human dignity. They are painful for the American Muslim community, which has sided with the President and our united country in our war against terrorism," said Dr. Nedzib Sacirbey, secretary of the board of AMC.

Federal authorities say they acted appropriately and that the raids were necessary to discover whether Islamic charities and organizations operating in this country were funneling money to militant organizations such as Hamas and Hezbollah in the Middle East.

Yet among those caught in the raids were people such as Sheikh Taha Jabir al Alwainy, a respected Islamic jurist with the Graduate School of Islamic and Social Sciences. Al Alwainy has lectured and written extensively against Islamic militancy and, as noted earlier, has even issued a religious ruling as the United States prepared to bomb Afghanistan saying it was the duty of American Muslims soldiers their to help defend their country against terrorism.

Raiding al Alwainy's offices was another sign of what Paz described as the ignorance about Islam and how to fight extremism that he found pervasive in intelligence and law enforcement communities.

"The intelligence community in the United States does not understand Islamic culture," Paz said. "I'm saying that after being in Washington for the past two years, I know they have so much information . . . but they can not understand it or use it."

But within the United States' borders were millions of people who could understand and interpret the information garnered from intelligence sources around the world. And Muslim Americans are the vital link in helping American law enforcement protect its borders. In fact, many are keen to serve as the country's first line of defense in the war against terrorism, to draw a clear distinction between the Islam they promoted as a religion of peace and al Qaeda's Islam of war.

There are signs that the FBI is beginning to understand that it needs to establish better relations with American Muslims. FBI Director Robert

Mueller braved a great deal of criticism from pro-Israel activists and their supporters in Congress for speaking to the eleventh annual convention of the American Muslim Council in Alexandria, Virginia.

"It is critically important for us to develop a strong relationship," Mueller told the gathering. He noted that many Muslim Americans had come forward to serve as translators and were even working with law enforcement authorities on Guantanamo Bay, Cuba, where the United States had transported Taliban and al Qaeda fighters captured during bombing raids of Afghanistan. And Mueller promised that as the FBI battled terrorism within U.S. borders, it would not abuse its powers by discriminating against Muslim Americans.

Mueller also said something that many Muslims at the convention had hoped to hear and sincerely hoped he meant: "We are out to address terrorists," he said. "This is in no way a war against Islam."

9

THE HATRED AND THE HOPE

SO, ALL OF THE REVEREND SMITH'S QUESTIONS ABOUT MARTYRDOM and September 11 boil down to this: Why do they hate us?

Men such as Mohammed Atta, Osama bin Laden, Ayman Zawahri, Munir al Makdah, and Abu Muhammad do indeed hate us. And they have dedicated their lives, and their deaths, to ridding the world of what they believe are the enemies of Islam. "They hate us," President Bush said shortly after September 11, "because of our democracy," and our "freedom of religion." But there are other reasons to consider:

- They hate us because of our wealth and power or rather, what they believe is our abuse of our wealth and power.
- They hate us because of our support of Israel, a country they believe was created on the blood of Arabs.
- They hate us because they believe we help Israel maintain control of Muslim holy places in Jerusalem.
- They hate us because our troops have "defiled" the holiest cities of Islam, Mecca and Medina.
- They hate us because their societies are still reeling from the effects of decades of western colonialism.
- They hate us because we support leaders in the Middle East whom they consider corrupt and despotic. But, though it may be little consolation, they probably hate Arab leaders even more than they hate us. They see people such as Egypt's president Hosni Mubarak and even the princes in Saudi Arabia's House of Saud as apostates, worthy of death.

- They hate us because they blame us for the suffering of the Iraqi people under U.S.-backed economic sanctions.
- And they hate us because they believe we control and exploit the resources of their region, especially their oil.

Such hatred is what led to the deaths of thousands of people on September 11 and that is still a threat to global stability. But there are other perplexing questions. Were Mohammad Atta and his partners the vanguards of Islam? Do Muslims consider them martyrs? And do Islamic militants want to destroy our world or take it over?

The truth is, men such as Atta, bin Laden, and Zawahri want less to destroy or take over our world than to get us out of theirs. But they have proven that they are capable of bringing their war to our borders.

Anger over these issues led some Muslims in the Middle East to turn martyrdom into a weapon of terror. But Islam does not have a monopoly on religious extremism or terror. Christians such as the Reverend Smith maintain that Christianity does not justify suicide, murder, and terror, despite the crusades, the mayhem in Northern Ireland, and the other atrocities that have been committed in the name of Christ.

Most Jews revile extremists such as the anti-Arab Kach movement but some Israelis idolize Baruch Goldstein as a martyr, even though he killed innocent Muslims as they prayed in Hebron, the location of Abraham's tomb, which is sacred to both Muslims and Jews. Goldstein's family wanted him buried in the Jewish Cemetery of the Martyrs in Hebron. Israel's government denied him that honor. He was buried in Kiryat Arba, a suburb of Hebron, where his grave has become a pilgrimage site for Jewish extremists.

We have seen that moderate Muslims prefer peace, and they argue that their extremists, like those within Christian and Jewish ranks, do not represent the truth of their religion. But despite their insistence that Islam is a religion of peace, to those who don't know its teachings, Islam can seem both violent and angry. The same holy book that some use to justify terror others use to argue against it.

Dr. Akbar S. Ahmed, former Pakistani ambassador to the United Kingdom and a respected expert on Islam, believes that Islam's manifestation in the modern world greatly depends on the quality of its leadership, the kinds of men and women who are shaping its ideology and relationship with the rest of the world. In a June 1999 article he argued that Muslim nations faced a "crisis of leadership" that would affect their relationship with the outside world.

> Osama, bearded, in his traditional Muslim clothes, and speaking in Arabic of jihad; and Jinnah, clean shaven, in his Savile Row suit, English accent, and Lincoln's Inn legal education—here, neatly, we have the two poles of Islam in direct opposition. The question is, which model will prevail in the next century? One of these two models will provide leadership for the more than one billion Muslims into the millennium.[1]

Despite the passion of their convictions that has galvanized a minority of Muslim from all over the world into jihad, bin Laden and his Taliban hosts could never be accepted by Islam's mainstream, Ahmed argued:

> With all their zeal for Islam, and their burning desire to impose their vision on society, the Taliban violated two basic tenets of Islam in a manner calculated to cause offence to many in and outside the country [Afghanistan]. Firstly, their discrimination against women and the beatings that they administer, contrast with the gentleness and kindness of the Prophet of Islam towards women. His famous saying that "heaven is under the feet of the mother" sums up the traditional attitude of Islam to women.
>
> Secondly, the harshness of the Taliban towards minority groups, the non-Pathans [also know as Pashtuns], is also against the spirit of Islam which encourages tolerance. The minorities of Afghanistan are also Muslims, but many non-Pathans have been discriminated against and treated with violence. This suggests an ethnic attitude rather than a religious one, although it may come under the guise of religion."[2]

Jinnah had a gentler view of Islam. He promoted women's rights in his vision of an Islamic state, insisted that Islam treat minorities and other religions with tolerance, and believed in the rule of law. But neither pole seems to adequately address the issues confronting today's Muslims.

Jinnah's way seems too Western for many Muslims, who view it as a denial of Islam's own culture and heritage. With anti-Western sentiment so pronounced in the Islamic world, Islamic leaders need to appear well grounded in their own civilization to effectively challenge the extremists and steer Islam into the new millennium.

"Most religious systems have suffered at one time or another from absolutist extremism, and Islam is no exception," wrote Khaled Abou El Fadl, an expert in Islamic law. "It would be disingenuous to deny that the Qur'an and other Islamic sources offer possibilities of intolerant interpretation. But the text does not command such intolerant readings. Historically, Islamic civilization has displayed a remarkable ability to recognize possibilities of tolerance, and to act upon these possibilities."[3]

It is true that all religions have experienced divisions, but Islam's schism over martyrdom and violence, which affects the loyalties of more than 1 billion people—a fifth of the world's population—has serious implications for world peace. The world has a vital stake in the resolution of Islam's internal turmoil.

Even before the disaster that struck the United States in the name of Islam, moderate and radical Muslim scholars had been engaged in a worldwide debate over the future of Islam and how the religion's precepts fit into the modern world. When he addressed the State Department's Open Forum in 1999 and warned of a terrorist attack on the United States, the controversial Sufi Sheikh Muhammad Hisham Kabbani drew a distinct line between the Islam he represented and that of militants. His stance angered many Muslims, including some in mainstream Islamic organizations in the United States. Kabbani castigated many Muslims leaders for supporting intolerance and jihad. His Islam, he said, was a religion of "moderation, tolerance, peace and justice . . . Islam, in general, is a religion that calls for respecting everyone and living together with everyone." After September 11, most Muslim leaders felt a new urgency to defend their religion against charges that it condoned terror and brutality and was the prime source of instability around the globe. After September 11 Muslims all over the world heard President Bush lay down the gauntlet, telling them the time had come to make one simple decision, whether they were "with us or with the terrorists."

The United States desperately needed moderate Muslims "with us." While the country can bomb its way around the world, in the end, the only way it can succeed in ending the threat of martyrdom as a weapon of terror is to effectively challenge the militants' message and undermine the anger that provides them support in many parts of the world. For that, the voices of the moderate Islamists are essential.

"The problem of extremism is a big danger, and it can be solved if the West better understands Islam and builds bridges with the moderate Muslims, the traditional Muslims," Kabbani said in his speech. "This way, the Muslim community will eliminate the extremist threat from within."

When Kabbani spoke out about the possibility of a terrorist attack, he put himself and members of his followers in the Islamic Supreme Council of America at risk from those on the other end of Islam's spectrum.

Most of the Muslims who oppose him do not so much disagree with his promoting Islam as a religion of peace as they did with his casting such a wide net in his alarmist statements alleging that 80 percent of American mosques were controlled by extremists:

> The most dangerous thing that is going on now in these mosques, that has been sent upon these mosques around the United States—like churches they were established by different organizations and that is ok—but the problem with our communities is the extremist ideology. Because they are very active they took over the mosques; and we can say that they took over more than 80% of the mosques that have been established in the U.S. And there are more than 3,000 mosques in the U.S. So it means that the methodology or ideology of extremist has been spread to 80% of the Muslim population, but not all of them agree with it. But mostly the youth and the new generation do because they are students and they don't think except with their emotions and they are rebellious against their own leaders and government. This is the nature and psychology of human beings. When we are students in university or college we always fight the government, whether they are right or wrong, we have to attack the government. This is how they have been raised.[4]

Kabbani also charged that militants have taken over many Muslim student organizations on college campuses in the United States. Kabbani is a polarizing figure, revealing the deep fissures within the Islamic group in the United States and around the world. After he spoke out, his organization said it received an onslaught of hate mail. Two letters, in part, read:

> You are an Israeli agent. We will destroy you. Die in Hell. Beware of your actions. . . . The Anti-Kabbani Coordinating Council is in the process of being formed. . . .

> I want to see you dead. . . . Let's just say it's a result of the recent tide of something that you have such a genuine fear of that you must warn your friends . . . [about] the extremist students . . . the last one you'll ever see."[5]

Kabbani, who insists on holding Muslims to the highest standards of kindness and tolerance, refused to stop raising the alarm about militants in

the United States and said he would continue to uncover extremism wherever he saw it, despite the risk to his own life: "If I kept quiet, a danger might
suddenly come that you are not looking for, so in preventing that danger
from coming, I am trying to sacrifice and give something to the Americans in
order that they understand that there is something coming up slowly. We
don't know where it is going to hit, it might be here, might be outside, might
be any country, and might affect the interest of the United States."[6]

Many Muslims would prefer to deal with their internal issues pri-
vately, without sending up alarms that could hurt everyone in their communities, as they fear Kabbani's speeches would do. But within the
mosques and religious organizations throughout the Muslim world, more
and more courageous people are beginning to stand up to the extremists,
in large part thanks to the horror of September 11. Their efforts were
sorely needed. Without the world's moderate Islamists working from
within to deter the jihadees, there is little hope of breaking the cycle of tit-
for-tat brutality that has consumed the Israelis and Palestinians. And without working with moderate Islamists, there is real danger that Americans
will find themselves embroiled in the same type of long-term guerrilla war
that the Israelis face, battling new generations of Islam's martyrs with the
death toll steadily rising.

Only respected, moderate Muslims can speak to the young men and
women who make up the backbone of the radical movements in order to stop
their flight into the ranks of the jihadees as a outlet for their rage. These
youths need to be convinced of the truth of another Islam. They need to be
convinced of Islam's preference for peace.

Moderate Islamists are also essential in helping the United States improve its standing in the Muslim world and refute the widespread belief, promoted by the militants, that the U.S. war on terrorism is really a war on
Islam.

"We need to find the intersection between moderate Islamic interests
and our interests," said John Sigler, a retired real admiral with the U.S. Navy,
in an interview in the winter of 2001. Sigler is researching ways to counter
terrorism at the National Defense University in Washington, D.C. "What is
really happening in Islam is the equivalent of the Christian reformation. This
is not a struggle of Islam against the rest of the world, although that's the
manifestation of it. This is really a struggle within Islam about what the future of Islam looks like."

Will it look like bin Laden's Islam of jihad? Like Jinnah's sophisticated, Westernized Islam of tolerance and rule of law? Or will Muslims find their true path somewhere in between?

Many Muslims are looking for a twenty-first century Saladin to resurrect their glorious past, but many of the African American Baptists listening to the Reverend Smith on that January morning less than four months after September 11, wished that Islam would find its own brand of Martin Luther King. They believe Muslims need someone with the courage, influence, and power to stand up to those who promote violence and hatred in the name of Allah; someone willing to boldly lead Islam's vanguard of nonviolence; someone, perhaps, brave enough to risk becoming Islam's martyr for peace.

Others might say that Islam needed its own Mahatma Gandhi, or, at least someone with the wisdom and restraint of a Nelson Mandela. But we should note that even Gandhi had his doubts about whether his nonviolent tactics would work anywhere else in the world and with any foe other than the British. And Mandela himself was once labeled a terrorist by the racists he opposed.

Dr. Ahmed and other Islamic scholars believe Islam does not have to reach outside its own rich history for answers to its modern dilemma. He argues that today Islam needs philosophers as great as those in its past who could meld its noble teachings to defend the weak and poor with the Qur'an's instructions for Muslims to treat non-believers with kindness; to be people of integrity, even in battle; and to be quick to forgive and eager to forge a just peace with even the most ruthless of enemies.

Islam has never promoted itself as a religion for pacifists, however. Muslims are required to battle injustice, even if it requires taking up arms to do so. "Muslims are not permitted by their faith to accept injustice," wrote Dr. Ahmed Yousef, executive director of the United Association for Studies and Research in Annandale, Virginia. "Muslims are obliged to seek peaceful solutions to injustice but are equally obliged to use physical force in self-defense when non-violent means fails to secure the basic human rights of both political and economic self determination and freedom of religion."[7]

That is not to say that there are not Muslims all over the world who daily promote tolerance, forgiveness, and peace. There are many notable examples in the United States.

Mahdi Bray, executive director of the Muslim American Society, Freedom Foundation, is a Christian convert to Islam. He leads an Islamic organization dedicated to dialogue with other faiths and to promoting Islam as a religion of peace, even as he condemns injustice wherever he saw it.

Ibrahim Remey, a Muslim member of the Fellowship of Reconciliation, which bills itself as the "largest and oldest interfaith peace organization in the United States," has written and spoken against all forms of violence, as a regular guest on Amin Radio, the Muslim Radio network in the United States. Remey is director of the Fellowship of Reconciliation's Peace and Disarmament program, an activist group promoting tolerance and nonviolence.

Amber Khan, a young Muslim peace activist, works with the Washington, D.C.-based Interfaith Alliance to promote a "positive and healing role of religion in public life." The organization includes members from more than fifty faiths, including Jews, several Christian denominations, Muslims, Buddhists, Bahais, Hindus, and Animists.

Dr. Maher H. Hatout, former chairman of the Islamic Center of Southern California, is a member of the board of directors of the Interreligious Council of Los Angeles and the Interfaith Alliance and works with both organizations to unite people of different religions.

Dr. Sulayman S. Nyang, a brilliant Islamic thinker who is a professor at Howard University, tries to serve as a bridge between the Muslim world and other religions. In a speech presented at Chizuk Amuno, a Jewish congregation, in Baltimore, Maryland, on November 27, 2001, at the invitation of the Institute for Christian & Jewish Studies, Dr. Nyang spoke eloquently about Islam's commonalities with Judaism and Christianity:

> To facilitate the task of knowing His Commandments, according to the Holy Qur'an, Allah dispatched 124,000 prophets to humankind over the centuries. The first Prophet was Adam, according to Islam, and the last of this long line of prophets was the Holy Prophet Muhammad. In between the first and the last, you have Noah, Abraham, Isaac, Ishmael, Jacob, Moses, Solomon, David and Jesus. You can see that the Islamic list of prophets includes persons, some of whom are on the Jewish and Christian lists as prophets. . . .
>
> Intellectual historians of the Muslim World and beyond may debate among themselves as to who influenced whom in the early history of Islam, but the fact still remains that Muslims benefited from the intellectual tools available to preceding civilizations and cultures. The different sects that arose in the first three centuries of Islam are the creatures of the interaction between their Islamic cultures and the neighboring Jewish, Christian and other cultures.[8]

Imad-ad-Dean Ahmad, president of the Minaret of Freedom based in Bethesda, Maryland, is another proponent of peace and cooperation between Islam and the West. In an article published in the *Middle East Affairs Journal* in 2001, Ahmad argued that Muslims needed to handle the matter as an offense against Islam:

> It is the moral duty of Muslims not only to condemn the attacks on non-combatant Americans (including hundreds of Muslims) . . . but to engage in a positive effort to identify the planners and material supporters of the attack, to confront them with the fact that their actions have violated the Sharia'ah [Islamic law] in a most egregious manner, to urge them to repent and to punish them if the families of the victims are unwilling to be merciful and accept compensation."

Dr. Ahmad also argued that bin Laden had no right or authority to speak for Islam and declare war on the United States.

> Let us begin by acknowledging that no state of war exists between Muslims and America. The 1998 declaration of war signed by bin Laden cannot be accepted as such. Bin Laden is not authorized to declare war on behalf of the umma [community]. . . .
>
> Even if a state of war had existed between the Muslims and the Americans on September 11, there can be no doubt that the attack on the World Trade Center would constitute not an act of war permissible under Islamic law but a war crime. . . . Thus it appears to be the consensus (*ijma*) of the *umma* as well as of the scholars that the act was a criminal act and therefore it is mandatory that the criminals be identified and punished."[9]

On the international stage, people such as Kamel al Sharif in Jordan, one of the founders of the International Islamic Council for Dawa and Relief, work within the Islamic world to resolve differences among Muslims that threaten to erupt into violence. Even political rebels have disavowed violence. For example, the Tunisian exile Rachid al Ghannouchi has dedicated himself to promoting democracy nonviolently and ending the monarchy that rules Tunisia. "Some Muslim people, militants, bear the responsibility of presenting a very bad picture of Islam, when it's linked with bombing and assassinations and plane hijacking." Ghannouchi said in a 1994 interview in London, where he lives in exile. "Even within Islamic movements, these violent groups represent the tiny minority of the whole body."

But this tiny minority has spread its message of war around the world, making "Muslim" and "fanatic" synonymous in the minds of people in the West.

Yet millions of Muslims around the world are dedicated to ending the association of Islam with violence and terror. Regrettably, their voices often go unheard in the western media because their message is neither provocative nor inflammatory, not the stuff that makes for eye-catching headlines. Peace mongers simply do not make news.

This is a serious failing within the American media, which too often values the sensational over accurate, balanced information. Terror makes news. War makes news. Flying airplanes into skyscrapers makes big news. And the soft-spoken, smiling bin Laden has become the world's biggest celebrity, gaining a sure spot on the evening news by summoning Muslims to jihad, even if only a few thousand out of the world's Muslims heed the call.

As newspapers, television, and radio shows promote bin Laden and his martyrs as Islam's warriors, the quiet, tolerant voices of Islam are muffled in the background, unworthy of the media spotlight. Far too many journalists working for radio, television and newspapers in the United States, know nothing of the basic facts about Islam and its teachings and are ill prepared to distinguish between a moderate and a militant. Yet these journalists are shaping American opinions about Islam and its followers, writing columns and engaging in lofty debates about Islam and terrorism that have no basis in the facts of the religion's teachings. Many Americans do not even know that Muslim moderates exist.

Less than a year after September 11, one well-informed retired executive was shocked to learn that Muslim leaders had condemned the attack. His response was common among Americans: "If they've condemned it, why isn't it in the papers?" he asked in disbelief.

Nobody knows it, because with so much news about terrorism threats, bombings in Afghanistan, suicide bombings in Israel, and Israeli warplanes assassinating Palestinians, there is no room and no air time left for the quiet, soothing statements about Islam's truth coming from Muslims moderates.

Yet these are the very voices that need to be heard, both in the Islamic world and the West. It is these very voices that U.S. policymakers need to engage to help shape American foreign policy toward the Islamic world. If the moderates are right, then America's war need not be with Islam. Muslims and Americans should be allies in the same war against intolerance, evil, and terror that not only has killed thousands of Americans but has sullied one of the greatest religions of the modern world. Moderate Muslims and the West desperately need to bridge the gap dividing them and find common ground to work together to defeat their common foe.

Some of the world's most influential Muslim voices have accepted the challenge. At the June 2002 conference of the Organization of Islamic Conference, an umbrella organization of Muslim countries, foreign ministers of fifty-seven countries met in Khartoum to address what Sudanese president Omar al Bashir called the "historic gap" between their world and the West. Press reports said Bashir called on Muslims to address forthrightly charges that Islam fosters terrorism. "If we fail to do so, we will become even more neglected and marginalized than we are at present," he said.

"We must listen to the voice of the contemporary world and adjust to whatever it has to offer that's beneficial and be in tune with the march of humanity," said Abdelouahed Belkziz, the conference's secretary general. "But we shouldn't, as we try to adjust, abandon our faith and Islamic civilization."[10]

This is the ongoing problem for the Muslim world: how to hold true to the precepts of Islam and maintain good relations with the West.

That same summer, a high-ranking delegation from the Muslim World League based in Mecca, Saudi Arabia, traveled to the United States on what they billed as a "goodwill tour." Led by Sheikh Abdullah al Turki, the organization's secretary general, the delegation sought to counter the prevailing view of Islam as a religion of fanatical martyrs-in-waiting. Their decision to meet their fears of anti-Muslim sentiment in the United States head-on is a sign of how alarmed many Islamic leaders are over what they see as a growing Western-Islamic divide.

"The events of September 11 have aroused some fear and mistrust between people in the Muslim World and the West," al Turki said. "We are all confronting a world crisis."[11]

The tension was pitting the Islamic world against the West, especially as the Bush administration has targeted many militant Islamic groups in its war against terrorism. Al Turki said much of the hostility between Muslims and the West stemmed from the false stereotypes that equate Islam with terrorism. "Today we have more than a billion Muslims throughout the world. Many of them, like any other people, make mistakes; they commit sins; they become extremists. . . . It is unfair to take such individuals as representatives of Islam and Muslims."

Al Turki and the other Islamic leaders reiterated the statements heard so often from moderates: Islam opposes terrorism and suicide bombings. But, in keeping with the feelings of most Muslim leaders, he said Israel's "oppression" of Palestinians provoked such actions.

Lest Muslims once again be misunderstood, Dr. Muzamil Sidiqi, former president of the Islamic Society of North America, stressed, "There is a difference between justifying something and understanding something."[12]

The Muslim World's League's delegation clearly addressed what might be the most crucial question for many Americans. Were the September 11 hijackers indeed martyrs for Islam?

Muslim scholars overwhelmingly say no. As Iran's Ayatullah Mohadghegh Damad, an expert in Islamic law, detailed, in Islam, martyrdom is an honor bestowed on the innocent who die from persecution or in battle; or upon a soldier who dies justly defending his home, his land, or his religion. It is a title of honor for Muslims, just as it is for Christians and Jews.

Finally, the world's preeminent Muslim scholars have concluded that Atta, bin Laden, and Zawahri were neither innocents nor soldiers fighting under the strict precepts of Islamic law. They were terrorists distorting their religion's true teachings. Many Muslims say the same thing about suicide bombers such as al Masri and their trainers who target women, children, and the elderly, actions that Muhammad clearly prohibited. They are not the vanguard of Islam. They are not defenders of the faithful. Few would disagree that they have done more to hurt the spread of Islam than to help it.

In the end, Muslims, Christians, and Jews can find common ground in this: Whatever their motives, their grievances, and their suffering, those who kill and maim the innocent are not what Islam praises as holy warriors. They are not shuhada. They are not martyrs.

EPILOGUE

SINCE THIS BOOK WAS PUBLISHED IN THE SPRING OF 2003 IN AN AT-tempt to answer the Rev. Smith's question, Islamic militants and, unfortu-nately a good part of the Muslim world, hate us even more. Much of the Middle East has become embroiled in outright war between Muslim mili-tants and the West, relations are soured between the United States and Eu-rope, and terrorists have had significant victories in their self-proclaimed holy war to purge all foreigners from their holy land. The situation is so grim that many people failed to appreciate one major piece of good news: By the summer of 2004, there had not been another terrorist attack on U.S. soil since September 11, 2001, although fears and threats persisted. America's war against Islamic militants was being fought away from American homes, schools and shopping malls, and in the streets, alleyways and bazaars of Baghdad, Fallujah and Kabul. Whether intentionally part of President Bush's plan or not, it was indeed a major achievement in the war against terrorism. And there were other developments of note.

Israelis had eliminated one of their greatest enemies. They assassinated Hamas' Sheikh Yassin, who joined the ranks of the *shouhada* he blessed for death. He had become one of Palestine's most revered martyrs, rallying his forces in death as he did in life. So even though Israel lost one major foe, it may have gained thousands more in making him a martyr. Yet no Islamic scholar of his weight and prestige had emerged to replace him and to stir the masses into jihad and suicide. Still, without Sheikh Yassin, much of the Mid-dle East is in an uproar and the attacks of the *istishhadi* have become almost de rigueur in the region, not only against Israelis, but now against American troops stationed in Iraq. Even Muslims are now being targeted by suicide bombers who see themselves in a battle to purify not only their land but Islam from the influences of infidels. And Central Asia seems to be shaping up as the next battleground for Islamic militants looking to overthrow dicta-torial regimes, especially those friendly to the West.

If Islamic militants needed another reason to hate the United States, they found it on March 20, 2003, when American planes began bombing Baghdad. The administration of George W. Bush sent American soldiers into Iraq, aided by a contingent of Brits and troops from countries that included Poland, Australia, Spain and the Philippines. He argued that the invasion of Iraq was part of the war on terrorism since Iraq possessed weapons of mass destruction, was willing to use them, and to pass them on for others to use again the United States. In his January 20, 2004 State of the Union Address, Bush explained:

> As part of the offensive against terror, we are also confronting the regimes that harbor and support terrorists, and could supply them with nuclear, chemical or biological weapons. The United States and our allies are deter-mined: We refuse to live in the shadow of this ultimate danger.
>
> The first to see our determination were the Taliban, who made Afghan-istan the primary training base of al Qaeda killers. As of this month, that country has a new constitution, guaranteeing free elections and full partici-pation by women . . .
>
> Since we last met in this chamber, combat forces of the United States, Great Britain, Australia, Poland and other countries enforced the demands of the United Nations, ended the rule of Saddam Hussein, and the people of Iraq are free.[1]

While the Bush administration took credit for bringing down two of the world's most despised regimes, ferreting Saddam like a scared rat out of a hole in the ground, it did not succeed in bringing peace, stability and democ-racy to either country. The Taliban indeed fell from power but it regrouped to wage guerrilla war against the U.S. backed government. And although the Bush administration formally returned sovereignty to Iraq in June 2004, many observers criticized the turnover as a sham since thousands of U.S. troops remained to help the U.S.-appointed government establish some sem-blance of security. That proved to be just as hard after the handover as be-fore. The formal change of national power did not appease the militants or many of the powerful religious leaders in the country, who wanted all foreign troops out of their region. Attacks against United States and allied troops continued. So while the Bush administration could rightfully boast that it brought down two of the world's most detested dictatorships, one religious and one secular, it also was blamed for unleashing mayhem in Iraq, instability in the region, and an increase in suicide bombings in Afghanistan and around the globe. Neither war ended or even diminished the threat of terrorism.

In May 2004 Islamic militants struck a train in Madrid, Spain, killing nearly 200 people and injuring more than 1000 just before the country's national election. Spaniards reacted in anger, not only against the people who terrorized them, but against the government of Carlos de Menem, which they blamed for getting them into the Iraqi morass with the United States. It didn't help that de Menem initially tried to blame the Basque separatist group known as ETA for the attack, fearing a backlash from a people who did not want to go to war in Iraq. Most of the people in the countries that entered Iraq with the United States also opposed the war, and did not believe that Saddam Hussein posed the immediate threat that Bush insisted he did.

Iraqis also did not welcome U.S. troops with parades and confetti as U.S. Secretary of Defense Donald Rumsfeld and Vice President Dick Cheney had anticipated. On March 16, Cheney said the war in Iraq would last "weeks not months," and he told NBC's "Meet the Press": "The read we get on the people of Iraq is there is no question but what they want to the get rid of Saddam Hussein, and they will welcome as liberators the United States when we come to do that."[2]

Jim Lehrer asked Rumsfeld in an interview on PBS's "The News Hour" in February 2003 if he thought the majority of the civilian population would welcome American troops into the country. Rumsfeld responded: "There's obviously—the Shiite population in Iraq and the Kurdish population in Iraq have been treated very badly by Saddam Hussein's regime. They represent a large fraction of the total. There's no question but that they would be welcomed. Go back to Afghanistan, the people were in the streets playing music, cheering, flying kites, and doing all the things that the Taliban and the al-Qaeda would not let them do."[3]

Even in Iraq, both Shias and Sunnis were initially happy at Saddam's downfall and some seemed grateful to the Americans for bringing him down. They took to the streets cheering, singing and knocking down statues of Saddam throughout Baghdad. Rumsfeld and Bush seemed to be right. But, as they did not envision, even the Shias who most hated Saddam would eventually turn with a vengeance against the American forces that brought their most hated enemy. In a sermon on July 24, 2004, Muqtada al Sadr, a Shia religious leader turned guerrilla in southern Iraq, berated American troops and interim Prime Minister Iyad Allawi whom the United States installed to run the country. "Damn him and damn the occupier," al Sadr railed in the summer of 2004.[4] It expressed the feelings of many Shias and many Iraqis who were fed up with the daily explosions and suicide bombings that killed not only Americans but Iraqi civilians.

Al Sadr had led his own terror campaign against American troops, until U.S. commanders were forced to try to negotiate a ceasefire with him to reduce further bloodshed. The bloodshed intensified, however. American soldiers as well as civilians now are being kidnapped and killed on a daily basis in Iraq, and they have become targets for Islamic militants throughout the region. While the U.S. promised shock and awe, cheering Iraqis welcoming American troops, and a quick transformation of a dictatorship into a model of democracy, the world witnessed a slow descent into chaos.

One of the lowest points for U.S.-led forces came when militants struck the United Nations headquarters in Iraq, killing 23 people, including Sergio Vieira de Mello, the U.N.'s special representative in Iraq. The attack on the United Nations was particularly significant in that the world body had opposed the U.S. invasion and had sent staff to provide humanitarian assistance to Iraq civilians. The militants were sending a clear message that they wanted to rid their world of all foreign influence, and that they made no distinction between American troops and foreigners in Iraq to help the Iraqi people.

The attacks prompted Bush to label the militants "enemies of the civilized world," vowing that the world as united against terrorism. But by the summer of 2004, the militants, after a series of kidnappings, beheadings and threats, had convinced the Philippines to withdraw its troops from Iraq. They also had convinced several companies doing business in the region to withdraw their representatives, and the resurgent Taliban fighters had created such a threat in Afghanistan that even Medicin Sans Frontier, the French medical aid organization, had decided to pull its staff out of the area. Overall, the United States and its ever-dwindling coalition seemed to be reeling under the advancing armies of Islamic jihadees who were surfacing all over the globe and attacking not only military forces, but also the economic underpinnings of the West. American officials were warning that Islamic militants were planning to attack financial institutions in New York, and they had already succeeded in destabilizing the oil industry.

In Iraq, American troops are being picked off daily, Arab fighters associated with both secular and religious groups are killing at random, and Muslim clerics are establishing their own militias to battle coalition troops. In addition, there is a real threat to the House of Saud in Saudi Arabia, which is now careening into its own showdown with militants bent on forcing foreigners out of the Hijaz.

From the perspective of Bin Laden and his colleagues, the war against the infidels is fully engaged and they have achieved some major victories. They have seen one of their most detested dictators unseated by the United States; they are directly engaging Western troops on two fronts, while opening another front in Saudi Arabia, and many Muslims around the world came to despise the United States and see it as the epitome of power gone mad. After several attacks on foreigners in Saudi Arabia, al Qaeda's minions brought about what they want most, a exodus of Americans from their holy land. The House of Saud, preparing for an all-out assault on the militants who would bring it down, offered amnesty to any al Qaeda supporters or activists who would surrender. But many people inside and outside of the region were not sure who would emerge victorious from the looming carnage. In a shocking development for Muslim Americans, in early August 2004, Abdurrahman Alamoudi, once considered as one of the leading moderate Muslims in the United States, confessed to being part of a Libyan plot to assassinate Saudi Crown Prince Abdullah, a charge that Libya denied. But the allegation revealed just how widely hated the House of Saud had become, even outside of the Arab world.

In May 2003, President Bush proclaimed that the mission in Iraq had been accomplished and that major fighting was over, but that statement came to be seen as both shortsighted and ridiculous, considering the carnage that ensued in the following months. By July 2004, the Associated Press estimated that 900 American had been killed, with another 6,000 injured. The Christian Science Monitor reported a year earlier than an estimated 5,000–10,000 Iraqi civilians had been killed in the fighting.[5]

And as the death toll for Americans and Iraqis mounted, officials investigations in both Britain and the United States concluded that the rationale both governments used to go to war was seriously flawed. Saddam Hussein did not possess weapons of mass destruction, was not poised to launch chemical and biological weapons, and did not collaborate with al Qaeda in the September 11 attack against the United States. Intelligence services in both Great Britain and the United States had gotten it tragically wrong, or the governments had lied. The U.S. Senate "Report on The U.S. Intelligence Community's Pre-War Intelligence Assessment on Iraq," concluded: "Most of the major key judgments in the Intelligence Community's October 2002 National Intelligence Estimate (NIE), Iraq's Continuing Program of Weapons of Mass Destruction, either overstated or were not supported by the underlying intelligence report. A series of failures, particularly in the analytical trade craft, led to the mischaracterization of the intelligence."[6]

Shortly after the Senate report was released on the failure or misinterpretation of intelligence in building the case for a U.S.-led war in Iraq, the National Commission for Terrorist Attacks Against the United States issued a scathing report that also blamed intelligence agencies and government for tragic failures. The report summarized its findings as: "Since the plotters were flexible and resourceful, we cannot know whether any single step or series of steps would have defeated them. What we can say with confidence is that none of the measures adopted by the U.S. government from 1998 to 2001 disturbed or even delayed the progress of the al Qaeda plot. Across the government, there were failures of imagination, policy, capabilities, and management."[7]

By the time both reports were released, CIA Director George Tenet had resigned, Bush's popularity was at a all-time low, and polls were consistently showing that growing numbers of Americans believed the war in Iraq had been a mistake. And what is worse, they believed that it had done little to either avenge the September 11 attack or prevent another one. In a poll released in July 2004, CNN reported: "Fifty-four percent of those polled said it was a mistake to send U.S. troops to Iraq, compared with 41 percent who expressed that sentiment in early June. Most respondents to the poll, 55 percent, also said they don't believe the war has made the United States safer from terrorism—rejecting an argument that President Bush has repeatedly advanced in his rationale for the war."[8]

In Iraq, public sentiment was even worse. Valentinas Mite, a reporter for Radio Free Europe/Radio Liberty, who spent several weeks during the summer of 2004 in Iraq, said most Iraqis were absolutely fed up with all of the foreign forces in their country, including Islamic militants fighting the United States. But they blamed the chaos and despair on the American invasion. Iraqis wanted security most of all, with a close second their desire for dependable electricity.

"They believe Americans can do anything and that Americans could provide security if they wanted to," Mite said. But many Iraqis suspect that the United States has a reason for keeping Iraq in turmoil and darkness, he said.

Many Iraqis believe the United States and Israel had colluded to rid the Jewish state of its most dreaded enemy in the Arab world, and steal Iraqi oil. Such widely held beliefs only increased the resentment many Iraqis felt toward U.S. forces as well as toward the Iraqis they accused of abetting the enemy. The behavior of some American soldiers toward the Iraqi population did not help matters, either.

"Overall, Iraqis have the feeling that the American troops don't respect them," Mite said. "I went on a raid with some other American soldiers who confiscated people's money, tore up toys looking for weapons while kids were crying, and it made people very angry. Most of the American soldiers were just tired and didn't understand the culture. Often they did not treat older people with the respect that is normally accorded them in Iraqi society," he said. "For example, some would open a door with their foot where an old man was sitting. And I heard a guy say several times, 'I'm tired of these monkeys.' All within easy earshot of angry Iraqi youth."

While Mite did not say this is the way the majority of American soldiers acted in Iraq, such actions by even a small percentage would have soured popular opinion toward U.S. forces even without a major development such as the al Ghraib scandal that erupted in the spring of 2004. The revelation that U.S. troops tortured and killed Iraqi prisoners seriously weakened America's moral authority and strengthened the arguments of Islamic militants who insisted that Muslims needed to fight the export of a bankrupt American culture to their world. The Arab press provided graphic details and photographs of naked Arab men forced to lay on top of each other in a human pyramid as their American soldier guards smiled for the cameras. In one photo, a young female soldier grinned and pointed at the genitals of one of her male captors. It was a spectacle that sickened people on both sides of the Arab-West divide, but in the Middle East, it was also another cause of outrage against the United States.

The militants made full use of this anger to rally more recruits and to taunt Islamic scholars who had spoken out against terrorism. In May 2004 a group linked to al-Qaeda that had claimed credit for the kidnapping and execution of American soldiers issued this statement as the Abu Ghraib scandal was unfolding:

Nation of Islam. Is there any excuse left to sit idly by? And how can free Muslims sleep soundly as they see Islam being slaughtered, honor bleeding, photographs of shame and reports of Satanic degradation of the people of Islam, men and women, in Abu Ghraib prison?

Where is the care, fervor and rage for the faith of God, where is the concern for the sanctities of Muslims and where is the revenge for the honor of Muslims in the crusader prisons? As for you Islamic scholars, you will answer to God. Do you not see . . . the Muslim youth who humiliated the greatest power in history, cut off its nose and shattered its arrogance? Do you not see that it is time for you to learn from them the meanings of responsibility and sacrifice? Until when shall you remain like women, excelling only in wailing and crying?

It was hard to see how things could get much worse, or better, from the perspective of a Muslim militant waging jihad against what he saw as the corrupt, evil American-led West.

Things did not always seem so grim. The initial U.S. invasion of Iraq proved to be a cakewalk, with American journalists gleefully tagging along behind U.S. soldiers as they rolled into Baghdad. It seemed a clean war at first. In the initial weeks, there were few American casualties, and journalists were kept neatly away from reporting on Iraqi dead. The thousands of dollars that both the military and media companies spent on chemical warfare seemed a foolish waste of money as no one found a trace of the stockpiles of chemical and biological weapons that the Bush administration insisted were inside Iraq. But in January 2004, David Kay, the man that the Bush Administration sent to find the WMD stockpiles in Iraq, resigned and concluded there were none to find. Kay told the press: "I don't think they existed. What everyone was talking about is stockpiles produced after the end of the last [1991] Gulf War, and I don't think there was a large-scale production program in the '90s."[9]

In his final report, Kay placed the blame on the intelligence community and said it had provided false information on which Bush sent the country into war: "I actually think the intelligence community owes the president rather than the president owing the American people," he said. "We have to remember that this view of Iraq was held during the Clinton administration and didn't change in the Bush administration," Kay said. "It is not a political 'gotcha' issue. It is a serious issue of 'How you can come to a conclusion that is not matched in the future?'"[10]

In the Middle East, and especially among the jihadees fighting the United States, the U.S. invasion of Iraq was always based on lies and was a deliberate attempt to takeover one of the Arab world's most oil-rich countries and one of Israel's biggest threats. That belief galvanized thousands of men and women allied with a myriad of secular and Islamic groups to make Iraq a battleground against the United States and its allies. The jihadees proved they were willing to use the most horrendous tactics to strike fear not only in the West but even among Muslims. The militants executed, even beheaded, civilians kidnapped in Iraq and Saudi Arabia, and they used the internet to publicize graphic videos of their killings.

The situation became so grave that militants professing to represent Islam routinely employed tactics that the religion's teachings expressly forbid—attacking people not directly involved in conflict, including fellow Muslims they deemed to be traitors to their people and to Islam by working with Americans in Iraq, Afghanistan and Saudi Arabia. Many of the fears expressed in the preceding chapters of this book about a U.S. invasion of Iraq and about the intensifying of the war within Islam have been realized in their most extreme.

Suicide bombers and jihadees, a combination of fedayeen Baathist fighters loyal to the imprisoned Saddam Hussein and Islamic militants, have won support throughout the Islamic world for their war with the United States and Britain. The Muslim street and a good part of the world is avowedly anti-American, the culmination of decades of resentment and anger over U.S. foreign policy in the region.

It is important to note here that since this book was published, the Israeli-Palestinian conflict has some surprising twists, with Prime Minister Ariel Sharon now intent on pulling Israeli troops out of Gaza. While the United States waged war in Iraq, Israel was free to hunt down its enemies in Palestinian ranks. Israel assassinated Sheikh Ahmed Yassin, the leader of Hamas, whom I interviewed in his offices in Gaza while researching this book, and months later, they also killed Yassin's successor, Abd al-Aziz Rantissi, who promoted suicide attacks not only against Israel, but against U.S.forces in Iraq.[11]

Marwan Barghouti, another Palestinian leader whom I also interviewed for this book, was sentenced in the spring of 2004 to five life terms in Israeli prison. Israeli agents captured him in a battle in the West Bank shortly after I met him in a vacant office building in Ramallah, and Barghouti stood trial on murder charges stemming from his association with suicide bombings and attacks on Israelis.

Israel has also threatened Hezbollah founder Sheikh Fadlullah, as well as its political leader, Hassan Nasrullah. And a cloud still hangs over the head of Palestinian Authority President Yasser Arafat who is a virtual prisoner in his compound in Ramallah. Near lawlessness exists in many areas of the West Bank as Arafat's security apparatus is ineffective, and should the Israelis assassinate him as Sharon has threatened, many fear chaos would ensue with Palestinian factions vying for power. Already there are signs of trouble as Palestinians in a renegade group called the Jenin Martyrs Brigade kidnapped several Westerners as a bargaining tool in demanding positions inside the Palestinian security forces. Arafat and his security honchos seemed helpless to control the increasing number of rebels inside Palestinian ranks. It was clear that Palestinians were headed toward another spate of internecine killing in a factional battle over power.

As if the Israeli-Arab conflict were not enough, there also is the prospect of instability inside Israel. After Israel reoccupied much of the West Bank and Gaza but the suicide bombers kept coming, Sharon decided to pull his troops out of Gaza, and build a controversial wall between the West Bank and Israel, confiscating some Palestinian land to do so. [12]Sharon's plan also called for closing settlements in Gaza, which has turned the most radical settlers against Sharon, with some even threatening to kill him. Israelis also were facing the possibility of internecine violence as a byproduct of containing the Palestinians.

With the prospect that Israelis could be forced to fight Israelis, it was also becoming increasingly clear that the war within Islam was well underway. In Iraq, al Qaeda claimed responsibility for the deaths of several leading members of Iraq's U.S.-backed transitional authority, and even after the transfer of titular sovereignty to the Iraqis, suicide bombers kept blowing themselves up to kill officials put in power by the United States. Militants were regularly targeting Iraqis who cooperated with Americans, even those who served as interpreters for civilian contractors and journalists.

Iraq's new President Iyad Allawi lived with the threat of death even as he vowed to annihilate his enemies. Yet in Iraq, it was unclear just who was the enemy, or how many enemies there were. Were they Shia militants wanting to push out U.S. troops and their secular Iraqi appointed government, or were they Saddam fedayeen intent on reestablishing Baathist control? Were they al Qaeda extremists or a combination of all three groups working at time independently and at times in coordination? Iraq had become the battleground not only for the war between Islamic militants and the United States, but also for the war within Islam. Al Qaeda's soldiers were fighting in the name of Allah but ignoring Muhammad's warnings not to allow their anger to push them past "the bounds of their religion."

The cries of moderate Muslims are almost drowned out in the chaos. Yet there were moderate Muslim voices decrying the denigration of their faith, and warning that Islam's teaching provided not justification for attacks against fellow Muslims. In November 2003, Saudi cleric Sheikh Saleh bin Humaid went on live television to condemn the attacks on foreigners in the kingdom, noting that many of them were expatriate Arabs. He castigated the militants for not sparing fellow Muslims and likened them to Israelis.

"Is the terrorism of Israel and the terrorism of those linked?" asked Humaid, who heads the kingdom's consultative Shura Council. "Is the purpose to kill more Arabs and Muslims and create more violence and instability? It is only inevitable to draw the comparison with the women and children who are being killed in Palestine and the homes that are being razed to the women and children who were killed in Riyadh while they were safe inside their homes."[13]

Humaid then called on Muslims to fight terrorism in the name of Islam, a call that was being repeated by more and more Islamic leaders as extremists seemed bent on finding new ways to shock and awe the West. They had definitely reached that goal with the emergence of the female *istishhadiyah* in the West Bank and Gaza in 2002. But the numbers of women killing themselves and others increased so significantly during the next two years that it stopped being worthy of special media reports. Women went to their deaths in Afghanistan, Chechnya, even Iraq, and in 2003 al Qaeda threatened to send female suicide bombers against the United States, noting that they had a better chance of success. The London-based al Sharq al Awsat publication carried a story in which it quoted a woman named Umm Usama, who said she was the leader of the group's female fighters.

"My duty is to supervise the training of the women fighters who belong to al Qaeda and the Taliban," she said in the interview with al Sharq al Awsat in March 2003. Um Usama said her group uses the internet to communicate, and she warned that female suicide bombers were being trained for operations in the West.[14]

Though she offered no Islamic credentials to support her interpretation of Islam's religious texts, Um Usama (Mother of Usama) spoke for herself and apparently for her army of al Qaeda women in declaring that "Islamic law permits the woman to stand by the man and to support him in the holy war." It's impossible to confirm Um Usama's standing within al Qaeda, but it is clear that even Islamic groups that have supported restrictive roles for Muslim women in society are now revising their positions and sending them out as jihadees, a role traditionally reserved for men.

But in late 2003, Hamas pushed the *istishhadiyah* phenomenon to greater heights by sending the first *istishhadiyah* mother to attack Israelis. Sheikh Yassin sanctioned Reem Raiyshi's mission shortly before his death, having overcome his initial reticence to allow women to serve as suicide bombers. Raiyshi's death made orphans of her two small children and many Muslims, including the leading scholars, were appalled at the development and many issued rulings against mothers serving as suicide bombers.

Columnist Dr. Ziyad Abu al-Hija expressed his outrage over the phenomenon of a mother dying as a suicide bomber in an article in *Al-Karamah*, a journal published by the Supreme Council's Information and Cultural Bureau of Arafat's Fatah organization:

> Who issued a fatwa [religious ruling] taking an infant's mother away from him? Who decided to add two more orphans to the list of Palestine's orphans? On the basis of what Qur'an verses and what hadiths [traditional Islamic writings] does a young mother leave her true place of jihad [holy war], which is raising the two children, one of whom still needs her milk? . . . The religious scholars of Islam, and particularly the religious scholars in Palestine, must make their point; they must clarify to all the position of Islam regarding operations of self-sacrifice, and the most recent operation in particular . . . Who can believe that a father or a mother rejoices at the martyrdom of their child? Oh religious scholars, raise your voices! Oh intellectual writers, raise your voices! There can be no more silence . . . [15]

Another Arab website, in an article by Dr. Hasan Mayy al-Nourani entitled "Hamas, Apologize to the Children," The Dunya al-Watan also castigated Hamas and Sheikh Yassin for sending a mother to die. Dr. Al-Nourani asked: "Have you apologized to the infant for letting its mother leave it forever? Sheikh Yassin, have you apologized to all the mothers for letting Hamas entice an infant's mother and drag her by her hair, pulling out her soft and milk-gorged nipple from between its lips?"[16]

He was describing his image of Raiyshi, a twenty-something resident of Gaza, who became the first known suicide bomber-mother for Hamas. She left a daughter, Doha, 18 months, and a son, Obedia, 3. Dressed in the Islamic hijab that is the hallmark of a religious Muslim woman, Raiyshi made a video before her December 2003 operation, suggesting that her suicide was a gift from God. She held an assault rifle and stood before Hamas flags as she declared: "I always wanted to be the first woman to carry out a martyr attack, where parts of my body can fly all over . . . That is the only wish I can ask God for."[17]

Like her female predecessors, Raiyshi did not look the part of a suicide bomber as she limped toward Israeli soldiers at the Eretz checkpoint. Pretending to be a sick woman, she got past their defenses and blew herself up inside their ranks. That a mother of two young children would undertake such an operation was a startling new development. As the mother of two young children, Raiyshi had every reason to live, especially from the viewpoint of a devout Muslim woman. In the video that Hamas released after her death, she felt it necessary to explain why she would orphan her babies: "I have two children and love them very much. But my love to see God was stronger than my love for my children, and I'm sure that God will take care of them if I become a martyr."[18]

Most Islamic scholars, even militants, have passionately argued a mother's first and holiest duty is to protect and rear her children. The Prophet Muhammad is reported to have said, "Paradise lies at the feet of mothers," and Muslim women are taught that their role is as important as that of a jihadee (holy warrior) in the defense and propagation of Islam. Yet, in what would appear to be a direct contradiction of Muhammad's teachings, both Hamas and Islamic Jihad, conservative Islamic organizations, are now vowing to send more women, even mothers, to kill and to die.

Yassin did not seem chagrined that Raiyshi's death made orphans of possibly dozens of children, including her own, but he justified the operation by proclaiming to the Arab press that "jihad is a duty for both men and women," making it likely that many other women, possibly more mothers, would join the ranks of the *istishhadiyah*. It is also within the realm of possibility that mothers will even be willing to die with their young children as they look for more surprising ways to strike out against the West.

Militants had long warned that the war between the West and their jihadees could last for decades, if not centuries. They are prepared to fight for generations, and are convinced that they ultimately will win. But many Muslims argue that eventually these forces that are defaming their religion will be stopped, but it will be Muslims dedicated to Islam who will have to defeat them. The greater Muslim world must stop seeing Americans as their enemy and recognize the radical elements inside their ranks as the greatest threat to the survival of Islam in the modern world. Many Muslims insist it will take more than public diplomacy to bridge the gap between Islam and the United States. They argue that it will take a change in U.S. policy and U.S. actions around the globe.

Citing Israeli and Western sources, Khorshid explained what is leading so many Muslims militants to become martyrs in attacks against the United States:

> From September 29, 2000 to March 10, 2004, 2,397 Palestinian civilians—of whom 460 were minors under the age of 18—were killed by Israeli security forces in the Occupied Territories, according to B'Tselem, the Israeli Information Center for Human Rights in the Occupied Territories . . . But the sufferings of the Palestinians are not limited to the period from September 2000 to the present, nor are they limited to killings; they go beyond that to house demolitions, detentions, humiliation at checkpoints, etc.
>
> . . . in Iraq, over 10,000 civilians were reportedly killed throughout the past year "as a direct result" of the US-led war and occupation, according to an Amnesty International [report] released on March 18, 2004 . . .
>
> Prior to the 2003 invasion, comprehensive economic sanctions were imposed on Iraq by the United Nations (sponsored by the US and UK governments) for more than 12 years, limiting the transfer of all goods and services to the country. The outcome was the loss of more than one million civilian lives, including 500,000 children under the age of 5. This number of victims is more than the victims of Hiroshima and much more than that of September 11.
>
> . . . in Afghanistan, the number of civilian deaths caused by the military operations has far surpassed the September 11 death toll. Muslims are also being slain in Chechnya, China, Kashmir, and the list goes on and on.
>
> The aforementioned facts might not necessarily justify why Muslim suicide bombings have rocked throughout the world, but they at least offer an explanation.[19]

Such thinking is now so widespread among Muslims that Americans, with all our military prowess, may not be able to win this battle against Islamic militants without the help of Muslim moderates. But the divide within the Muslim world is now so great that even a drastic change in U.S. foreign policy may not immediately convince many Muslims to openly confront the militants, and it certainly will not appease the hardened followers of bin Laden's al Qaeda. Yet Americans can not win the war against terrorism unless the millions of good Muslims throughout the world declare a true jihad against the militants who are destroying the image of Islam. Unfortunately, many Muslims argue, that American actions in Iraq and Afghanistan, the on-going Palestinian-Israeli struggle, and U.S. support of non-democratic Arab regimes prevent Muslim moderates from standing with the West against the radicals. They warn that if the United States does not learn from the mistakes committed in Iraq, it will only increase al Qaeda's numbers, and further weaken the forces of moderation within Islam.

The previous generation thought the Cold War might bring the end of creation, but the West now faces a determined, disciplined and persistent enemy that is not only willing to die, but cherishes death as a path to martyrdom. The wrong weapons in such hands would not only threaten Western civilization, but would aggressively seek to annihilate it. There is a very real possibility that such plans are already in the making. At this writing, U.S. intelligence officials are warning that American financial institutions are being targeted for the next major al Qaeda attack, possibly in New York; Christian churches have been attacked in Iraq; and explosions have gone off outside American and British embassies in Tashkent, Uzbekistan, signaling another battleground for al Qaeda. Many people in Central Asia are worried that Hizb ut Tahrir, the powerful Islamic group in the region that had a platform of spreading Islam around the world, might have teamed with al Qaeda to terrorize Central Asia and overthrow undemocratic regimes. Yet even as they Hizb ut Tahrir members were persecuted throughout Central Asia, they had not resorted to violence. The fear was that this could be changing, and that Central Asia might provide another breeding ground for Islamic militants, much as Afghanistan once had. What is undeniable is that since September 11, the war in Iraq has provided new fodder for the fires of hatred burning against the United States in much of the Islamic world. The battle between Islamic militants and the U.S.-led West is fully engaged, Islamic militants, like the biblical plagues of locusts, are swarming around the globe, secretly recruiting, organizing and planning their next attack. They have at their beck and call a weapon more lethal than even the Cold War's atomic bomb. They have scores of men, women and children ready to fight the West and to die as martyrs.

NOTES

CHAPTER 1

1. E. Van Donzel, *Islamic Desk Reference* (E. J. Brill, Leiden, The Netherlands, 1994) p. 251.
2. John Kelsay, *Islam and War: A Study in Comparative Ethics* (Westminster/John Knox Press, Louisville, Ky. 1993) p.48.
3. Karen Armstrong, *Jerusalem* (New York, Ballantine Books, 1996, 1997) p. 274.
4. The Pew Research Center, "Public Opinion Six Months Later" (March 7, 2002). Text available at: http://people-press.org/commentary/display.php3? AnalysisID=44.

CHAPTER 2

1. United Nations Press Release Press Release SG/SM/7586 "Secretary-General Says News of West Bank Violence "Chilling," (October 12, 2000). Text available at: www.un.org/News/Press/docs/2000/20001012.sgsm7586.doc.html.
2. Defence for Children International,"Violations of Palestinian Children's Rights Stemming from the Israeli Occupation, (March 2002). Report available at: www.dci-pal.org/english/reports/factviol.html.
3. Justus Reid Weiner, "The Use of Palestinian Children in the Al-Aqsa Intifada," (Jerusalem Center for Public Affairs, Nov. 1, 2000). Report available at: http://www.jcpa.org/jl/vp441.htm.
4. Saud Ibn Muhammad Al-'Aqili, "Muslim Criticism of the Use of Children in the Intifada," *Al Hayat* (April 18. 2001). Article available at: http://memri.org/bin/articles.cgi?Page=archives&Area=sd&ID=SP2060.
5. Young Men's Christian Association Rehabilitation Program, "The Stories of Palestinian Children." Report available at: www.east-jerusalem-ymca.org/stories_of_palestinian_children.htm.
6. Kathryn Westcott, "Children Bear Scars of Mideast Conflict." Article available at: http://news.bbc.co.uk/hi/english/world/middle_east/newsid_1951000/1951569.stm.
7. Ibid.
8. UN Commission on Human Rights resolution, Economic and Social Council, "Question of the violation of human rights in the occupied Arab territories, including Palestine," March 21, 2001. Available at: http://domino.un.org/ UNISPAL.NSF/5ba47a5c6cef541b802563e000493b8c/0fb9dea61c1179f4852 56a2500517b09!OpenDocument.
9. UN Commission on Human Rights resolution, Economic and Social Council, "Question of the violation of human rights in the occupied Arab territories, including Palestine," April 11, 2001. Available at: http://domino.un.org/

UNISPAL.NSF/561c6ee353d740fb8525607d00581829/610f67470f91433585
256a330064a91a!OpenDocument.

10. Ibid.

11. Photos and interview with Haya Schijveschuurder by Israeli Ministry of Foreign Affairs; available at: http://www.mfa.gov.il/mfa/go.asp?MFAH0kb90.

12. Nomi Morris, "Suicide Bomber Strike Jerusalem;" August 10, 2001; Knight Ridder/Tribune News Service; International News; KR-ACC-NO: K376.

13. Sharon's speech available at: http://www.israelemb.org/articals/2002/April/2002040900.html.

CHAPTER 3

1. Robert Payne, *The History of Islam*, 1959, (New York: Barnes & Noble Books; 1959), p. 126.

2. Moojan Momen, *An Introduction to Shia Islam*, (New Haven, Conn.: Yale University Press; 1985), p. 30.

3. "The Ashura Uprising" in *The Words & Messages of Imam Khomeini*, (Tehran: The Institute for Compilation and Publication of the Works of Imam Khomeini, International Affairs Department; 1995), p. 11.

4. John Simpson, *Inside Iran*, (New York: St. Martin's Press; 1988), p. 243.

5. International Affairs Division, Imam Khomeini Cultural Institute, "Pithy Aphorisms, Wise Sayings and Counsels of Imam Khomeini;" www.irna.com/occasion/ertehal/english/saying/.

6. Article available at: www.irna.com/occasion/ertehal/english/will/.

7. Ibid.

8. Kauthar, An Anthology of the Speeches of Imam Khomeini, Vol. 2 (Tehran: The Institute for the Compilation and Publication of the Works of Imam Khomeini, 1995) pp. 362–363.

9. Article available at: www.iranian.com/Times/1999/Marchd/Mamasani/rights.html#261.

10. Article available at: www.irna.com/en/tnews/020313133216.etn01.shtml.

11. Article available at: www.metimes.com/2K/issue2000–42/reg/iranian_schools_to.htm.

12. Text available at: http://usinfo.state.gov/topical/pol/terror/02040106.htm.

13. Article available at: http://iran-pressservice.com/articles_2001/sep_2001/iran_terrorist_attacks_us_12901.htm.

14. Article available at: http://www.rferl.org/nca/features/2001/10/03102001120634.asp.

15. Article available at: www.rferl.org/nca/features/2001/10/03102001120634.asp.

16. Article available at: www.abbc3.com/tehranconference/eng.htm.

17. Article available at: www.irna.com/occasion/ertehal/english/will/.

18. Article available at: www.arabicnews.com/ansub/Daily/Day/990515/1999051539.html.

CHAPTER 4

1. Boaz Ganor, "A New Strategy Against the Terror." Article available at: www.ict.org.il/counter_ter/isct_article.cfm.

2. Future News The Daily, "Suha Bishara, Lebanon's Symbol of Resistance Against Occupation Has Been Released, (September 3, 1998). Article available at: www.future.com.lb/news/archive/1998/e0309.htm.

3. Australian Broadcast Corporation, Four Corners: Debbie Whitmont, "Interview with Kamil Idris." Transcript available at: www.abc.net.au/4corners/stories/s584946.htm.

4. Seattle Times News Service, "West Bank violence angered Palestinian woman bomber," (January 31, 2002). Article available at: http://seattletimes.nwsource.com/html/nationworld/134397898_bomber31.htmlhttp://archives.seattletimes.nwsource.com/cgi-bin/texis.cgi/web/vortex/display?slug=bomber31&date=20020131.

5. Article available at: www.khaleejtimes.co.ae/ktarchive/020202/middleeast.htm.

6. Sandra Mackey, *Lebanon: Death of a Nation* (New York: Congdon & Weed, Inc., 1989), p. 30.

CHAPTER 5

1. Text available at http://abclocal.go.com/ktrk/news/100401_news_will.html.

2. Ibid.

3. Extracts from Dr. Ayman Zawahri's *Knights Under the Prophet's Banner*, available at www.fas.org/irp/world/para/ayman_bk.html.

4. Text of Osama bin Laden's statement is available at: www.usatoday.com/news/world/bomb096.htm.

5. Text of fatwa available at: www.almuhajiroun.com/fataawa/16–09–2001.php.

6. Ibid.

7. Text available at: http://www.ict.org.il/articles/fatwah.htm.

8. Ibid.

9. Sheikh Abdullah bin Muhammad bin Humaid, *Jihad in the Qur'an and Sunna*, (Maktaba Dar-us-Salam, Riyadh, Saudi Arabia, 1995) p.10.

10. Ibid: Surah 22: 39, 40.

11. Partial translation of Sunan Abu-Dawud, Book 14 available at: www.usc.edu/dept/MSA/fundamentals/hadithsunnah/abudawud/014.sat.html.

12. Syed Muhammad Hussain Shamsi, *The Prophets of Islam*, (Alhuda Foundation, Inc. Englewood, N.J. 1994), p. 93.

13. Sayyid Qutb, *Milestones* (The American Trust Publications revised translation, Indianapolis, 1990), p. 53.

14. "Jerusalem Blast Suicide Bomb Kills 18, Wounds More Than 70 in Downtown Pizzeria" : http://abcnews.go.com/sections/world/DailyNews/jerusalem010809.html.

15. Maryam Jameelah, "Shaikh Izz-ud-din Al Qassam Shaheed: A Great Palestinian Mujahid" (Mohammed Yusuf Khan & Sons, Lahore, Pakistan) p. 5.

16. Ibid., p. 6.

17. Dan Rubin and Michael Matza "Bomb on Jewish Sabbath kills at least nine in Jerusalem," Copyright 2002 Knight Ridder/Tribune News Service, March 3, 2002.

18. Text available at: www.missionislam.com/islam/conissue/palestine.htm#top.

19. Muhammad Hamidullah, *Introduction to Islam*, Paris, 1959, Centre Culturel Islamique, p. 79.

20. Muhammad Ali Alkhuli, *Traditions of Prophet Muhammad*, Al-Farazdak Press, Riyadh, Saudi Arabia, 1984, p.70–71.

21. Translation of comments by Sheikh Abdel Aziz Bin Abdallah Al Sheikh, Grand Mufti of the Kingdom of Saudi Arabia available at: www.chretiens-et-juifs. org/ISLAM/Palazzi_against_suicide_bombing.htm.; and at http://www.ict. org.il/articles/articledet.cfm?articleid=214.

22. Translation of article available at: http://www.ahram.org.eg/weekly/2001/532/ eg8.htm.

23. Ibid.

24. Ibid.

25. Text available at: http://thetruereligion.org/terror.htm.

26. Text available at: http://usinfo.state.gov/topical/pol/terror/01101611.htm.

27. Text of fatwa available at: www.unc.edu/~kurzman/Qaradawi_et_al.htm.

28. Ibid.

29. Sayyid Qutb, *Milestones*.

30. Ibid., p.49.

31. Ibid., p. 50.

32. Op cit; see note 3.

CHAPTER 6

1. Dr. Eyad Sarraj, "Why We Have Become Suicide Bombers." Article available at: www.missionislam.com/islam/conissue/palestine.htm#top.

2. Ibid.

3. Alfonso Chardy, "Parents try to stop children from becoming suicide bombers." Article available at: www.realcities.com/mld/krwashington/3331761.htm.

4. "Palestinian bomber hinted about becoming martyr," (*USA Today*, August 10, 2001.) Article available at: www.usatoday.com/news/world/2001/08/10/ bomber.htm#more

5. The Qur'an: Surah 3: 169.

CHAPTER 7

1. Report of the Secretary-General prepared pursuant to General Assembly Resolution ES-10/10 (Jenin); full text available at: www.un.org/peace/jenin/.

2. Ahmad Rashad, Hamas: *Palestinian Politics with an Islamic Hue* (Annandale, VA, United Association For Studies and Research, 1993); p. 4.

3. Ibid., p.4.

4. Boaz Ganor, "The Islamic Jihad: The Imperative of Holy War," Jan. 1, 1993. Full text available at: www.ict.org.il/articles/islamic.htm.

5. John Kelsay, *Islam and War* (Louisville, KY, Westminster/John Knox Press, 1993), pp. 106–7.

6. Terrorism list is available at: www.ustreas.gov/offices/enforcement/ofac/sanctions/terrorism.html.

7. Matthew Kalman, "Hamas: Israel to Pay 'Heavy Price.'" (*USA Today*, March 4, 2002.) Article available at: www.usatoday.com/news/world/2002/03/05/usat-mideast.htm.

8. Rosemary Sayigh, "No Work, No Space, No Future: Palestinian Refugees in Lebanon," (*Middle East International*, August 10, 2001). Full text at: www.arts. mcgill.ca/mepp/PRRN/papers/sayigh2.html.

9.   Human Rights Watch report available at: www.hrw.org/press/2001/06/isr0622. htm.

CHAPTER 8

1.   Human Rights Watch, "Trials of Civilians in Military Courts Violate International Law Executions Continue, No Appeal of Death Sentences to Higher Court," vol. 5, Issue 3, (July 1993). Full text available at:www.hrw.org/reports/1993/Egypt/.
2.   Ibid.
3.   Extracts from Dr. Ayman Zawahri's *Knights Under the Prophet's Banner,* available in English at: www.fas.org/irp/world/para/ayman_bk.html.
4.   Ibid.
5.   "Traif Tactics," *Middle East Peace Report*, Vol. 3, Issue 31 (February 25,2002); text available at: www.peacenow.org/nia/peace/v3i31.html.
6.   Henry Siegman, "The Saudi Initiative: Future Visions of the Middle East"; Text and audio of speech available at: www.fpa.org/topics_info2414/topics_info_show.htm?doc_id=105744.
7.   Ibid.
8.   Edward Said, "Is Israel More Secure Now?" *Counterpunch* (January 4, 2002); Text available at: www.counterpunch.org/saidsecure.html.
9.   Ibid.
10. "*Al-Sharq Al-Awsat* Publishes Extracts from al Jihad Leader Ayman Zawahri's New Book" (December 2, 2001); Text in English available at: www.fas.org/irp/world/para/ayman_bk.html.
11. Daniel Pipes, "Mistakes Mistakes Made the Catastrophe Possible," *The Wall Street Journal* (September 12, 2001); Article available at: www.danielpipes.org/article/63.
12. Gareth Evans, "Building International Defenses Against Terrorism: A Comprehensive Strategy," *Georgetown Journal*, Volume III, Number 1 (Winter/ Spring 2002): p. 131.
13. Ibid., p. 131.
14. Daniel Pipes, "Mistakes Made the Catastrophe Possible," The Wall Street Journal, (September 12, 2001). Text of article available at: www.danielpipes.org/article/63
15. Sheikh Muhammad Kabbani, "Islamic Extremism: A Viable Threat to National Security," (January 7, 1999). Text of speech available at www.islamic-supremecouncil.org/extremism/islamic_extremism.htm.
16. Seth Borenstein, "Experts Think Bin Laden Tape Is Authentic," Dec. 14, 2001. Article available at http://www.s-t.com/daily/12–01/12–14–01/a01wn013.htm.
17. Reuven Paz, "Hamas Responds to Counter-Terrorist Laws," (June 1998). Article available at www.ict.org.il/articles/Hamas_art3.htm.

CHAPTER 9

1.   Akbar S. Ahmed, "Islam's Crossroads: Islamic Leadership," (June 1999). Article available at: www.islamfortoday.com/akbar02.htm.
2.   Ibid.
3.   Khaled Abou El Fadl, "The Place of Tolerance in Islam: On Reading the Qur'an—and Misreading It." Article available at: http://bostonreview.mit.edu/BR26.6/elfadl.html.

4. Sheikh Muhammad Kabbani, "Islamic Extremism: A Viable Threat to National Security," (January 7, 1999). Text of speech available at www.islamic-supremecouncil.org/extremism/islamic_extremism.htm.

5. Islamic Supreme Council press release, "National Muslim organizations incite modern day lynch mob," (March 2, 1999). Copy of press release available at: www.islamicsupremecouncil.org/media_center/Releases/lynchmob-March_2_99.htm.

6. Sheikh Muhammad Kabbani, "Islamic Extremism: A Viable Threat to National Security," (January 7, 1999). Text of speech available at www.islamic-supremecouncil.org/extremism/islamic_extremism.htm.

7. Dr. Ahmed Yousef, *The True Clash of Civilizations: Zionism As Seen Through Islamist Eyes*, (Annandale, Va.: United Association for Studies and Research, May 2002), p. iii.

8. Dr. Sulayman S. Nyang, "God, Man and History: An Islamic Perspective." Full text of speech available at: www.icjs.org/scholars/nyang1.html.

9. Imad-ad-Deen Ahmad, "Islam Demands A Muslim Response to the Terror of September 11," (Middle East Affairs Journal 7 #2–3, Summer-Fall 2001), p. 1. Article available at: http://www.minaret.org/response%20to%20terror.pdf.

10. Speech of his Excellency Omar Hassan Ahmed Al-Bashir president of the Republic of the Sudan at the twenty-ninth session of the Islamic conference of foreign ministers available at: www.oic-oci.org/press/english/june2002/al-bashir.htm.

11. Joyce M. Davis, "International Muslim Leaders Warn Against Anti-Muslim Sentiment," (Knight Ridder Newspapers, July 8, 2002); Article available at: http://www.realcities.com/mld/krwashington/3623892.htm.

12. Ibid.

EPILOGUE

1. http://www.whitehouse.gov/news/releases/2004/01/20040120-7.html
2. http://msnbc.msn.com/id/3080244/
3. http://www.pbs.org/newshour/bb/middle_east/jan-june03/rumsfeld_2-
4. http://english.aljazeera.net/NR/exeres/4424B681-13CC-4745-B9DD-BEFDC596793B.htm
5. http://www.csmonitor.com/2003/0522/p01s02-woiq.html#
6. http://intelligence.senate.gov/conclusions.pdf
7. http://www.9-11commission.gov/
8. http://www.cnn.com/2004/ALLPOLITICS/06/24/poll.iraq/
9. http://globalsecurity.com/weapons_of/ex-us_arms/ex-us_arms.htm
10. http://cgi.cnn.com/2004/WORLD/meast/01/25/sprj.nirq.kay/
11. www.us-israel.org/jsource/biography/Rantissi.html.
12. http://electronicintifada.net/v2/article2648.shtml
13. http://www.iht.com/articles/96629.html
14. http://www.cbsnews.com/stories/2003/04/01/attack/main547237.shtml
15. http://www.middleeastinfo.org/forum1331-1
16. Ibid.
17. http://www.guardian.co.uk/israel/Story/0,2763,1123305,00.html
18. Ibid.
19. http://www.islamonline.net/English/Views/2004/04/article08.shtml

INDEX